The Net Effect

School Library Media Centers and the Internet

Edited by
Lyn Hay and James Henri

The Scarecrow Press, Inc.
Lanham, Maryland, and London
1999

SCARECROW PRESS, INC.

Published in the United States of America
by Scarecrow Press, Inc.
4720 Boston Way
Lanham, Maryland 20706
http://www.scarecrowpress.com

4 Pleydell Gardens, Folkestone
Kent CT20 2DN, England

ISBN 0-8108-3601-7 (pbk: alk. paper)

CONTENTS

---

* Submitted and accepted as a refereed conference paper.

---

* Submitted and accepted as a refereed conference paper.

---

* Submitted and accepted as a refereed conference paper.

---

* Submitted and accepted as a refereed conference paper.

---

* Submitted and accepted as a refereed conference paper.

Introduction

As we move towards the new millennium, leading edge schools, as well as those facing crisis upon crisis, are experimenting with forms of working and the organization of teaching that demands a fundamental reassessment of the role of learning in schools. Senge (1990) reflecting on the same developments and challenges in the business world named this phenomenon the learning organization. When applied to schools the gentler notion of learning community is sometimes preferred. The idea of a learning community and its contrast with the traditional idea that we have of pre-adult education can perhaps be seen in the collision of two powerful forces. The first is that immovable object known as schooling (all the structures and ways of doing things at school by way of classrooms that have changed little during the twentieth century). The second is the irresistible force known as learning (all that is needed to equip those at school students and teachers -- to have a personal understanding of what it means to be human and to have the skills and competencies, and the desire to continually relearn for a future that is becoming almost uncomfortably different from the present). The challenge of the Information Age is to find ways to address the challenge posed by this collision.

Watkins and Marsick (1993) talk of six action imperatives underpinning a learning community. Teachers:

1. create continuous learning communities;
2. promote inquiry and dialogue;
3. encourage collaboration and team learning;
4. establish systems to capture and share learning;
5. empower people towards a collective vision; and
6. connect the organisation to its environment.

These imperatives provide some understanding about the actions that are needed to sculpture the learning community. In a similar vein, Henri (1995) coined the phrase the "information literate school community" in an attempt to highlight the key role that information plays in this learning community. Two touchstones embedded in this concept are:

1. just in time learning; and
2. desktop learning.

These touchstones are at the heart of the learning community because they allow for adaptation at the workplace just in time for the next learning adventure. Traditional approaches such as formal courses of study, face-to-face lectures, workshops and seminars, certainly remain important. But to the extent that they are separated from the main business of the organization and taken at arms length, their value for the organisation, rather than for the individual, is diminished.

Among the vast array of teachers, school library media specialists* have been at the forefront of schools renewal and information technology innovations, advocating and modelling these touchstones, and along with principals, they provide the best exemplars of what is possible.

There are in excess of forty papers included in this title, brought together under ten topics, namely:

- Censorship: More Problems. Possible Solutions?
- Children's Literature and the Internet: Issues and Services
- Critical Thinking in the Electronic Age
- Electronic Collection Development: Selection and Management Issues
- More Hot Spots for TLs
- MOO Trek: Using MOOs in Education
- Multiple Personalities?: Teacher Librarian, Cybrarian, Director of Information Services
- Process and Product: How Do We Assess Students Work?
- Professional Electronic Networks for TLs
- The School Library Home Page

Many of these presenters are household names in the field of school librarianship and all are concerned in one way or another to address the needs and concerns of learning communities. The cast includes academics, consultants, writers, school library media specialists, webmasters, cyberspace activists and librarians. Writers come from Australia, Canada, Iceland, the United Kingdom and the United States of America. The viewpoints of key stakeholders such as the International Association of School Librarianship, LM_NET, and OZTL_NET are voiced. Each writer addresses key issues such as

---

* Read Teacher Librarian for Canada and Australia. Read School Librarian for the United Kingdom.

censorship, professional development, collection development, and assessing learning, and relates these to the milieu of the digital world.

Certainly the range of topics is broad and the debate is solid. An objective reading of these papers would sensitize even the most hardened sceptic to the viewpoint that school library media specialists across the world are at the cutting edge of education; that issues are the same or similar the world over; and that there is a range of viable viewpoints and possible solutions. This is part of the rich tapestry of life in the complex and ever changing Information Age.

These presentations were made as part of a Virtual Conference conducted in 1997[+]. This conference was the second such international conference conducted by the editors and demonstrated the ground breaking role of those working in school librarianship to deliver an international conference from the desktop.

A short biographical note is appended to each paper, and you are encouraged to talk up the debate with one another by making use of the proffered email address.

Those readers who wish to be included in the 1999 Virtual Conference to be held over two weeks in July should email to <jhenri@csu.edu.au> or <lhay@csu.edu.au>.

Lyn Hay and James Henri[‡]
ITEC VC'97 Information Services Strand Coordinators

[+] Copies of the proceedings of the first conference Hay, L. and Henri, J. (eds.). *A meeting of the minds: ITEC Virtual Conference '96 proceedings.* Belconnen, ACT: ASLA. Available from ASLA Press, PO Box 450, Belconnen, ACT, 2616. ($AUD32.00 incl. postage and handling).

[‡] **Lyn Hay** is Lecturer and **James Henri** is Senior Lecturer in Teacher Librarianship with the School of Information Studies, Charles Sturt University, Wagga Wagga, N.S.W., Australia. Lyn may be contacted via email at **<lhay@csu.edu.au>**. James may be contacted via email at **<jhenri@csu.edu.au>**.

References

Henri, J. (1995). The information literate school community: Exploring a fuzzy concept. *Scan*, 14 (3): 25-28.

Senge, P.M. (1990). *The fifth discipline*. Sydney: Random House.

Watkins, K.E. and Marsick, V.J. (1993). *Sculpting the learning organization*. San Francisco: Jossey-Bass.

Topic A

Censorship:

More Problems. Possible Solutions?

The Role of Reviewing and Commentary in Children's Literature: A Subtle Form of Censorship?[*]

Maureen Nimon[†]

Overview

This paper argues that high profile reviews and commentary on children's literature in the media encourage censorship because they feature the exceptional and groundbreaking title rather than the typical. Items published in the last 12 months, which have this potential, are discussed. All professionals have a responsibility to keep the public informed of the general situation as well as new trends and unusual books.

Reviewing and Censorship

Censorship aims to limit intellectual freedom and is therefore decried in our society. But while fighting censorship is an important principle, its implementation is difficult. Where diversity of opinion is tolerated, one person's stand in defence of core values will be perceived by others as an attempt to censor

Accepting that consensus on many titles is unlikely; we guard against censorship by being as explicit as possible as to the basis of our judgments. We expect the same of reviewers and commentators since it is they who set the agenda for debate. The following discussion is based on a small number of recent, high profile articles, which have raised key issues in regard to Australian children's books. Ireland, for example, claims that modern books ignore ethical boundaries proper to children's literature (1996a,b). Her influence is reflected in Legge's article (1997:10) which argues that "life sucks" in today's teenage fiction. Since morality and ideology are such emotive issues, discussion of these aspects of the literature in isolation is alarmist. When such a stand also dominates reviews, as it did recently (Hunter 1997), then the danger of censorship increases.

Ireland, Hunter and Legge are entitled to voice what they see as significant matters. Nor are they alone in their views. As a result of extended research into Australian children's literature of the past three decades, Scutter (1996:4-5) concludes that "in the speculative

---

[*] Submitted and accepted as a refereed conference paper.

[†] **Dr Maureen Nimon** is Senior Lecturer with the School of Communication at the University of South Australia, Magill Campus in South Australia. Maureen may be contacted via email at **<Maureen.Nimon@unisa.edu.au>**.

dystopic fictions of the 1980s, the adult world is dismissed...the parent generation...is rejected as models of entity". She observes that in Australian books of the 1990s, "there is a blinkered view that if realism is the genre that aims to represent 'reality'..., then 'real' realism takes the most extreme and exceptional cases and represents them as, somehow, typical..." (Scutter 1996:7). Legge (1997:13) is right when she states "the need for hope is central to the debate over youth fiction".

The problem is how to address this need. Legge (1997:10) implies an answer when she asserts that the debate is not about "morality nor ideology but...a particularly bleak (honest?) strain of social realism for young adults". Her statement suggests that the situation may be resolved by censoring the more extreme examples.

Books dealing with the most disturbing aspects of life should be rejected if they offer nothing more than shock value. Yet there should always be books which disturb in order to force the reader to think through questions of moral responsibility. *Sleeping Dogs*, intended for adolescents on the brink of adulthood, deals with incest, challenging the reader to decide whether this crime matches Griffen's bitterness, the central evil destroying the Willow family.

Moreover, Legge errs when she represents the debate as being about a bleak view of life rather than morality or ideology. Morality and ideology are inescapably part of constructions of reality. More importantly in this context, so is 'hope'.

Here is part of the dilemma. If people expect more 'hope' in juvenile literature, what is it they wish to see? Consider the problematics of representing hope. What should authors promise the next generation or say about the meaning of life?

Some of the bleakness of adolescent literature arises from the fact that when authors do tackle the evils present in the world, reviewers and commentators find their solutions to be unconvincing in proportion to the degree in which authors set their stories in 'imaginary' or 'real' worlds. Many seem prepared to accept the conclusions of fantasy writers as affirming and uplifting, but those in scenarios approximating familiar societies are "trite", "tendentious" and "sad" (Hunter 1997:8).

To illustrate the way in which a particular emphasis taken in a review article may heighten a perception of bleakness, take Hunter's (1997) recent reviews of four adolescent titles, three of which put their characters in peril of their lives. One, *Outside Permission*, she damns for being based on the "paranoid supposition" that authorities may manipulate people's lives in order to extend their understanding of human behaviour. This view of the world is "sad" and "fostering an acceptance that there is always someone outside to blame." Yet she praises "the many lessons" of Kelleher's *Firedancer* in which the protagonists are similarly endangered by the authorities. Why does the same plot device merit such different treatment in each case? Again, Hunter finds that Kelleher offers hope, putting forward the "antidote" of the earthy lives of Neanderthals "to the ills of a consumerist technological age". Kelleher's "antidote" of necessity must be interpreted in a very loose fashion by contemporary readers. More importantly, Hunter either does not notice or ignores what Nilsson offers as answers to the question of whether death, especially an early death, renders life pointless. Similarly, she dismisses *The Climb*, a book in which a boy, caught up in a fascist society, must make choices which will affect not only his own safety but also that of others. Hunter condemns *The Climb* as a literary failure. That is a proper judgement for a reviewer to make, but given the emphasis she places on the political and social pictures which the four authors portrayed, not to examine or even mention the writers' answers to the social ills described, casts two of the three books about 'bleakness' as indulgences in extremity apparently just for the sake of drawing an audience. If 'lessons' are to be the justification for novels about dire dilemmas, why does the reviewer not consider the lessons offered in all cases?

Hunter appears vulnerable here to a phenomenon many are prone to - the ability to find comfort in distant scenarios, while being unconvinced by solutions put forward to those that are more familiar. Scutter (1996:4-5) notes how many contemporary books offer a retreat into pastoral romanticism as a remedy for modern ills. The point to be made, however, is that the weight of the comments on political and social ideology in Hunter's review[‡] could be

---

[‡] I have exchanged correspondence with Linnet Hunter about my concerns with her review which I have elaborated in this paper. It should be noted by readers that Hunter believes that I have placed an emphasis on part of her review which distorts the whole and I think, that in my concern with the general trends in public commentary on children's literature this year, she has a point. I also wish to point out that it is not the job of reviewers to be concerned with how their words may be used by would-be censors. Nevertheless, I wish to draw attention to how discussion of the novel and ground-breaking title may led to a public impression that the body of adolescent literature is far more radical than is the fact. (The correspondence with

redressed by paying more attention both to questions of genre and audience. Ottley's book would not seem so inappropriate if it were viewed as farce, nor *The Climb* so negative if it were seen as a book for those in the senior high school, rather than the younger adolescents satisfied by *Firedancer*. Thus the values of the work of reviewers to professionals is inestimable, but a balanced view of the field of children's literature must be maintained if censorship is to be kept at bay.

References

Hunter, L. (1997). Only one ace in the pack. *The Australian, The Weekend Review*, Feb 22-23: 8.

Ireland, J. (1996a). Are they the best books of the year? *Reading Time*, 40 (2): 18-20.

Ireland, J. (1996b). Written for children? Letter to the Editor. *Quadrant*, 40 (10): 330.

Legge, K. (1997). Life sucks, Timmy. *The Australian Magazine*, March 8-19: 10-18.

Scutter, H. (1996). Representing the child: Postmodern version of Peter Pan. In *Writing the Australian Child*, ed. by Clare Bradford. Nedlands: University of WA Press: 1-16.

Linnet Hunter grew out of this article so I think it only fair to reflect what we discussed. Personally, I'm pleased to see Hunter getting a fairly regular spot in the *Weekend Australian*.)

Censorship in Saskatchewan's Public School Libraries[*]

Elizabeth Roberts[†]

A recent survey of Saskatchewan's public school libraries conducted under the auspices of the Saskatchewan Writers' Guild revealed that censorship is indeed not only occurring, but flourishing in this province's schools. In the three year period 1992-95, approximately 250 challenges were brought against resources in the libraries of our public school system. Clearly, censorship is a part of life for today's librarians, but what does the term actually mean in an educational context, and what are the ramifications of its prevalence in our schools? A definition of censorship that is particularly useful to educators was developed by Reichman (1988). Reichman (1988:2) defined censorship as:

the removal, suppression, or restriction of literary, artistic or educational materials -- of images, ideas and information -- on the grounds that these are morally or otherwise objectionable in light of standards applied by the censor.

Allowing censors to have free reign in our schools could prove to be devastating to schools in an information rich society, where the effective implementation of a resource based curriculum depends upon students and teachers having access to a myriad of resources that express diverse viewpoints. It is therefore critical that both educators and the public they serve develop an awareness and understanding of the relationship between censorship, teaching and learning. Bryson and Detty (1982) claim when censorship enters the public school system it not only "limits the students' right to read, to learn and to be informed [but also] the teachers' right to academic freedom". Limitations such as these are clearly unacceptable in a democratic society.

---

[*] Submitted and accepted as a refereed conference paper.

[†] **Liz Roberts** has taught most grades in school, worked as a teacher librarian, a library and curriculum consultant and principal of a K-12 school with the Saskatchewan Department of School Education in Canada. Liz has worked on province-wide initiatives for the improvement of school libraries including an assessment project, a resource based learning project and has also served as President of the Saskatchewan School Library Association. Liz may be contacted via email at <haywir@orion.sk.sympatico.ca>.

An Historical Perspective

Surprisingly, censorship has not been a major problem in public school libraries until fairly recently. However, with the marked increase in the number of challenges to school resources during the last three decades, it has emerged as a crucial issue among educators. Cutts (1983:7) noted that:

from 1972 through 1979 more episodes of censorship or attempted censorship were reported than in any comparable earlier period. It has been reported that book banning in the United States has increased 400% [from 1980 through 1983].

McCarthy (1993) confirmed that this increase was the beginning of a trend in American schools; one that has been closely paralleled in Canadian education. "According to the People for the American Way, the number of reported incidents [of censorship] was 50% higher in 1991-92 than in the previous school year." (McCarthy 1993:55). Several factors have contributed to this growing statistic. Prior to the 1960s, schools generally contained an ethnocentric student population. In addition, because the curriculum, texts and supplementary resources were prescribed by departments of education and rigidly taught and adhered to by the teachers of the day, few if any challenges were brought against school resources. It was also true that in all but the largest schools in metropolitan areas, centralised libraries did not exist. Instead, the library consisted of a few shelves of innocuous books located at the back of each classroom.

With the 1960s came political upheaval, a sexual revolution, changing societal norms and experimental forms of education. Values that were once entrenched and static began to be questioned and reassessed. In recent years, the shift toward interactive curricula in education, the development of centralised school library collections, and the change in the nature of the communities served by schools have resulted in an upsurge in censorship activity in public school libraries. Specifically, conditions such as the following have fostered an increase in the concern over school resources:

• the switch in English Language Arts courses from teaching an approved canon of literary works to a curriculum whose objectives include personal growth and reader response. This "engagement model" incorporates a broad spectrum of works, many of which picture teenage characters in realistic situations facing difficult personal decisions, often related to controversial societal issues.

- the inclusion of a wider range of multi-media resources containing diverse and often conflicting viewpoints in the teaching of all school subjects.

- the implementation of Social Studies, Health and Science curricula that reflect the moral, ethical and ecological dilemmas of modern society but whose "politically correct" values may not conform to those values introduced in students' homes.

- the development of centralised libraries that have incorporated a multi-media approach to collection building and not only present diverse opinions on many real life issues but reflect our multi-cultural society and espouse ethnic diversity.

According to Cavanagh and Styles (1981), parents who once taught their children that what the teacher said was always right now attempt to influence what the teacher does in the classroom and what their children learn. As our society has become more literate, parents have begun to read, criticise and censor materials their children read and study at school. Parents are increasingly concerned about the exposure of their children to controversial issues and images and to certain innovative instructional strategies. They believe schools can and should improve the ability of young people to create a better society, and in a world of absentee parents pursuing careers, they expect schools to become surrogate parents. Part of that 'parenting' includes passing on the cultural and historical heritage which will help make their children decent, respected citizens. Finally, Cavanagh and Styles (1981:124) suggest that although most parents willingly accept responsibility for the upbringing of their children, a small minority equate this responsibility with controlling their children's lives, in school and out. The increase in censorship activity reflects the fact that this desire for control extends to the selection of the resources used in their children's classrooms and libraries.

Who Censors? Why?

Generally speaking, censors operate along a continuum that runs from the ultraconservative to the extreme liberal. Extremists at both ends of the spectrum feel they are right in insisting that specific topics or ideas be kept from children. Two active groups of extremists are largely responsible for the fear that causes both censorship and pre-censorship to flourish in our public school libraries. Right wing censors object to materials that: contradict traditional values and lifestyles; encourage political viewpoints antithetical to the conservative mainstream; or present religious viewpoints other than their own. "Some groups [find] any material or strategy that does not promote reliance on Biblical absolutes offensive". (McCarthy 1993:60). "Because of this sincere belief, any resource becomes open to challenge by right wing groups. Any materials that encourage students to clarify values -- in other words, to become more active learners -- are alleged to represent an anti-theistic belief." (McCarthy 1993:52). The *Quest* health materials and the *Tactics for Thinking* program, used in many Saskatchewan schools, as well as *Reflective Teaching and Roleplays, Games and Simulations*, titles from the province's instructional strategies series of booklets, have run afoul of right wing censors. These resources have been objected to because they allegedly teach relative values, encourage students to make their own decisions or teach students to indulge in self-hypnotic trances. In addition to rejecting the broad curriculum, conservative, fundamentalist groups also object to specific course offerings such as:

> *sociology, psychology, health and biology as well as instruction pertaining to values clarification, self-esteem, multi-cultural education, evolution, AIDS education and global education. [They] are being contested as anti-Christian, anti-American and otherwise inappropriate... Collaborative learning and thematic instruction are being challenged because they shift to students some of the responsibility that was formerly lodged with the teacher.*
>
> (McCarthy 1993:56)

Topics such as the aforementioned are liberally scattered throughout Saskatchewan's new curricula and receive support from the resources of our public school libraries. It is these resources that are often the target of right wing censors.

Left wing censors, on the other hand, insist on political correctness, objecting to any author who derides minority groups or creates sexual, racial or cultural stereotyping. Their objective is to oppose educational materials and other media that exhibit a traditional white male Anglo-Saxon orientation (Simmons 1994:58-59). The Council on Interracial Books for Children (CIBC), a group of American authors, editors and historians is illustrative of left wing organisations. The organisation promotes children's literature that reflects a multicultural society. To assist teachers and librarians in selecting resources, it publishes a journal that rates children's books according to a set of established criteria. The focus of the evaluation, however, is on the content rather than on the literary and artistic values of the works. Amey (1989) points out the problems inherent in this approach. The journal allows the reviewer to analyse, rate and tabulate a book's artwork and text for signs of ageism, conformism, escapism, and elitism, as well as sexism, materialism and conformist and escapist tendencies.

The thrust of this sort of critical approach to children's literature may differ in focus and detail from past practice, but it connects with a long history of attempts to use children's books to indoctrinate the young. This censorious slant...grew out of early attempts to structure children's books along didactic lines (Amey 1988:17-18).

Roxburgh, publisher for Farrar, Straus and Giroux, agrees that left wing censors regard books as instruments "to help correct the behaviour of individual children as well as the social problems of the culture into which they are born" (Roxburgh 1994:121). The problem with censors, whether they have left wing or right wing leanings is the same. They all demand that only one point of view be offered to children. At neither end of the spectrum is there any regard for children as rational, thinking individuals capable of making carefully considered, responsible decisions. Nor is intellectual freedom regarded as a student right by either group.

Censorship and Writers
As the level of censorship has increased in public school libraries, those who publish or produce materials for children and those who recommend and select materials for school libraries have all been affected by the 'chill of the challenge'. Quite naturally, authors want their books to be published. Producers want their works to be seen and heard. However, if authors or producers are aware that including prohibited words, discussing forbidden subjects or making unacceptable references will cause their works to be rejected by publishers or potential buyers, creativity is affected by a form of self-censorship. Economic realities often dictate that a compromise be made. Writers and producers continually have to ask themselves if the economic reward is worth changing a word? changing a character? altering a plot? disrupting dialogue and subtly distorting the original message? If writers continually answer "yes", there is a

danger that the resources our schools depend upon will become stilted, artificial and didactic. Our libraries will contain material which fails to challenge a reader, listener or viewer, but which will satisfy the censor.

Similarly, in order to retain economic viability, people who publish or produce materials for children often exert 'soft' or voluntary pre-censorship by avoiding the production of both materials on sensitive or politically incorrect issues, and materials for which they foresee a limited market, such as works by and for minority groups (Steptoe 1993:94). Voluntary pre-censorship is also possible at the post-production stage. Reviewers who feel they should warn teacher librarians about possible censorship problems that may arise with the purchase of an item may use a simple descriptive phrase in a review such as, "the strong, colourful language used in this novel", that effectively limits the chances of that novel being included in many school library collections. In addition, some libraries ban specific authors from their collections, regardless of what they have written, simply because their work is routinely challenged. Once a work is purchased, pre-censorship or 'soft censorship' (censorship exercised without any outside pressure having been exerted) may still occur. Library staff, teachers or administrators, afraid of offending a parent or creating controversy in the community may spontaneously remove a resource before it becomes accessible through general circulation.

Several American studies cited in McDonald's *Censorship and Intellectual Freedom* (1993) indicate that although teacher librarians and administrators profess a belief in intellectual freedom, in actual practice, in the face of public disapproval, they lack the confidence to support their principles, and summarily remove resources they feel might meet with opposition from a segment of the school community (Burress 1984:60-61; Woods 1981:102-108; Fiske 1959:70). This finding may account for the large amount of soft censorship that exists in Saskatchewan's public school libraries.

A second possibility is that where school libraries are staffed by non-professionals, there is little understanding of the difference between censorship and good selection practices. Non-professional staff are certainly the norm in the majority of Saskatchewan's rural schools. Asheim (1983:181) defined clearly the unique responsibility of the selector of library resources:

The mass agencies of communication think in terms of large, faceless audiences. The common denominator, not the individual differences, becomes the criterion. A library... strives to assure that while the interests of the majority are being met, the interests of the many minorities are being protected... the individual, the special case, has rights too... One segment of the library's total constituency should not be permitted to interfere with another segment's rights and it is part of our responsibility to protect the rights of all.

Effective, responsible selection requires that library personnel have full knowledge of the library collection; the resources that are available; the reputation and reliability of authors, publishers, and producers; the community the library serves; the curriculum and students in the school; the values and beliefs that guide their own lives. The commitment to responsible selection means:

...not allowing our biases and prejudices to influence our decisions, and... that the decisions we make we try to make on the basis of knowledge, not on personal opinion. Our task in building collections... is, rather, to show our staff, our students and our community that we are competent enough to be trusted with this responsibility.

(Hambleton 1987:6)

To protect a school library from the actions of would-be censors, school divisions need to develop comprehensive selection and reconsideration polices which they adhere to rigorously. Selection policies are the method used by Boards of Education to legally devolve the responsibility for the selection of library resources to professional school staff. They provide the guidelines for the selection practices in each school, and ensure that the process of choosing resources is undertaken by personnel with training in selection. A selection policy is a Board's means of stating publicly its belief in intellectual freedom for children. In addition to providing an objective process for dealing with requests for reconsideration, this statement acts as a warning to would-be censors that sound selection practices are supported in the school division. The anecdotal comments of the respondents to the survey questionnaire in the recent Saskatchewan study indicate that this message has not been clearly articulated in the school libraries across our province.

The Saskatchewan Survey
The comments indicated that the practice of soft censorship is prevalent in our public schools. Of the ninety-two comments

recorded, forty-seven (51%) were statements describing and justifying this practice. A number of reasons were given by library staff for pre-censoring materials. The first reason was because of budgetary considerations. As one teacher librarian stated, "With our limited budget, we can't afford anything we're not very sure will support our curricula without being 'socially acceptable'. We have had very few questions".

Other respondents cited pressure from fundamentalist religious groups as a reason for practicing soft censorship. This pressure is reportedly exerted in several ways. One rural teacher librarian was requested to compile a bibliography of "books which dealt with anything related to sexuality" for review by members of her local school board. Later, she had to defend the library's role of providing "appropriate information on sensitive topics" for students. Another rural teacher librarian made a conscious choice not to buy Robert Munsch's book, *Giant*, in order to avoid "a hassle". She reported, "The public library has this available therefore, I 'chickened' out. This decision was based on the religious aspect of the book and the fundamental tone of the town". An urban teacher librarian was forced by public pressure, to bypass any selection criteria and collection building principles that had been established because "a religious group carefully monitors books added to the collection" and adds materials they feel are suitable for the library although the literary quality of the works is questionable. Finally, in one instance, censorship insinuated itself throughout an entire public school via the coercion exerted by a number of staff members. "One of the schools where I work has a staff where several members, including the principal, share common religious beliefs that condemn the observance of Halloween and the use of books and materials referring to ghosts and the supernatural. This subtly acts as a censorship device since school themes are planned to exclude these topics and teachers are discouraged from using materials that deal with these topics". Still other respondents claimed to use soft censorship as a method of fostering morality among the students by monitoring the collection. "Personally," wrote one rural aide, "as the individual in charge, I'm very cautious in selection -- I do not approve of substandard literature in the library nor do I support the current 'trends' kids desire. I have no R.L. Stine, Babysitter Club or Degrassi". Another aide stated, "In selecting books, the basic policy is to avoid those with profanity or obscenity". Still a third, in the library of a K-12 school noted, "Any titles containing detailed sex, party, drinking scenes and/or negative attitudes towards [morality] (ie. Planned Parenthood) found by staff, or on a cursory [review] by myself are removed and kept off the shelf. Some titles (ie. Stephen King) are available for reading by Grade XII students only". Stephen King's works are available, though with some obvious reluctance, in the previous school. Other respondents were not so charitable. A rural technician in a composite school states that in her school, "We have been very fortunate in having virtually no challenged material in our library. However, I am careful!... I feel there is a broad distinction between school libraries and public libraries. I, for example, don't put Stephen King books in the library... no 8 year old needs to read Stephen King... Stephen King is full of violence and swearing, so I'm trying to make the point that there is a difference between proper selection and censorship". Other respondents have made comments such as the following indicating the person concerned strongly viewed his/her actions simply as "good selection practice."

I choose not to purchase books on Satanism or demonic fiction.

We try to choose books that are not likely to be offensive.

We approach the 'challenge challenge' by avoiding it. In other words, we don't order those materials which we know would be a source of conflict.

We use selective censorship when selecting materials -- ie. we try not to order 'adult' materials for our middle school.

The teachers, principal and library technician usually do screen most of the materials in the library.

The conservative values present in the communities served by these libraries are clearly an incentive for this protective pre-censorship. As one rural teacher librarian stated very blatantly, "I am careful to order materials which are appropriate for the ages of the students in our school. I try to be aware at all times of materials with cultural or gender biases and of the standards of the community in which this school is located." These are good selection practices, but the cautionary tone indicates a librarian who is unsure of the support that would be available should a challenge occur, and who is not about to push the boundaries of the community in any way. Library staff are not the only soft censors active in Saskatchewan school libraries. One respondent, an urban teacher librarian, spoke of "a novel that our principal objected to because of language... I pulled it and gave it to the public library." Another teacher librarian in a city school noted "We have author readings in our school every year and twice in the last 4 years the principal has moved to censor the readings." Other teacher librarians reported that, "In my fourteen year career most challenges have come from staff -- particularly the principal", and "I find more challenges coming from school staff and administrators than from outside the school". This same sentiment was echoed by an aide in a rural school who claimed "The only censorship that has occurred since I have worked in the library has come from within the school (school staff)." Statements such as these enhanced the statistics provided in this study which indicate that the second largest group of challengers after parents and guardians are members of the school staff. Because not all respondents added comments to their submissions, one can only speculate that the practice of removing resources, perceived by school personnel as being controversial, is even more prevalent than the limited number of comments received indicates. The practice of soft-censorship appears to be based on fear -- fear of repercussions within the home community (this is particularly true where pressure groups are active censors); fear of losing a job should a challenge escalate into a public confrontation; fear that support from school administrators would be nonexistent if the library staff attempted to stand up for the principle of intellectual freedom.

As one teacher librarian blatantly stated, "Because I am not sure what support I would receive from the administration via the challenge policy, I 'select' carefully." Comments from library colleagues would suggest that perhaps her fear is not unfounded. In addition to the instances of soft censorship, a large part of the censorship activity in Saskatchewan's public school libraries consists of formal challenges to the resources. The Saskatchewan Writers' Guild survey was distributed to 546 public schools and replies were received from 342 libraries -- a response rate of 62.5%. Reports from a total of 97 school libraries in the final sample indicated that challenges had been initiated against one or more of their resources during the past three years. Thirty-three of these school libraries were in urban schools while 64 were in rural areas. In other words, almost twice the number of reported challenges occurred in rural schools compared to urban schools. Contrary to what the literature on censorship in general would have led one to believe, the majority of the censorship activity in Saskatchewan was in the elementary (K-8) schools with 60 (61.9%) of these schools reporting challenges. The second largest category reporting challenges were the composite (K-12) schools. However, in these schools, the majority of the titles challenged were ones generally used in elementary grades. Only 14.4% of the censorship took place in secondary schools. In public school libraries throughout the province, 151 resources were challenged during the three year period of the study, many of them repeatedly, so that in all, approximately 250 formal challenges were initiated. The resources challenged included children's books, young adult novels, non fiction titles, periodicals, videos and drama scripts. For the purposes of this study, the resources were grouped into two categories, one category for books, and a second for periodicals and non-print resources. Figure 1 includes the titles of the ten most frequently challenged resources in each category, while Figure 2 summarises the various reasons for the challenges (these are displayed in order of frequency, the ten most common reasons, province-wide, for challenging resources).

Figure 1: Ten Most Frequently Challenged Resources in Rank Order of Frequency

Resource	Author
1. Goosebumps	R.L. Stine
2. Giant or Waiting for the Thursday Boat	R. Munsch
3. Pigs	R. Munsch
4. Witches	R. Dahl
5. Baby Blues	P. Kropp
6. Fear Street Series	R. L. Stine
7. Bumps in the Night	H. Allard
8. Revolting Rhymes	R. Dahl
9. Sweet Valley Romance, title unspecified	F. Pascals
10. The Stupids Step Out	H. Allard

Periodicals and Non-print Titles
1. Windscript
2. Young and Modern
3. MacLeans Magazine for "Sex in the Vatican"
4. Flare
5. Pro-life News
6. Spin
7. Teen
8. Sports Illustrated for "Swimsuit" issue
9. Disney videos
10. Song of Superman video

Figure 2: Ten Most Frequent Reasons for Challenges

1. Witchcraft or use of the supernatural
2. Materials inappropriate to the students' maturity level
3. Violence
4. Inaccuracy of information
5. Explicit sex
6. Profanity
7. Obscenity
8. Defiance of authority
9. Nudity
10. Racism and/or religion

Depending on where the library was located, the ranking of the reasons varied as is shown in Figure 3, which illustrates the most common reasons for challenging resources in both urban and rural libraries. The majority of people challenging the resources were the parents or guardians of the students. This group was closely followed by classroom teachers and school principals as illustrated in Table 1.

Figure 3: Reasons for Challenges - Urban and Rural

Urban	*Rural*
1. Violence	1. Witchcraft
2. Inappropriate to Maturity of Student	2. Inappropriate to Maturity of Student
3. Racism	3. Explicit Sex
4. Morality	4. Morality
5. Obscenity	5. Violence
6. Profanity	6. Profanity
7. Nudity	7. Defiance of authority
8. Explicit Sex	8. Obscenity
9. Religion	9. Nudity
10. Sexism and Stereotyping	10. Religion

The same situation existed whether the school library was located in an urban area, and whether the library was in an elementary, secondary or composite school. Approximately one-third of all challenges were the result of actions by the school staff. The Education Act in Saskatchewan stipulates that all school divisions in the province have a selection policy in place and that this policy should provide a mechanism for handling challenges to any school resources. Despite this fact, 30.9% of the responding libraries had no such policy. Many library aides responding to the questionnaire indicated that they were unaware of the existence of a policy in their school division and thus could not respond to the question.

Table 1: Sources of Challenges to Resources

Source	Number of Challenges
Parent/Guardian	69 (62.2)*
Student	1 (0.9)
Teacher	9 (20.7)
Principal	7 (6.3)
Administrator	3 (2.7)
Board Member	2 (1.8)
Librarian	4 (4.1)
Other Library Staff	2 (1.8)
Total:	111 (100.0)

* In all tables, the percentages appear in parentheses. Numbers of challenges are greater than 97 since resources may have been challenged more than once.

Clearly, many library personnel faced with challenges were not only unaware of the proper procedures to follow, but also of the availability of support in a potentially emotional and trying situation. These factors most certainly affected how these people dealt with challenges occurring in their libraries. Unfortunately, whether or not a policy existed seemed to have little bearing on the resolution of a challenge. As Table 2 points out, in the majority of cases either a selection policy did not exist (21.4%) or was not used (29.4%).

Table 2: Use of Selection Policy During Challenges

Use of Policy	Number of Challenges
No Policy	43 (20.87)*
Used Extensively	33 (16.01)
Used Somewhat	66 (32.03)
Policy Not Used	59 (28.64)
No Response	5 (.02)
Total:	206 (97.57)

* Percentages do not total 100 due to missing cases.

When the policy did exist, it was used extensively in only 16.4% of the cases. About a third of the time a policy was only partially used. This indicates that where selection policies exist, they are not likely used with staff members, and they are probably used sporadically in the case of challenges brought by the public. This is unfortunate, since school libraries with effectively implemented selection policies and challenge procedures experienced fewer challenges. The lack of use of a selection policy is reflected in the results of the challenges to the resources.

Table 3: Results of Challenges to Resources

Results	Number and Percentages
Resource Retained	83 (41.9)*
Resource Removed	81 (40.9)
Use Restricted	27 (13.6)
Resource Altered	7 (3.5)
No Response	8 (.03)
Total:	206 (99.93)

Table 3 reveals that 41.9% of challenged resources were retained in the library collections while the remainder, 58%, were either removed completely (40.9%), were restricted (13.6%) or altered in some way (3.5%). It is difficult to know if these data reflect an inability to protect resources through the use of the selection policy, a fear of the turmoil that can be caused by censorship activists, or a pro-censorship stance being assumed by library staff. The comments of the respondents indicate that the prevalence and acceptance of soft-censorship probably had some bearing on the outcomes of the challenges.

Other factors also influence the number of challenges a school library receives. In Saskatchewan, libraries are generally staffed either by teacher librarians (usually in urban schools) or teacher-aides (in rural schools). Teacher librarians handle approximately 20% more challenges than the next largest category of staff. This is undoubtedly related to the fact that professional staff are more likely to select and include in their collections a wider variety of materials on diverse topics. The collection is thus open to more demands for reconsiderations. In addition, because teacher librarians have been alerted to censorship issues through their professional training, they are more likely to resolve a challenge to a resource through an accepted process. Teacher-aides, on the other hand, are more likely to consider the right to remove resources as a function of the professional staff in a school and comply with requests for the removal of resources made by teachers or administrators without using the challenge process. In addition, the study found that on the whole, school libraries in the province use very few reliable sources in selecting resources, with rural schools using fewer selection aids than urban schools. It was disturbing to note the heavy reliance on publishers' catalogues indicated by many respondents. These catalogues are purely a means of advertising a product and are in no way meant to offer discretionary or critical reviews that evaluate materials according to educational or literary standards, yet they are the second most commonly used selection aid, with resource displays placing first. It is difficult to defend resources that have not been chosen according to established criteria and literary standards.

Two additional relationships that affect the number of challenges in a school library should be noted. There is a relationship between the type of school, the qualifications of the staff, and the amount of time library staff are allocated to perform their duties. Schools with secondary students (K-12 or 9 12) are more likely to have qualified, professional staff in the library, for longer periods of time. In the final sample, 44.7% of secondary school libraries were staffed by teacher librarians (the next largest category being teacher-aide at 21.4%). This is possibly related to the perception that research is an activity of higher level learning and therefore, secondary students require assistance in handling information for research papers. Where teacher librarians were employed as library staff, challenges to resources were generally handled through an established challenge procedure, and the resource was generally retained. The retention rate dropped sharply where non-professional staff were employed.

Finally, indications are that censorship is not growing in the province. Generally speaking, challenges have not increased since 1992, and in some instances may have decreased slightly. This might seem to be an encouraging statistic but one must question whether the present level of censorship is acceptable, and one must also be aware that the prevalent incidence of soft censorship is not included in this statistic.

Implications for Saskatchewan Education

There are several implications for present day education arising from this study. Whenever and wherever censorship occurs, it will narrow horizons, limit thinking and diversity, and create a restrictive, closed attitude in the classroom. Such an atmosphere Such an atmosphere directly contravenes the spirit and intent of Saskatchewan's Goals for Education and the province's attempt to implement a resource based curriculum. Saskatchewan Education intends that students will develop an acceptance of a multi-cultural, global environment; tolerance for multiple viewpoints; and awareness of political, economic, social and artistic diversity among people and countries. It expects that students will not only develop the ability to think critically and creatively, but be able to find, examine, evaluate, generate and apply information gleaned from various sources in a variety of formats.

Students are also expected to develop the ability to learn independently and accept responsibility for their own education. These goals are difficult to attain where censorship limits access to conflicting ideas, opposing world views, differing cultural milieus, or divergent lifestyles because they may be controversial or because they exist outside the community norm. Students need to develop those skills which will allow them to become discriminating consumers of information. This will not be possible where access to resources is limited or restricted.

Equally, teachers will find their instructional strategies restricted where censorship occurs. It is difficult to teach students to "analyse", "contrast and compare", for example, where only one dominant viewpoint exists in a library collection. It is also difficult to individualise instruction and to retain flexibility in teaching methods when library or teaching staff have decided that certain ideas and information are inappropriate for the maturity level of the students. Jonathan Green, in *The Encyclopedia of Censorship* (1990) comments, "Censorship assumes people are stupid, gullible, weak and corrupt." In other words, censors assume students are unable to discriminate between accurate and inaccurate information, discern bias and prejudice, identify rational and irrational ideas.

One has only to visit an elementary class taught by an open, inquiring teacher to recognise that this is a misconception. Early in their school life, children can be taught to question the reliability of a resource, evaluate literary works, question the actions and emotions of fictional characters, react in a discerning way to an author's ideas, appreciate well-developed characters, plots, and themes, and reject resources that do not meet high standards. Censorship prevents students from developing a personal value system by making the comparisons and evaluations that allow them to decide what is 'good'.

It was clear from the comments of respondents in the study that the restrictive economic climate may be partially responsible for the amount of censorship presently occurring in education. Where budgets are limited, a decision may be made to concentrate on purchasing materials that support one aspect of a topic rather than spreading the resources thinly across an area to support two opposing views. The choice of 'how to think' about a subject is thus, inadvertently, made for the student. No matter how restricted a library budget is, the principles of good selection can still be followed, the balance in the library collection maintained, the concept of inclusion rather than exclusion adhered to, and the needs of both the curriculum and the individual student considered.

A restrictive stance toward resources also has implications for a future that will be characterised by an expansion in the volume of information that reaches our communities and schools as they are bombarded from cyberspace. The Internet looms large on all horizons. In recent months, the media have been flooded with the news that first Germany, and more recently Thailand, were attempting to censor the use of the American Internet feeder, CompuServe, throughout their countries because they deemed some of the programs to be pornographic in nature. While the attempts were unsuccessful, they did force CompuServe to modify its delivery system.

Schools and parents have also been frantically investigating ways to put 'Nannies' in place; restrictive menus that prevent children from gaining access to unsavoury information. While restrictive menus may be worthwhile for schools in terms of focusing learning during instructional time and conserving financial resources paid out for each minute a student is 'online', there is simply no way to completely protect students from information. Teaching students to manage information wisely and competently is a more reasoned approach. Unlike the woman who recently confessed on radio to almost killing her prize cat by changing its diet to pure calf's liver on the advice of a fellow traveller on the information highway, students need to become questioning, discriminating handlers of information. Teaching the skills necessary to achieve this solution should perhaps become the focus of teaching in all schools. The restrictive attitude of the censors, both inside and outside the school, can prevent educators from reaching this goal.

Censorship stifles creativity -- artistic, scientific, or philosophical. By restricting the access to information, censors impair a student's ability to become a discriminating, thoughtful participant in a democratic society. In contrast, by advocating effective selection practices supported by qualified professional staff, educators encourage students to grow intellectually, to develop and affirm a personal system of values, to become responsible, discerning thinkers. For while censors attempt to narrow and restrict knowledge and conform to preconceived ideas and values, effective selectors attempt to spread before their students a banquet of the choicest portions of information and to teach them to choose, digest and assimilate, wisely and thoughtfully, from the feast.

References

Amey, L. (1988). Pyramid power: the teacher librarian and censorship. *Emergency Librarian,* 16 (1): 15-20.

Asheim, L. (1983). Selection and censorship: a reappraisal. *Wilson Library Bulletin,* 53 (3): 180-183.

Bryson, J.E. and Detty, E.W. (1982). *The legal aspects of censorship of public school library and instructional materials.* Charlottesville,Va.: Michie.

Burress, L. (1983). *Newsletter on intellectual freedom,* 1 (1), 8.

Cavanagh, G. and Styles, K. (1981). The many faces of censorship. *Canadian Library Journal,* 38: 123-125.

Fiske, M. (1959). *Book selection and censorship: a study of school and public libraries in California.* Berkeley, Ca: University of California Press: 70, 102-111.

Green, J. (1990). *The encyclopedia of censorship.* New York: Facts on File: vii-ix.

Hambleton, A. (1987). Literature worth the name does not lie: Selection and censorship. *The Medium,* 31 (4): 26-30.

McCarthy, M. M. (1993). Challenges to the public school curriculum: New targets and strategies. *Phi Delta Kappan*, September, 75: 55-60.

Reichman, J. (1988). *Censorship and selection: Issues and answers for schools.* Chicago: American Library Association.

Roxburgh, S. (1988). In M. I. West (ed.). *Trust your children.* New York: Neal-Schuman: 121-122.

Simmons, J. (1994). 'Political correctness -- the other side of the coin.' In J. Simmons (Ed.), *Censorship: A threat to reading, learning, thinking.* Newark, Delaware: International Reading Association: 57-61.

Steptoe, J. (1988). In M. I. West (ed.). *Trust your children.* New York: Neal-Schuman Publishers: 94.

Woods, L.B. and Salvatore, L. (1981). Self-censorship in collection development by high school library media specialists. *School Media Quarterly*, 9 (3): 102-108.

Some Discussion Questions

Discussion No. 1

> No library exists as a repository for all ideas. In point of fact, this whole idea of whether or not parents should be allowed to participate in this process is very hypocritical. The very fact is that many choosings and limitings have occurred on the part of other elements in this mix and the question now is should parents be allowed to participate. All sorts of genuine, true, real censorship has occurred, including that practiced by the librarian.
>
> (Ronald Godwin, Vice President, Moral Majority)

- Do you agree with this statement? Is there a difference between censorship and selection? If there are differences, how does one explain these differences to a parent, colleague or school administrator? If no difference exists, why are the two terms used by librarians?

- How can a librarian respond to a majority of the community who say they don't want their tax dollars spent on materials containing ideas they oppose? Does a teacher librarian have a duty to expand the horizons of students in a school in such a community despite the stated objections, or is it a librarian's job to build a collection that will reflect the community's values?

- How can a dissident individual or group in the school respond to a library whose collection reflects only the views and tastes and values of the majority in the school community?

- Should the teacher librarian consult teachers, the principal, and parents before selecting a potentially controversial book? Who should have the final word?

Discussion No. 2

The library represents the storehouse of our culture. It is the place in the country where information covering all points of view is available to anyone who needs or wants them. All sides of every issue should be represented in the library.

(Judith Krug, American Library Association)

Suppose they went out and bought a book teaching genocide. Suppose -- I mean, just this principle that every idea is fine and can be in a library. Suppose they glorified Hitler or preached mass murder of Jews. Or suppose they had in a library a book which white children were borrowing that was preaching inherent inferiority of blacks and it was disrupting things in the school. You have to have some limit on what you want kids to read. Don't you really? I mean, do you really want them to read a book preaching genocide?

(Judge Ralph Winter, U. S. Court of Appeals, Second Circuit)

- Are all libraries really neutral storehouses of knowledge and experience as Ms. Krug suggests? Or are school libraries, in particular, part of an overall educational apparatus whose goal is to mould young minds?

- With the availability of unlimited information on the Internet, are cultural groups worldwide in danger of losing the specific value system(s) they wish to inculcate in their young citizens? Should this be prevented? How?

- Do school library collections and public library collections differ from one another? How?

Discussion No. 3

Children belong to parents and the parent and the school should work harmoniously together where possible. And there has to be pragmatic cooperation. But quite literally the parents' wishes should prevail.

(Ronald Godwin, Vice President, Moral Majority)

No one here is talking about kids. They're the ones who are going to be able to read these books or not able to read these books and they have very clear ideas about what they want to read and why.

(Judy Blume, Author)

- The parents, society and the child all have an interest in the education and upbringing of the child. Where do the rights of one leave off and the other's begin?

- What should be the role of parents, school officials, (elected and appointed) teachers, taxpayers, education professionals, and students themselves in the selection of educational materials? Who should have input? How much? Who, if anyone, should have a veto?

Discussion No. 4

It's the context in which the resource is used and the context in which the material is taught, the relationship between the teacher and the student... Some people think if we study something in a book, film or tape that we condone it. There is no reason to think that because something is portrayed in a book or film that the school is sanctioning that attitude.

(June Berkley, Department of English, Ohio State University)

- What is the role of public education in a democratic society? To what extent should the schools teach critical and independent thinking, and to what extent should they inculcate the community's values? Who defines these values?

- How far should an educational program go in introducing provocative ideas, or even controversial themes? If a line is to be drawn, who should draw it and where?

- Where does education end and indoctrination begin?

Acceptable Use of the Internet in Schools: What would YOU do?

*Georgia Phillips**

In order to discuss the applicability of library standards to education information technology services, I have fabricated the following scenarios, and included some of the library principles, Australian and American, which seem relevant. This idea comes from Jamieson McKenzie's article, 'Creating Board Policies for Student Use of the Internet' in *From Now On: A Monthly Electronic Commentary on Educational Technology Issues*, 5 (7), May, 1995 at <http://fromnowon.org/fnomay95.html>.

What would YOU do?...

Case #1 Explicit Language
You are teacher librarian and system administrator at Gum Valley High School. HSC students at your school are studying a novel which has been the subject of much controversy of late. Material about this book is available on a discussion group which has been downloaded to the Intranet for student use. A parent complains about the explicit language when a print out of this material is taken home. The principal asks you to remove this material from the server. Should you remove this material?

The Australian Library and Information Association, *Statement on Freedom to Read*, states:

> *A librarian should not exercise censorship in the selection of materials by rejecting on moral, political, racial or religious grounds alone material which is otherwise relevant to the purpose of the library and meets the standards, such as historical importance, intellectual integrity, effectiveness of expression or accuracy of information which are required by the library. Material should not be rejected on the grounds that its content is controversial or likely to offend some sections of the library's community.*
> <http://www.alia.org.au/policies/freedom.to.read.html>

---

* **Georgia Phillips** is a teacher librarian, currently holding the position of Technology Project Officer with the Training and Development Directorate, New South Wales Department of School Education in Sydney, N.S.W., Australia. Georgia may be contacted via email at <pngphillips@illawarra.starway.net.au>

The Australian School Library Bill of Rights states:

The responsibility of the school library is: To place principle above personal opinion and reason above prejudice in the selection of materials of the highest quality in order to assure a comprehensive collection appropriate to the users of the library.

(Does this statement help?)

The American Library Association's statement on 'Challenged Materials' says:

[I]t is the responsibility of every library to have a clearly defined materials selection policy in written form which reflects the LIBRARY BILL OF RIGHTS, and which is approved by the appropriate governing authority.

<http://www.alia.org.au/policies.html>

You should clarify your authority, create a selection policy consistent with intellectual freedom, and apply it fairly.

Case #2 Software Filters

You are a Social Studies Head Teacher and have heard that many racist groups maintain sites on the Net. You would like your Year 10 class to critically examine these 'hate sites' in order to further their understanding of bias. The ICP says you can not access these sites as they are restricted by SmurfPatrol. What do you do?

The Australian Library and Information Association, *Statement on Freedom to Read*, states:

3. The functions of the librarian include: to promote the use of materials in the librarian's care; to ensure that the resources of the library are adequate to its purpose; to obtain additional information from outside sources to meet the needs of readers; to cater for interest in all relevant facets of knowledge, literature and contemporary issues, including those of a controversial nature; but neither to promote or suppress particular ideas and beliefs.

<http://www.alia.org.au/policies/freedom.to.read.html>

The US 'Library Bill of Rights' says:

Materials should not be proscribed or removed because of partisan or doctrinal disapproval.

<http://www.ala.org/work/freedom/lbr.html>

The Australian Centre for International Research on Communication and Information Technologies (CIRCIT) - Conclusion 10 states:

The Commonwealth Government should actively promote teaching skills in the critical assessment of the content of on-line services. The increasing use in education of content derived from electronic networks introduces new issues such as authentication of authorship and puts new slants on issues such as copyright and plagiarism.

The Reading and Viewing strand of the national English profile includes the teaching of critical assessment of print, film and television material. This needs to be expanded to ensure that students are able to understand the range of ways in which content is placed on electronic networks and how to critically assess this content.

<http://teloz.latrobe.edu.au/circit/>

So, don't deny access to something just because it is offensive to many or even to yourself. If you believe that the principles of intellectual freedom developed for libraries apply to educational computer sites, you should override the restriction to the material in order to use it for the purposes of studying bias. Assurance must be made that all students learn to discriminate and think critically.

(Lastly take a look at Jamie McKenzie's parody of filters at <http://fromnowon.org/smurf.html>).

Case #3 Student Publishing
You are a Webmaster at Lake Paluka High School and have had students designing and creating the school web site. They have used an aesthetically pleasing leafy background for the school's main web page. A parent complains that the leaf used is a marijuana leaf. The principal orders you to take off the entire school web site and deny access to the 'offending' students. What do you do?...

It is the responsibility of your school to develop guidelines for publishing on the school's web site, and to have them approved by the school administration or other appropriate authority. These guidelines should include student publishing. As long as these are adhered to, student involvement should be welcome.

Identify the leaf. Have students change pattern if necessary and show to principal. Refer to your school Acceptable Use Policy which should state consequences of publishing 'inappropriate' material.

Case #4 'Libel' on Mailing List

You are a system administrator at Clamsville School. Your site has a mailing list for community members. You have just received email from Paulette McHanson, local fish shop owner. She says she is suing your school because students have "libelled, slandered, and defamed her character" and caused her "great emotional stress, and problems with her family and friends." List discussion participants spoke up. They said they did talk about racism and unsubstantiated slurs made by Ms. McHanson. They said this was legitimate and should not be censored. What do you do?...

The Australian Library and Information Association, *Statement on Freedom to Read*, states a librarian should uphold the right of all Australians to have access to library services and materials and should not discriminate against users on the grounds of age, sex, race, religion, national origin, disability, economic condition, individual lifestyle or political or social views.

You should get advice from legal counsel. No action should be taken because of a one-sided legal threat.

Case #5 Filtered Sites

The state Department of Education Internet computers have been delivered with a software package already installed which Internet blocks access to a great many seemingly innocuous sites, including a World War II site needed by history students at your school. This has been done without any consultation within the educational or wider community, and without any accompanying guidelines or policies. You are the School Internet Manager. What do you do?

The Australian Library and Information Association, *Statement on Freedom to Read* says:

> *A librarian should not exercise censorship in the selection of materials by rejecting on moral, political, racial or religious grounds alone material which is otherwise relevant to the purpose of the library and meets the standards, such as historical importance, intellectual integrity, effectiveness of expression or accuracy of information which are required by the library concerned. Material should not be rejected on the grounds that its content is controversial or likely to offend some sections of the library's community.*

<http://www.alia.org.au/policies/freedom.to.read.html>

The ALA *Library Bill of Rights* says:

A person's right to use a library should not be denied or abridged because of origin, age, background, or views.

The ALA's *Free Access to Libraries for Minors* says:

. . .[P]arents - and only parents - have the right and the responsibility to restrict the access of their children - and only their children - to library resources. [...] Librarians and governing bodies cannot assume the role of parents or the functions of parental authority in the private relationship between parent and child.

The ALA's *Access for Children and Young People to Videotapes and Other Nonprint Formats* says:

ALA acknowledges and supports the exercise by parents of their responsibility to guide their own children's reading and viewing.

The ALA Intellectual Freedom Statement says:

With every available legal means, we will challenge laws or governmental action restricting or prohibiting the publication of certain materials or limiting free access to such materials. Don't stop access by minors unless your competent legal adviser says you must.
<http://www.alia.org.au/policies.html>

Case #6 *Student's Personal Details*
You are a teacher working with students who are publishing their work with biographical sketches on your school web page. The department's technology section has visited your site and noticed that you have published student photos with their names. They have asked you to remove your site. What do you do?

Draft guidelines for publishing on the New South Wales Department of School Education (NSW DSE) Web site state that "it is the policy of the DSE not to disclose personal details of students or DSE staff without prior approval." (NSW DSE, *Protocols and Guidelines for Publishing on the DSE Internet Service,* 11 December 1996 Draft)

Delete names. Leave the site up. Ensure parental and student approval obtained. Abide by school publishing guidelines. Ensure student safety.

Case #7 *Unsupervised Use*

An elementary teacher extremely enthusiastic about the Internet encourages students to browse through the Internet during 'free time'. He feels Year 5 are old enough to make reasoned judgments about materials and he warns them to stay away from certain sites. One day a group of his parents descend upon your office (principal) to complain that their children have been browsing Danish pornography in the back of the classroom while the teacher corrected papers in the front of the room. Your action? Over to you!

Case #8 *Defamation of School*

An Assistant Principal at Mount Black Primary School has found a site on a university server which lists educational facilities. This site has defamatory statements included about him and his school. He gets in touch with his district Technology Adviser and complains. You are the Technology Adviser. What do you do?

Refer to the Director, School Technology, to contact the University regarding their guidelines for publishing. They are responsible. Legal counsel could be contacted if necessary.

A useful reference is *Guidelines for the development of policies, regulations and procedures affecting access to library materials, services and facilities* located at <gopher://ala1.ala.org:70/00/alagophx/40728008.document>.

Lastly, I strongly recommend reading Jamie McKenzie's article 'A Dozen Reasons Why Schools Should Avoid Filtering' in *From Now On*, 5 (5), March/April 1996 located at <http://fromnowon.org/march96/whynot.html>. Then suggest where we in NSW go from here. Every school has now been provided with an Internet computer pre-loaded with CyberPatrol, a greatly invasive and restrictive software filtering package. No consultation took place within the educational community nor the wider community.

What would YOU do?

Developing a School Acceptable Use of the Internet Policy: the Process

Kerry Wellham[*]

Most Department of School Education schools across New South Wales can now offer their students access to the Internet. While the Internet offers an overload of information, it should be our aim to guide children, parents and staff in making informed decisions about the use of the Internet and the value of the information they discover. It is also our challenge to encourage our students to transform this information into knowledge, this knowledge into learning and this learning into wisdom. To apportion responsibility for using the Internet in schools, acceptable use policies must be developed in schools.

What to find in an Acceptable Use Policy

As with other school policies that describe acceptable student behaviours, an acceptable use policy should clearly outline expectations for staff, students and parents. It should be linked to other standards for students' rights and responsibilities. It can help educate stakeholders on what to expect of the Internet, the boundaries of behaviour, and consequences of violation. Including contracts for students, parents and teachers, this policy can honour freedom of speech, privacy, copyright and equal access to information for all.

An Acceptable Use Policy should include:

- an explanation of the Internet (including some of its benefits)
- a rationale (purpose) for the policy
- scope of the policy
- the beliefs underlying the policy, relating to the Internet and its use
- responsibilities which outline unacceptable use
- consequences and repercussions of breaches of the contracts
- Student contract
- Parent contract

---

[*] **Kerry Wellham** is a teacher librarian, and at the time of writing was seconded as a TILT Facilitator for the New South Wales Department of School Education, Newcastle District, N.S.W., Australia. Kerry may be contacted via email at <kwellham@norfolk.nf>.

- Teacher contract
- Management procedures (including make up of an 'action group' to create, implement, oversee and assess the policy), the responsibilities of the action group, procedures for violation and assessment procedures
- a strategic plan,
- and a bibliography.

The Process: a Strategic Plan

Action 1: Define the need for a policy and its possible scope.
Personnel: TL, School Executive, District Technology Team.
Responsibilities: To raise awareness for the need of this information policy, to ensure procedures are in place to support the creation of this plan, to ensure school has all correct DSE documentation.
Resources: appropriate DSE documentation.
Cost: Nil.
Time: 5 weeks.

Action 2: Clarify involvement of personnel and resources. Form action group.
Personnel: Action group (Principal, Classroom teacher, TL, parent).
Responsibilities: Clarify actual roles and responsibilities within the group, clarify types of support needed to write and implement policy.
Resources: as above.
Cost: Nil.
Time: 5 weeks.

Action 3: Locate possible support (services and materials, including other policies, publications, articles, Internet sites...)
Personnel: TL.
Responsibilities: Create thorough list of possible resources, articles, support services and personnel, acquire copies of all necessary documentation and articles/ sites.
Resources: Release time, access to Internet, indexing and abstracting services.
Cost: $380.
Time: 3 weeks (but continually updated).

Action 4: Identify within these services, good examples and useful information. Create a comprehensive list.
Personnel: Action group.

Responsibilities: Read and note suitable terminologies, references, find other possible sources of support, use Internet itself to gain overview of how best to implement into classroom use.

Resources: Collated documentation, release time, Internet service and online time.

Cost: $360.

Time: 10 weeks.

Action 5: Identify and classify key issues to be included. Select suitable information from support materials.

Personnel: Action Group.

Responsibilities: Classify keyword guides, what should be included in policy, how policy should be worded.

Resources: Above documentation.

Cost: Nil.

Time: 10 weeks (same 10 weeks as above).

Action 6: Write draft policy, including budgetary implications and school beliefs in relation to the Internet. Make it clear and brief.

Personnel: Action group, school assistant.

Responsibilities: Using above guidelines, brief draft to be formulated, write actual policy with references (TL using wordprocessor), edit and format draft policy.

Resources: Knowledge gained so far, paper, use of word processor, release time.

Cost: $90.

Time: 10 weeks.

Action 7: Present draft policy to stake holders (parents, staff, students)

Personnel: Action group, Technology Adviser, TILT Facilitator for district.

Responsibilities: Conduct staff meetings, conduct parents awareness night, conduct sessions for staff on use of Internet in classroom.

Resources: Copies for all staff, publicity, TILT component No 2.

Cost: Nil.

Time: 4 weeks.

Action 8: After feedback, publish and disseminate policy.

Personnel: Action group, School Assistant.

Responsibilities: Decide on any necessary changes, rewrite any necessary changes, rewrite any necessary changes, send copy to National Library, collate final product into professional document.
Resources: Paper, binding machine.
Cost: Nil.
Time: 3 weeks.

Action 9: Implement policy: send home contracts, create file to house contracts....
Personnel: Staff of school.
Responsibilities: Ensure all students who could be using the Internet have read and signed the appropriate policy and contract. Contracts to be housed in file in Library.
Resources: Copies for students, parents, file for contracts.
Cost: $12.
Time: 3 weeks for initial implementation, and then as necessary.

Action 10: Assess success and further needs/ directions.
Personnel: Action group, school executive.
Responsibilities: Conduct appropriate assessment procedures, write notes and observations, evaluate implications, ensure brief report is ready for Annual School Report.
Resources: Discussions with students, parents, teachers, possible questionnaires, photos, record any infringements and actions taken, procedures for notifying Department of extreme breaches or external threats.
Cost: Nil.
Time: Continual.

Action 11: Include assessment in annual school report:
Personnel: Principal, District Assessment Team.
Responsibilities: Prepare for meeting with District Assessment Team, Add evaluation of policy to Annual School Report.
Resources: Analysis of successes and problems, assessment results.
Cost: Nil.
Time: 15 weeks.

Action 12: Commence planning for Information Literacy Policy, Procedures and lesson plans:
Personnel: New Action Group (Principal, TL, Technology Committee members).

Responsibilities: Commence planning for the creation of follow up policy on Information Literacy (use of technology and the Internet in the school and wider community).

Resources: Appropriate literature searches, articles, Internet sites, actual policies.

Cost: From next policy budget.

Time: 12 to 18 months (at about same time as action 6 commences).

References

Anderson, J. (1996). Internet Use - a primary perspective. *SCAN,* 15 (4): 27 - 29.

ALIA. (1996). ALIA/ASLA joint statement on library and information services in schools. ALIA Policy Statements Online. Available <http://www.alia.org.au/alia/policies/services.in.schools.html>. Accessed 5 January, 1997.

Beasley, Aja A. (1996). Hot list for 'Acceptable Use' policies. Acceptable use policies. Available <http://199.205.20/WebPages/ DLL/ConsultantsAja-B/AcptUse.htm> Accessed 2 January, 1997.

Bennetto, E. and Manning, M. (1996). *Learning for the future: Developing information services in Australian Schools - Teacher Resource Kit.* Belconnen, ACT: ASLA.

Chaparro, C. (1996). Policy and Censorship on the Internet Online. Available <http://trfn.clpgh.org/Internet/Policy/policy.html>. Accessed 2 January, 1997.

Dillon, K. (1996). Management of student access to the Internet: Issues and responsibilities. *SCAN,* 15 (4): 32-35.

Franklin Web Team. (1996). Acceptable Use Policy. Ben Franklin Middle School Home Page. Available <http://fms.crcmedia.com/ policies/aup.html>. Accessed 2 January, 1997.

Haughton, Sally. (1996). 'Acceptable Use Policies' The Internet in the Classroom Online. Available <http://www.ucalgary.ca~mueller/ aup.html>. Accessed 3 January, 1997.

Loosely, Stephen. 'Internet code of practice.' 3 February,1997. Online posting. <Oz-Teachers@owl.qut.edu.au>. 4 February, 1997

NSW Department of School Education. Technology in Learning and Teaching. (1996). Available <http://dse.nsw.edu.au/tilt/detail/comp.html>. 16 December, 1997.

Simeone, P. (1996). The challenge of the Internet across curriculum. *Access*, 10 (4): 27 - 29.

What you need to know about acceptable use policies. Acceptable Use Policies (1996). Available <http://www.covis.nwu.edu?AUP-archive/CoVis-AUP.html>. 31 December, 1996.

Topic B

Children's Literature and the Internet:

Issues and Services

Visiting Authors on the Web

*Ashley Freeman**

Traditional 'live' author visits have generally proved to be a popular and successful way of motivating and extending students with regard to their own writing and their recreational reading. They have themselves also shown to be a positive way of promoting the library within the school community. Such visits normally involve the teacher librarian, or a group of teacher librarians, investing a considerable amount of time and effort in arranging for an author to visit a school or cluster of schools. The author or illustrator then arrives, speaks to and responds to students about her or his life and work and departs leaving behind (if all goes well) inspired and delighted students and teachers and a tired but happy teacher librarian. An associated issue is cost. Authors generally survive on surprisingly low incomes, but they still need to be able to eat. Hence their travel, accommodation, and sometimes a fee, frequently need to be paid.

The question thus arises; as there are an increasing number of author pages appearing on the World Wide Web can they offer a viable and relatively cheaper and effortless way of achieving much the same results as 'live' author visits? Obviously it is not possible to provide a definitive answer to such a subjective question, but hopefully this paper will provide some perspectives from which to view it.

It is certainly true that there is an expanding number of author home pages on the Web. One only has to visit sites such as the *Children's Literature Web Guide* <http://www.ucalgary.ca/~dkbrown/index.html> or Vandergrift's *Children's literature page* <http://www.scils.rutgers.edu/special/kay/childlit.html> or to search using terms such as 'children's authors' on search engines such as Yahoo to find a number of author home pages.

---

* **Ashley Freeman** is a lecturer in Teacher Librarianship with the School of Information Studies at Charles Sturt University, Wagga Wagga, New South Wales, Australia. At the time of writing Ashley was also the Reviews Editor for *Reading Time: Journal of the Children's Book Council of Australia*. Ashley may be contacted via email at <afreeman@csu.edu.au>.

As this paper originates in Australia, the home pages of Australian authors are considered first. There are surprisingly few. A number of searches resulted in only the following hits:

Graeme Base
<http://www.penguin.com/usa/childrens/bios/base/base.html>

Mem Fox
<http://www.friend.ly.net/user-homepages/j/jorban/scoop/biographies/mfox.html>

Morris Gleitzman
<http://www.ozemail.com.au/~andrewf/morris.html>

Paul Jennings
<http://people.enternet.com.au/~jennings/>

John Marsden
<http://www.ozemail.com.au/~andrewf/john.html>

Natalie Jane Prior
<http://www.gil.com.au/~dragon/>

Tim Winton
<http://www.ozemail.com.au/~andrewf/tim.html>

Also worthy of mention is the Australian Authors of Children's Books section from *OzLit* <http://www.vicnet.net.au/%7Eozlit/children.html> which lists a number of Australian authors, giving the names of their works and a link to their home page, if they have one. The entry for Ursula Dubosarsky is noteworthy in that it contains considerably more information on this author and her work than the other entries.

It is also pertinent to include *Colin Thompson's homepage* <http://www.ozemail.com.au/~colinet>. While British, he is currently resident in Australia and created his latest work, *Tower to the Sun* here.

There are probably other Australian author home pages which I have not yet found (please let me know of any of which you are aware) and there are a few fringe sites which I have chosen not to include, such as the *Norman Lindsay Appreciation Site* <http://www.real.com.au/~ncoates/NLINDEX.html> where the focus is not on Lindsay as a children's author. There are also false trails; the Margaret Clark home page, for example, turned out to be the home page of an academic at the University of Melbourne - Dr

Margaret Clark. Searching on the Internet can almost be as time consuming as organising a 'live' author visit!

The content of these home pages varies considerably. Natalie Jane Prior's home page is disappointing in its brevity and lack of anything substantial (I gather this site is soon to be extended). At the other end of the scale, Colin Thompson's page (created by himself) is full of the type of pertinent material that is part of a successful 'live' author visit such as an insight into the ideas and inspiration behind his works, his plans for the future, examples of his intricate art work, the opportunity to communicate directly with him (via email), his whims and humour, and current information (his page is regularly updated). Sadly (and rather oddly) the home page of the creator of *Animalia* (Graeme Base) is straight text, while Mem Fox's page is basically a short fun letter format (auto)biography with a photograph of her and a few commercial links. The remainder tend to be enjoyable, well presented and informative pages, especially those of Gleitzman and Jennings, but not to the standard of Thompson's page.

The implications of this is that the 'live' author visit is still by far the better option for interacting with and being inspired by Australia's children's (and young adult) authors. Indeed in most cases it is the only option. This is not to say that Australian author home sites, where they exist, do not have value, at the very least they provide some information on that author and/or the author's work. While currently they do not, overall, compare with the availability and input of a live author, an increase in the number and quality of sites would be very desirable and of benefit to the authors as well as students, teachers and teacher librarians.

The greatest advantage of author home pages for Australian schools is the access provided to information on, and occasionally through email to, overseas authors. Here, where there is little possibility of 'live' visits, student access is obviously increased through the power of the Internet. While the lists of authors online provided at the *Children's Literature Web Guide* and Vandergrift's *Children's Literature Page* look impressive, in actuality they would represent only a very small percentage of all authors. It is also important to note that several of these sites are for deceased authors and are created and maintained by fans, enthusiasts or publishing interests. (This does not necessarily diminish their value.)

While numbers may be relatively small there are nonetheless some well-known names and impressive sites. Well-known authors present include:

Eric Carle
<http://www.eric-carle.com/>

Roald Dahl
<http://www.nd.edu/~khoward1/Roald.html>

Tomi dePaola
<http://www.opendoor.com/bingley/mywebpage.html>

Herge
<http://www.du.edu/~tomills/tintin.html>

C.S. Lewis
<http://cslewis.cache.net/>

Katherine Paterson
<http://www.terabithia.com/>

Beatrix Potter
<http://www.wwwebguides.com/authors/society/potter/beatr.html>

R.L. Stine
<http://place.scholastic.com/goosebumps/index.html>

Among the more highly acclaimed sites (as indicated on the *Children's Literature Web Guide*) and well worth inspection as indicators of the access possible through 'virtual visits' are:

Virginia Hamilton
<http://www.virginiahamilton.com/>

Kevin Major
<http://enterprise.newcomm.net/kmajor/>

J.R.R. Tolkien
<http://www.csclub.uwaterloo.ca/u/relipper/tolkien/rootpage.html>

Thus, it is unlikely that virtual author visits will eclipse live author visits in the short term. Ideally the two forms will not only coexist, but will increasingly compliment each other. Author home pages are increasing the access available to authors, and to information on authors, and have the potential to increase significantly in number and to be enjoyable, innovative and informative sources. It will be interesting to see to what extent this potential is realised.

The Fear of Surfing

Colin Thompson[*]

At the beginning of 1994 I was invited, as one of about fifty children's authors and illustrators, by my UK publisher Random House, to attend a multi-media conference. This was about CDROM development rather that the Internet, but what happened applies equally to both.

We were all shown a CDROM from Random House in America and we all thought how clever it was that you could click your mouse on a door and it opened. We thought it was wonderful that the characters sang and danced and we could interact with them. But five minutes after the demo had finished the general excitement had turned to gloom. *"It's the end of life as we know it,"* people were saying. *'No one will ever buy books again."* *"We're too old to change,'* some said, as they saw their careers vanishing overnight.

Of course this attitude was ridiculous. I've no doubt exactly the same thing was said by everyone in radio when television started, but of course they were all missing the point. What was happening was something new, something that would stand alongside what already existed, not replace it, except maybe in certain areas of reference books. You couldn't curl up in bed and read a CDROM and how many people had home computers, and how many would want to pay three or four times the price of a book to get something that when you looked at it dispassionately, was far less sophisticated than stuff that Disney had been doing sixty years before?

The reason everyone was frightened was because it was all new. Of the fifty authors and illustrators I seemed to be the only one who had ever seen any of this stuff before. One or two used wordprocessors but most still wrote by hand or worked on typewriters. I was the only one who was interested in all the new computer technology. I had a computer since the early eighties, well before I had been a children's author.

---

[*] **Colin Thompson** is an English author and illustrator, now based in Australia. Colin can be contacted via email at **<colinet@atlantis.aust.com>**. Colin's WWW homepage is also available at **<http://www.atlantis.aust.com/~colinet>**.

What most people at the meeting failed to realise was they weren't alone in their Luddite attitudes. Apart from the two people making the presentation, all the other Random House employees there, felt the same way about these new developments. The difference was that they kept quiet about it.

The point of the meeting had been to 'introduce us to the future' and see what ideas we could come up with for CDROMs. I couldn't wait to get started. As far as I was concerned CDROMs combined all the things I was good at with all the things I liked. I could write, illustrate and play around on my computer and, if what Random House were telling us was true, I could also become a millionaire extremely rapidly. This was better than perfect!

A week later I went back to them with several ideas. This was three years ago and the number of CDROMs produced by Random House UK so far hasn't quite topped zero. Compared to books, CDROMs are very expensive to produce, far more than they need to be. This has been used as the excuse for inaction but in reality it's because like all publishers, with one or two exceptions, they are terrified of the technology. In their hearts they do believe that it will mean the end of life as they know it, that no one will ever buy books again.

You see a huge modern building with a big publishing conglomerate's name on the front and you assume that inside, everything runs on super-efficient oiled wheels. Well it doesn't. It runs on obsolete equipment that is incompatible with that in the next office. If you offer to supply your text on a disk, they say thank you and then re-type everything by hand. Even though most of the small publishers have been swallowed up by these large groups, and are run by accountants rather than people who love books, they still seem to operate the same as they did before but without taking the risks their forefathers did. Publishing is the career of gentlemen and technology is what people in factories do. I have only just had my first email from a publisher and they were as pleased with themselves as my daughter was when she learnt to tie her shoelaces. I'm sure that really important stuff is still sent by pigeon or a man with a message stick.

Over the next few years CDROMs as such will largely be replaced by online material available over the Internet. Most homes will have a box connected to their TV and through this box you will be able to get movies on demand, surf the Internet, send email, shop, follow the stock exchange and many, many other interactive things. These boxes already exist. They are cheaper than computers and will undoubtedly become as commonplace as video recorders are now.

Unless today's book publishers change their attitudes and embrace all this new technology as something exciting that can expand their markets, they will be left behind. And what is worse, they will be pushed aside by new companies that have none of the experience that publishers can offer, and our children will be offered lower and lower quality products, ninety percent of which involve killing something before it kills you. Software engineers are, by and large not the people who should be producing this stuff. They may be brilliant at making little people leap over tall buildings, but they are not always the best people to create the people or the buildings or decide why they want to leap in the first place.

It's perpetuating the endless divisions between creative ideas people and those who actually have to make those ideas come to life. How many buildings, machines, cars have been sketched out on paper only to be cut down and modified by those who have to make them because of practical considerations caused by lack of communication. Too often the result is mediocrity and unless publishers make the effort to put authors and illustrators together with software people a great opportunity will be lost and ultimately a lot of people will be put off by the poor quality of what's on offer. After all, not all of us want to eat greasy burgers in bland buns.

The point is that the Internet offers the possibility for something entirely new and publishers seem unable to realise this. The majority of CDROMs for children are tired old books, that should have been pulped years before, being recycled with as little effort as possible, into 'multimedia' products. Adding a few whistle and bells does not make a good CDROM, just a fast short-term buck. The initial novelty of CDROMs has worn off a lot and many people are now realising that what they thought was wonderful was really no more than mutton dressed as lamb. A good CDROM should be something that does not, or cannot, exist as a book, or at least takes a book and enhances it like many of the excellent products put out by Dorling Kindersley.

I have recently created my own site on the Internet where children (and adults) can find out all about my book and even answers to the big eternal question, not - 'What is the meaning of life?' - but - 'Where do you get your ideas from?' People can send me email from the site and there is a link to a bookshop in Sydney, Australia where they can order any books they can't get hold of locally. I had a great time creating the site which took me about a week to set up and in the few weeks it's been running I have had a wonderful response from all over the world. From now on, my homepage and email addresses will be printed in all my books too. It's a lot quicker and cheaper for me to type ten emails than it is to type ten letters and envelopes, stick stamps on them and go to the postbox. Also publishers have a terrible habit of hanging onto letters for up to three months before forwarding them by which time the children have assumed that you can't be bothered writing back to them, which I always do. One child in America wrote with a list of questions because she wanted to do a school project on me. By the time I got the letter it was six weeks too late. With the Internet, individual children or adults or whole school classes can send me messages and get a reply within a couple of days.

How many publishers do you know that have a site on the Net? One or two at most and they are generally patchy and very incomplete. Two years ago I came to live in Australia and here there is a higher percentage of people on the Internet than any other country in the world (so I have been told). The Australian people welcome modern technology with the sort of enthusiasm that publishers now need to be showing.

Right now I am in the middle of final editing for my next picture book. This means couriers rushing out colour prints of the pages from the UK which takes about four days and no doubt costs a small fortune. If my publishers would take advantage of the technology that is actually sleeping on their desks, they could email the pictures to me in a couple of hours. I suppose it's like the shampoo advert - it won't happen overnight, but it will happen.

Finally, please join with me in demanding that the words - edutainment - and - infotainment - be made illegal and punishable by five years in jail being forced to watch Flopsy, Mopsy And Cottontail Get Interactive.

Meandering in Cyberschool

*Kay E. Vandergrift**

The World Wide Web (WWW) is powerful both as a teaching tool and as a metaphor for teaching itself. The interactivity, the versatility, the non-linearity, and the multiple alternatives available to learners on the WWW seem to me to be the very essence of what teaching is all about. In fact, the WWW may serve as a model for the workings of the human mind as a complex design process relating new knowledge to what is already known. The specific knowledge gained is often not as important as the empowerment of the learner exercising at least some degree of intellectual control in making connections between and among what is available on the Web and what already exists in the mind. If the responsibility of the teacher is to compose learning environments to foster that sense of empowerment and of joy in discovery that encourages lifelong learning, the WWW is an ideal teaching tool.[†] Content, context, and community, essentials of teaching and learning, take on whole new dimensions on the Web.

Teachers develop and shape content, place it in multiple contexts, and assist in building learning communities[‡] whether that occurs in a self-contained classroom or in cyberspace. Using the Web in teaching, curricular content is not bound by textbooks, traditional teaching materials, or the individual teacher. Specific content may be designed and direction given, but the learner is free to explore alternative pathways to new content.

This is not to say that teaching and learning are characterised by aimless wanderings or lack of purpose, although some of our most inspiring discoveries are found as a result of intellectual twists and turns with no fixed direction in mind. Even when one enters the Web for a particular purpose or to access specific information (and it is certainly possible to do so), the acquisition of data or satisfaction of a need may lead to a new, unanticipated route. Often the desire to reach a set destination gives way to a sense of destiny as encountering new ideas or meeting new minds assumes priority. In this way, each student creates individual learning paths, shapes

[*] **Kay E. Vandergrift** is a Professor in the School of Communication Information and Library Studies at Rutgers University, New Brunswick, New Jersey, USA. An electronic version of her paper is available at <http://www.scils.rutgers.edu/special/kay/entrance.html>.

personal meanings, and can share ideas or validate new knowledge with others in the virtual world as well as within the classroom community. Encountering Web content or the creators of that content from different perspectives encourages the recognition that there is no one right way to perceive the world and helps students to break out of the limiting contexts of a particular teacher, classroom, discipline, region, or nationality. Thus, teaching is less about control and more about helping students sort out, select, and make sense of many alternative meanings.

At its best, the creative use of WWW technologies blurs the lines between science and art and is an ideal way to extend young people's involvement with literature. Like a picture book, the Web combines text and illustration to create a virtual world that can be experienced in many different ways and from many points of view. Critics study literature by examining authors, audiences, and the external world recreated in a work, as well as the text itself and that text within the author's canon, a particular genre, or the larger literary canon. Each of these approaches to a literary work is enhanced by access to information and ideas on the WWW. Most readers enjoy learning about the authors of favourite books, and this is certainly confirmed by the popularity of author websites.[§] The focus on audience reception or reader response theories of literary criticism[**] has always been important in teaching and has achieved scholarly importance in recent decades. For those involved in this kind of literary study, the Web vastly expands the interpretive community and facilitates the examination of factors that influence response and interpretation. Simultaneously, students begin to break out of the personal and cultural confines of their own responses as they discuss literature with others in that expanded interpretive community.

Teachers have long used stories to extend and enhance understanding of history and of other cultures; but, with the WWW, that understanding can be extended exponentially. Imagine, for instance, US students in a community with almost no cultural diversity discussing a story about Japanese-American Internment camps[††] during World War II with Japanese-American students from around the country. Since many Japanese students study English, and novels such as *Journey To Topez*[‡‡] have been translated into Japanese; it would be possible to extend the discussion to students in Japan. Young people from other nations could also add their perspectives in a truly international forum about one of many aspects of American history frequently ignored[§§] in the authorised curriculum. That forum could be enlarged to include historians and other adults who lived through the internment camp experience. What has been true of older technologies is also true of the WWW. Students must be taught to be enlightened consumers and critics, as well as creators, of the products delivered through that technology. Certainly one of the most frequently raised questions surrounding the Web is that of authority. It is true that anyone with adequate resources can create a webpage, but the same might be said for the publication of a book; and few of us would consider that reason enough to bar young people from bookstores. Instead, we can capitalise on interest in the Web to teach critical skills that will enable students to identify and benefit from the very best websites.

Assuming access to the WWW and an excitement about its possibilities for teaching and learning, there are still many questions to be considered before deciding to develop a website. The first considerations must be educational. Who is the intended audience? What is the purpose of the website?[***] What content is most appropriately placed on the Web? How is true inquiry built into the site rather than just activity? Can websites be designed to meet personal learning styles? How does a teacher imbed fundamental philosophical beliefs into a website? For instance, how are gender-fair and multicultural principles communicated to website users? How can the WWW be encompassed into the ongoing learning environment rather than being used only for 'enrichment' or 'reward'? At what point do graphic and technical elements (illustration, sound, animation, etc.) cease serving as an integral part of the content, as enticement, or as enhancement and become distractions from content? How can we be certain that images, especially clip art images representing racial, ethnic, national, religious, or cultural groups, are not stereotypical or offensive?

Other questions have to do with the allocation of resources, both personal and technological. How much time and energy can a teacher devote to a website without shortchanging students in the primary learning environment? Is there enough Web access for students to benefit not only from the local site but from global resources? How are anticipated users likely to access the website and how does this influence web design? If students participate in developing websites, how involved should they be and how is this work justified as an aspect of their learning? How does a teacher balance quality control of the site with authentic learning and fair evaluation of each student's work? How does one attribute authorship when students do initial work but the teacher verifies and adds to the site and assumes responsibility (perhaps with future students) for maintenance and updating? Once the intellectual content and design is achieved, is it a legitimate use of students' school time to work on the technical aspects of preparing materials for the Web?

After a website is mounted, new questions come to the fore. Of critical concern to the educator, now Webteacher, is: How much time can be allocated to the maintenance of the site? Even the most simple sites often require updating and/or enhancement and those with external links must be verified regularly to assure that the sites linked are still functioning and that the content is still appropriate. Many sites also generate a great deal of email. Interactivity is one of the greatest advantages of the Web, of benefit to the creator as well as to the consumer. Confirmation and compliments are gratefully received, as are some suggestions for additions to a site. It becomes clear, however, that many users assume that the availability of a website means its creator is also available as a reference librarian, a bibliographer, or a research assistant to anyone who can relate a personal project even tangentially and remotely to the content of the website. It is essential to consider where the teaching responsibility ends. As a teacher, one may be able to distinguish among sincere but naive inquiries, students from other institutions trying to enlist someone to do their homework, trivia questions, and interesting intellectual challenges. All of these require time, if only the reading time, and most present teachable moments. The problem is that the number of those moments is so great that responding can become, literally, a full-time responsibility.[†††]

While the technology is still young, it is important to think through the educational possibilities and implications of the WWW. The name itself suggests one of greatest possibilities. The Web is truly a global medium, allowing users to reach beyond geographic boundaries to share information and ideas and to engage in dialogue with people throughout the world. Those of us with English as our primary language are fortunate that many other language communities study English and are willing to accommodate us in communicating. Although there will undoubtedly soon be programs for simultaneous translation on the Web, perhaps this global electronic sharing will encourage English speakers to learn other languages to more fully understand and appreciate cultural nuances.

Those interested in children's literature might use the Web to do more collaborative work, both nationally and internationally. There are many children's literature websites,[‡‡‡] but there is abundant duplication among them. To some extent, this is of value as users encounter different approaches to a topic or different titles selected for a bibliography on that topic. On the other hand, we might present a fuller and more useful picture of the field if we could agree to work on different aspects of the general body of knowledge and then share areas of specialisation based on geography, personal history, or professional expertise. On the international scene, we might begin by encouraging the listing of award winning books and key authors and illustrators from every nation. The ability to see a bookjacket and read a brief annotation would at least create an awareness of existing works worldwide and, hopefully, stimulate interest and exchange. Of course, there are problems of translation too numerous to discuss here; but, even within the English-speaking world, there is far too little of this kind of sharing.

Teachers will continue to be concerned about authority, plagiarism, copyright, censorship, and child protection on the WWW. This is essential, but it is also essential that we see the Web clearly for its possibilities as well as its limitations and its dangers. Never before has it been so easy for students and teachers to expand intellectual boundaries and become active participants in a global community. Well used, the Web offers a wealth of scientific, aesthetic, and cultural information that can be personally tailored for and quickly delivered to individual learners. Literature has always been one of the ways human beings reach out to each other across time and space. The WWW also breaks those barriers and, in so doing, increases the capacity of users not only to gain information, but to understand and appreciate others.

[†] This first excerpt is taken, with permission, from my 'Building a Web Site with a Brain', *School Library Journal*, 42 (4), April 1996: 26-29. "Those concerned with helping young people develop inquiry skills might also want to consider matching teaching and learning styles with various resources and approaches to content. At present, most websites concentrate on providing resources, but some do provide commentary, opinions, questions, or interactive capabilities. School or library sites, for instance, might set as their purpose any of the following:

To offer additional resources that supplement existing curricular materials, either for greater depth or for alternative perspectives on a topic.

To select a particular event in history and look at that event from multiple perspectives, raising a variety of questions and providing resources as a model for approaches that students might take in their research. For example, the incarceration of Japanese-Americans in re-location camps during the Second World War might be explored from the personal perspectives of the incarcerated as well as of those in government and the military. It might also be examined as an example of mass hysteria, bigotry, opportunism for monetary gain, and the vilification of those who appear different. [Footnote: Readers will find an additional example on Christopher Columbus in my *Power Teaching*. Chicago, IL: American Library Association, 1994, pp.60-65.]

To fill in gaps of knowledge that may extend the understanding of a literary text. For instance, young people who read and enjoy *Lyddie* may gain both greater appreciation of that story and of U.S. history by learning about the New England mill girls, labor conditions, and views of women in that setting. Readers' responses to science fiction and works of authors such as William Sleator may be enhanced through learning about the scientific principles underlying the stories.

To develop opportunities for students to explore topics that are neglected or given only superficial coverage within the school curriculum. For instance, a Web page or pages might be devoted to specific instances of historical controversies related to human rights such as the trials of Joan of Arc, the Chicago Seven, Emma Goldman, the Rosenbergs, and Sacco and Vanzetti. [Footnote: An early exploration of hypermedia in relation to a literary text that also focuses on the Sacco and Vanzetti case is found in my article, 'Hypermedia: Breaking the Tyranny of the Text', *School Library Journal*, 35, November 1988: 30-36.]

To help young people realise that there is no one right answer to frequently asked questions by examining how such answers are skewed by different resources, different media, different perspectives and different points in time.

To match and extend the content of an existing website with additional content or an alternative approach. For instance, a fifteen-year-old girl wrote about women in Arthurian legends for the Booklook website, [Footnote: This can be found at <http://bcn.boulder.co.us/library/bpl/child/booklook/women.html> Boulder, Colorado Public Library, which matches and extends Edward Sullivan's Medieval World homepage.]

To develop the kind of bookwebs now being created by students and teachers in whole language programs. [Footnote: For those unfamiliar with book Webs, see my *Power Teaching*. Chicago, IL: American Library Association, 1994, pp.50-53; 77-100.] as sites on the world wide Web.

To demonstrate how to search a wide range of biographical tools and reviewing media for information and commentary about favourite authors and books.

After considering these questions one must still recognise that to create a website a decision depends on many additional factors, such as, knowing what is already available on the Web, identifying a potential audience, [Footnote: Given the global nature of the WWW, the audience may be anyone in any place in the world. The primary audience, however, may be a local community accessing a particular website for information relevant to that community. Languages may also be a primary concern for a website in a community where more than one language predominates.] determining sufficient quality content for that audience, and accessing a server for a new website. [Footnote: The organisation that provides access to the Internet can usually also function as the Web Server. Web browsers such as Netscape are available free to schools and public libraries. It is important to note that direct access to the server, that is, loading and removing Web pages, may be tightly monitored by managers of net servers. Information on servers, including commercial servers, is available in many of the books in the bibliography.]

‡ Readers might find the following useful in looking at sharing literature: <http://WWW.scils.rutgers.edu/special/kay/sharelit.html>.

§ The author page I have in my website contains over 400 authors/illustrators, including many from Australia: <http://WWW.scils.rutgers.edu/special/kay/author.html>.

** Readers might find the following of help: <http://WWW.scils.rutgers.edu/special/kay/readerresponse.html>.

†† Information on the Japanese-American Internment camps is found at: <http://WWW.scils.rutgers.edu/special/kay/internment.html>.

‡‡ The citation is provided to the original book written in English and also included is a transliterated citation to the Japanese translation of the book. Uchida, Yoshiko. *Journey to Topez: A Story of the Japanese-American Evacuation.* New York: Scribner, 1971. Uchida, Yoshiko. *Topazu e no Tabi: Nikkei Shojo Yuki No Monogatari.* Yaku Shibata Kanji. Tokyo: Hyoronsha, 1975.

§§ To examine a number of Websites that explore issues in American History, often neglected in teaching, see: <http://WWW.scils.rutgers.edu/special/kay/americanhistory.html>.

*** This second excerpt is taken, with permission, from 'Building a Web Site with a Brain', *School Library Journal,* 42 (4), April 1996: 26-29.

Determining a purpose for a website depends upon institutional and/or personal goals and on the interests and knowledge of the persons involved in its creation. It also requires careful thinking and design strategies, including a discussion of questions such as the following to help in the decisions concerning purpose.

• What is the anticipated benefit to both creator and consumer?
• Is public image of quintessential importance so that establishing a homepage best addresses image building, either for a person or an institution? For instance, a school library might decide that a website highlighting young people's accomplishments is the best way to build community support for funding for technology.
• Is 'missionary zeal', that is, the desire to stimulate interest in a topic or share a personal passion, the prime motive?
• Is establishing a website critical for equalising use of resources in a world increasingly dividing rich and poor in access to information? Or does it further divide the information rich and the information poor?
• Is providing possibilities for locating alternative views and significant numbers of resources a prime motivation?
• Is thinking and communicating globally a cardinal value to be developed through a website?
• Is creating a website that excites, entertains, provokes, entices, or intrigues a user a driving force?"

††† I have a large number of examples of email correspondence that demonstrate all of the above issues and problems.

‡‡‡ To locate a number of available websites on children's literature visit: <http://WWW.scils.rutgers.edu/special/kay/childlitWebs.html>.

Book Raps: an Internet Project

Jenny Stubbs[*]

Introduction

In *Booktalk*, Aiden Chambers quotes from a letter he received from a teaching colleague, the words of an 8 year old girl telling her class that, "We don't know what we think about a book until we've talked about it." This reflected Chambers own opinion that "the act of reading lies in talking about what you have read." Agnes Niewenhuizen also recognised this and to promote youth literature in Melbourne has established a programme called 'Book Gigs', which encourages participation by readers to help them to come to a deeper understanding and appreciation of the text and to introduce new literature to a wider audience. Book Circles and book discussion groups have been around for years, but with the introduction of the Internet a new dimension has been added to the meaning.

To quote from Chambers again, "It is psychologically impossible to read something without experiencing a response." Chambers says that this leads to two things. Firstly the reader wants to talk about it with a friend. Children sometimes want to draw or act out what they felt. Secondly they enjoy the experience of reading so much they want to have it again.

What is a Book Rap?

A Book Rap is a book discussion conducted via email but can contain one element of a 'Book Gig' in that the author can sometimes be involved in the discussion. Book Raps began in term one 1996 as one of the online curriculum projects -- *Oz-Projects*. Groups of students or individual students can discuss scheduled books or nominate books of their own choice. Guests for the Book Rap can sometimes involve authors, illustrators and other experts relating to the content of the book. Book Raps have generally been aimed at the upper primary and secondary areas of schooling. 1997 sees the introduction of a rap for children 5+ with Stellaluna and extends the discussion range to an international audience.

---

[*] **Jenny Stubbs** is Teacher Librarian, Ipswich District, Education Queensland and President, Children's Book Council (Qld Branch), Qld., Australia. An electronic version of her paper is available at <**http://www.schools.ash.org.au/schools/jstubbs/bookrap.htm**>. Jenny may be contacted via email at <**jstubbs@gil.com.au**>.

Purpose

Book Raps aim to encourage reading for pleasure and to promote talk about books. As this was an Australian project it also aimed at promoting Australian children's literature via the Internet, although international authors were not excluded.

Teachers have for years been devising various ways to motivate students to read. Everything from innovations on book trees to one hundred and one ways of doing a book report have been attempted to stimulate and motivate children's reading. How many times have these attempts to stimulate reading actually had the opposite effect? Here is a way of developing a love of literature by sharing books with children and having them share with each other that may challenge some of the traditional methods of the past.

Advantages of Rapping

- Students are generally motivated by programs that involve computers in their learning.

- Rapping is interactive as opposed to just using the web for gathering information. The student changes from a consumer to a producer.

- Shared reading experiences allow students to respond to others' thoughts and feelings and empower the students as learners.

- The immediacy of email allows students to maintain their interest.

- The structure of a Book Rap encourages everyone to participate because all responses are accepted. There is no censoring by list managers, although there may be guidance at the school level.

- Students can feel secure that their opinions will be heard. They will often express their points of view and express more challenging ideas via email than in a classroom situation.

- Discussing the book with their peers gives them more security and enables them to consider the differing views of others and to revise their opinions if necessary.

- As more authors and illustrators come on line there is a greater opportunity for students to discuss their reading experiences with them than ever before. The tyranny of distance will be a thing of the past.

Stellaluna - The Rap

Stellaluna was first mooted as a suitable title to rap by Cherrol McGhee, a classroom teacher who had participated in the Connecting Teachers Project funded by Education Queensland. Cherrol taught a composite class of Year 1-4 students and wanted to do a rap with them. Until then, the only raps had been aimed at upper primary and secondary students. She approached her local teacher librarian, Libby Daly and together with myself, Lindy McKeown from *Oz-Projects* at Queensland University of Technology (QUT) and undergraduate Venessa Lean who had conducted some research on Book Raps held an initial brainstorming session to plan the rap.

Cherrol then approached the publishers of *Stellaluna* in America and received a great deal of support including an email address for the author, Janell Canon. Much work followed in locating bat sites online, and bat experts online such as Jill Morris, author of *Australian Bats*. Other resources that could be used in an integrated unit on the book were collected.

More meetings were held to decide on the rap points to be used for discussion by the students and to plan a '*Stellaluna* Web Site' with links from the 'Book Rap Site'. Book Raps in the past have not had web sites attached to them, but it was felt there was so much support material available that a web site was the best way to share the information. It was decided that the rap could be of interest to a greater audience than was initially planned and so junior and senior raps were decided upon.

After the planning it was time to advertise, so emails were sent to all major lists to notify potential participants of the rap. Although the first rap point posting date was 21 April, teachers needed to be aware of what was coming so they could plan to integrate it into their programme. Information about the book and how to join the rap was therefore emailed to the lists a few weeks prior to this date.

Schools began immediately to introduce themselves in preparation for the first rap point. Sample letters may be obtained from the web site at <http://www.schools.ash.org.au/schools/jstubbs/bookrap.htm>.

Story Synopsis

Stellaluna is a picture book written by Californian author, Janell Canon. It tells the story of a young fruit bat separated from her mother and raised by a family of birds. She has to learn to adapt to the different way of life, habits, food and rules of the nest in order to survive.

Themes covered include friendships, comparisons between birds and bats, being lost, and foster families. *Stellaluna* is also available on a CDROM in the Broderbrund *Living Books* series.

Sample Rap Questions

Rap Point One

(a) Name and describe any types of bats living in your neighbourhood.

(b) As you receive messages from other rappers, mark the location and any other information on a world map.

(c) Ask other rappers questions about their local bats.

(d) Send unanswered questions to the bat experts on line at <bat_info@owl.qut.edu.au>.

Rap Point Two

(a) Why do you think mother bird looked after *Stellaluna*?

(b) Tell us about a lost or orphaned animal that you have looked after.

(c) Tell about any animal that you know about which has been fostered by a different animal family. This could be from real life or a book or film.

There will be four Rap points over four weeks, with additional rap points for the CDROM rappers.

How to Get Started:
From the email inviting teachers to join the rap:

You can register now and up to 21 April 1997. The first rap point will be posted on or near then. A rap point will be posted each week with the rap wrap up at the end of May.

To participate, join the list/s which best suits the age of your class.

stellaluna-junior (for young classes 5-8 years)
stellaluna-senior (for older classes 9-12 years)
stellaluna-teachers (for teachers on line help about book raps and resources)
bat-info (sending information about bats and asking questions of our bat experts)

How to Rap:

1. Join the list/lists. To do this, address an email message to <majordomo@owl.qut.edu.au>.

Leave the subject blank. In the main body of the message, type: subscribe (list name)

For example if you wanted to join the junior book rap type: subscribe stellaluna-junior

2. After you receive a succeeded message, it is time for your students to send a message of introduction addressed to:

<the (list name)@owl.qut.edu.au>

For example: <stellaluna-junior@owl.qut.edu.au>

Use the subject : Introducing (your-school-name)

Include: (a) an introduction of your class or group, (b) the name of your school, (c) the location of your school (town or city, state and country).

Please send ONE message for your group.

3. Check the mail daily and mark the other participants on your Rap Map. This is a blank map of the world with the major countries marked. You may need an atlas to help locate the Rappers locations. Use one big map for junior children. Older children may have their own individual ones as well.

4. Read *STELLALUNA* by Janell Cannon.

5. On or near the 21 April read the first rap point and prepare a response.

Mail your response to the address used for your introduction.

6. Check the mail daily and read other Rappers responses.

7. Respond to other Rappers via the list.

8. A new rap point will be posted each week for the next 3 weeks.

9. The rap wrap up will happen at the end of May.

More Stellaluna Book Rap details are available at:

<http://owl.qut.edu.au/oz-teachernet/projects/book-rap/ stellaluna.html>

Lists available for subscribing are at:

<http://owl.qut.edu.au/common-cgi-bin/oz-students/ listsavail.html>

Who to contact for more information on the *Stellaluna* Book Rap:

<cmcghee@b022.aone.net.au> (Cherrol McGhee)

<jstubbs@gil.com.au> (Jenny Stubbs)

<ldaly@gil.com.au> (Libby Daly).

Interested in running a Book Rap yourself? Look in *Oz-Projects* for more information about how to be a coordinator. For more general information on Book Raps and a link to the calendar go to the Book Rap Page. Here you will find archived information on the raps from 1996 such *as Space Demons, Swashbuckler, Over Sea Under Stone* and the Book of the Year Awards.

The Future

I recently attended a QSITE workshop on IRC (Internet Relay Chat) and immediately saw the potential for applying it to the Book Rap Project. It is a bit like combining the Writers On-line project run via Keylink in 1990 with a Rap. A web site could be created for an author and students could then rap about the books by that author. The author could join the online rap and at a set time participate in an IRC (or CU-See-Me) session. Isolated schools who have little chance for author visits can experience a virtual visit. I suppose what is really needed is people with the time and expertise to coordinate these projects.

One international project that is running now is the 'Read In' which is linking up global readers and giving them the opportunity to chat to each other and authors online.

References

Chambers, Aiden. (1985). *Booktalk: Occasional Writing on Literature and Children.* London: Bodley Head.

Topic C

Critical Thinking in the Electronic Age

Multiple Pathways to Knowledge: Empowering Learners for the Information Age.

Karen Bonanno [*]

As we enter the 21st Century it is becoming more apparent that the focus will be information on demand. For the social and economic development of Australia, people will need to acquire knowledge and learn new skills for the future of our nation in a global world of production and exchange, in particular, the production, distribution and use of knowledge.

"Literacy has an effect on people's capacity to adapt to economic change, to participate actively in political processes, and to avail themselves of lifelong learning." (Chapman 1996:21). Literacy can be defined as "using printed and written information to function in society to achieve one's goals and to develop one's knowledge and potential." (Chapman 1996:21).

Literacy can no longer be bound by a traditional focus on reading, writing, listening and viewing, but needs to evolve and expand as the information world becomes more complex. The advent of new technologies has facilitated the move towards more complex literacy skills that will empower the learner as they cooperatively develop literacy competencies through the interactivity of information technology and the ability to communicate effectively with a wider world of creators and shapers of information.

Why? - Setting the Futures Scene
Judith Chapman has indicated that there are some significant trends in the economic and social spheres of worldwide activity that will have serious implications for future educational developments as nations move towards the 'knowledge economy' and the 'learning society' (Chapman 1996:12-25).

(A summary of Chapman's comments appear below with additional information to supplement the trends.)

---

[*] **Karen Bonanno** is Director of the library consultancy firm, Queensland Library and Information Services and currently holds the position of National President for the Australian School Library Association (ASLA). Karen can be contacted via email at <kbonanno@bigpond.com>, or via snail mail at PO Box 255, Moranbah, Qld 4744. This paper was presented at the EduNet97 conference in Melbourne during the Library Information Resources strand on Friday 18 April 1997.

Economic Factors

Nature and pattern of employment

High youth unemployment is occurring across the world leading to the young never gaining job-related skills and failing to secure employability. This lowers their self esteem, has an impact of their health and well-being and interferes with their relationships and integration into the social and community fabric of society. Aspects of crime related activity, substance abuse, youth suicide and poverty are emerging.

In 1997 it is anticipated, in Australia, that 24% of workers will be employed on a temporary or contract basis. (Herrigan 1996:28). The traditional work patterns of full-time, permanent employment will be available to a select few operating as the 'professional core' of an organisation. There will be a shrinking of the 'corporate' world as businesses become lean, mean, low cost, low overhead machines. The second layer of the Australian workforce will comprise the highly paid, highly skilled specialists who will be employed by companies on an outsourcing basis. The third layer will be the temporary and contract personnel. Even though Australia's conversion from temporary to permanent staff is a low 2%, Herrigan says that the figures are changing. "Many people find temporary work to be a useful bridge into full-time employment, enabling them to try out a job before committing themselves to a permanent position." (Herrigan 1996:28).

Population trends

Across the nations there is an ageing labour force. Coupled with the growth industries that are highly skilled, technologically based and service oriented, education of the workforce has extended beyond the K-12 parameters to a K-80, lifelong learning focus.

The face of Australia is changing as our population absorbs an increased Asian migration. It is predicted that by 2030 our population will be 56% of Asian origin.

Changing labour force

The worldwide labour force is experiencing an increase in women in employment, a decrease in men and youth in employment. In Australia alone, approximately 97% of all businesses are small business operations, catering for the self-employed and providing for a growing increase of women in the workforce. Gone are the days when a person entered the workforce at one level with one organisation and stayed with the organisation for their working lifetime. Constant job changes and periods of unemployment are evident. To be able to be employed one will have to be retrained every 4 to 6 years to survive in the new global economy.

Technological change

Computers have changed the way we live and the way we work. What we have seen in the last 20 years will be nothing compared to the changes in the next 10 years. The computer, telephone and television as we know it now will merge.

These changes will alter the type of jobs available. Education and training will need to focus on the development of a highly technologically literate and skilled workforce.

Globalisation

Internationalisation is being replaced by globalisation, not just in the information world, but globalisation has become an integral part of the twenty-four hour cycle of production and exchange.

Societal Factors

Changes in family structure and relationships

There is increasing single parent households, increasing single parent-never married and increasing divorce rates. This has an impact on the income generated per household, influencing the poverty level and therefore assisting in determining those who have access to financial, educational and family activities compared with those who don't. Also, several parents may have a say in a child's education.

Children 'at risk'

These children can be identified as those who are unsuccessful in reaching standards in school, who become drop outs and fail to make the transition to adult life and be fully integrated into the normal accepted patterns of social responsibility in the work force and family life. Contributing factors are linked to poverty, family relationships, low literacy and lack of support. They attain low levels of achievement, experience low satisfaction and self-esteem, indulge in truancy, become behaviour problems, and turn to substance abuse and use of drugs, early pregnancy and crime to sustain an 'identity'.

Underclad

Chapman defines the underclad as 'a class of people who are perceived as living outside society's norms and values and who are separated not only from the more affluent in our community but also from the traditional working classes and others on low income" (Chapman 1996:20). Contributing factors to the development of the underclad are unemployment, changing family structures and poverty.

The working poor, casual, permanent part-time and welfare-dependent make up most of the underclad society.

Non-work related/'leisure' activities
All the above lead to new relationships between work and leisure. For example, unemployment provides extended time for non-work activity. Also, the move to fewer working hours and working from home is fuelling a trend to seek self development, self fulfilment and aesthetic and intellectual orientations.

There will be a need for our current schooling system and methods of delivery to be re-designed around the electronic text of the evolving 'knowledge economy' and 'learning society'. The changes and trends that will occur in the next 5 to 10 years will provide opportunities for the creative thinkers.

> *We are the last generation to be reared within a culture in which print is the primary information medium. Because we have grown up and become skilled in a print-based community, we have developed certain ways of making sense of the world. We are, to some extent, what print has made us. And now we have to change.*

> (Spender 1995:xv)

The new technologies and the changing trends of our global world will challenge the way we 'do' education. It will change the relationships between teachers and students in their pursuit for lifelong learning. The education sector will be challenged by the transition to globalisation, the changing skills of the workforce and employment patterns, technological changes and the social challenge of a national identity.

Lepani has indicated that the result of these developments will create a new architecture of learning. "Eight key principles can be identified which must now inform the new learning architecture for the design of educational services in the knowledge economy.

- *Lifelong Learning* - no longer front-end school learning but continuous across the life cycle to facilitate flexible career paths and enhanced personal development;

- *Learner Directed Learning* - the learner takes increasing control of the learning process with the teacher becoming the facilitator of learning and the diagnostician and therapist of learning difficulties, to enable the learner to achieve optimum learning outcomes;

- *Learning to learn* - developing the capability in individuals and groups to understand and more effectively plan and realise their own learning strategies - the so-called meta-cognition skills of learning;

- *Contextualised Learning* - locates theoretical learning and competencies in different contexts through real life-learning environments and simulations, including action learning - the convergence between academic and vocational learning;

- *Customised Learning* - products and services are designed to meet different learning preferences or cultural/ organisational situations and can be appropriately modified by the learner to meet the particular needs of individuals and groups,

- *Transformative Learning* enables learners to challenge and change belief systems and behavioural patterns, through constructivism, to meet new needs and opportunities, and to overcome disabilities and disadvantage, with particular attention to the development of higher order thinking skills associated with epistemic cognition - the understanding of how knowledges are constructed;

- *Collaborative/Cooperative Learning* - enables groups as well as individuals to learn interactively across time and space;

- *Just-in-Time Learning* - learning opportunities are available from the global learning 'supermarket' when and where learners need them to meet their learning needs - whether these learners are students, their parents, teachers or principals."

(Lepani 1996:22)

A new form of information literacy and management driven by the interactive, multimedia, information learning technologies of the day will need to emerge. Students will need to develop an ability to effectively define, locate, select and organise information to then share and create their reconstructed knowledge in a variety of formats that include text, image and sound.

DATA
↓
Researching
Accessing
Comprehending
↓
INFORMATION
↓
Critical & Creative
Thinking
↓
KNOWLEDGE
↓
Linking
Conceptualising
Synthesising
↓
EDUCATION
↓
Application
Judging
Philosophising
↓
WISDOM

What? - Considering Multiple Pathways

Early perspectives on 'library skills' tended to focus on 'the library' and paid little attention to the fluid and evolving process of the development of information literacy skills. Over the years many of the professional associations of teacher librarianship in Australia have developed information literacy frameworks which are a part of a holistic process and non linear in nature allowing the learner to develop an information-gathering model that reflects their own learning style and searching process. The emergence of electronic information technologies and associated resources, together with information management systems in Australian schools, has required a change from the strategies traditionally used with print resources.

An Australian national information processing framework was developed in 1993 and published in *Learning for the future:*

Developing information services in Australian schools (1993). This framework incorporates the non linear steps of:

- defining,
- locating,
- selecting,
- organising,
- creating/sharing and
- evaluation.

The learner is able to return to earlier steps as the need arises as they progress through the search and retrieval process. The framework also integrates the interactive skills of literacy (reading, writing, listening, speaking, viewing, drawing), critical thinking and problem solving skills.

In 1994 the Australian School Library Association(ASLA) received funding from the National Professional Development Program (NPDP) Strategic Initiatives Element to develop an interactive multimedia CDROM professional development program entitled *Teaching Information Skills* The nationally developed information processing framework provided the backbone for this program. The CDROM content demonstrates, in real-life case study situations, effective teaching and learning strategies for resource based teaching and learning of information skills and competencies. The CDROM addresses an Australian need for all teachers and teacher-librarians to obtain professional development so that they can integrate information skills and competencies into the curriculum in similar terms to those presented in the National Statements and Curriculum Profiles.

In the USA similar information processing frameworks have been developed. At the *Big Six* Web site <http://ericir.syr.edu/big6/> the six steps that make up the Big Six model and components are as follows:

1. Task Definition
    Define the information problem
    Identify information needed in order to complete the task (to solve the information problem)
2. Information Seeking Strategies
    Determining the range of possible sources (brainstorm)
    Evaluate the different possible sources to determine priorities

3. Location and Access
        Locate sources (intellectually and physically)
        Find information within sources
4. Use of Information
        Engage (eg.) read, hear, view, touch) the
        information in a source
        Extract relevant information from a source
5. Synthesis
        Organise information from multiple sources
        Present the information
6. Evaluation
        Judge the product (effectiveness)
        Judge the information problem-solving process
        (efficiency)

Another USA model, the Follett (1994) information skills model incorporates:

- appreciation/enjoyment,
- presearch,
- search,
- interpretation,
- communication and
- evaluation.

Within this model learners can develop an overview of the task, integrate broad concepts, locate information providers, identify information resources and tools, search for relevant information, interpret information, organise and format information, share new knowledge and evaluate the product and process.

Within all these frameworks/models learners will develop their literacy skills and will also develop abilities to formulate, summarise, explore, identify, select, filter, infer, evaluate, assess, compare, contrast, analyse, classify and synthesise information. They will be able to communicate and share their new knowledge by creating, speaking, writing, demonstrating, designing, composing and presenting through appropriate formats.

The information literacy skills embedded in these frameworks/models will enhance the 'new learning architecture' defined by Lepani.

Other associated issues that will need to be addressed are acknowledging sources from within an information rich environment. Students will need to be encouraged to develop habits of giving credit where credit is due. By monitoring each stage of the research process it is possible to determine the authenticity of the students work in conjunction with their individual writing style and their level of ability. This can be linked very closely to the development of Acceptable User Policies (AUP) as students begin to access digital information via worldwide networks. It is the responsibility of the school to develop such a policy to assist students to make informed decisions about the information they are gathering. Visit the Acceptable User Policy Web site located at <http://www.newlink.net/education/help/aup/>.

When? - Determining Points of Access
A recent experience with a group of first year education students during a tutorial class revealed their lack of understanding of the complexity of the information process. Having walked them through the process in relation to their prescribed assessment task, their outcry was, 'Why didn't someone teach me this when I was at school?' Probably, they did, but was it within a context for learning or as an isolated incident?

Young children enter their formal schooling years with a curiosity for learning. They come to the classroom with a baggage of learning experiences on which teachers can build. Often the recognition of prior learning is not accommodated in these early years and knowingly or unknowingly teachers undo the learning and knowledge base.

Take this story as an example:

> By the time Emma Camille Schwartz was five years old, she knew high-tech. At the age of two she had mastered the buttons on the VCR at home in Chicago. By three she could manipulate the mouse that operated her mother's Macintosh computer. Soon she was calling her friends and her grandmother on her father's car phone and contacting her father on his pencil-size pager. Emma knows how to operate the family's CD stereo (though she's not allowed to). She records her own songs on a Radio Shack tape recorder and uses a play calculator to experiment with numbers. At play group she can easily converse with the other preschoolers about the video worlds of 'The Little Mermaid' and 'Bambi'.
>
> In the Fall, when Emma starts school, she is in for a culture shock. When she walks through the schoolhouse doors, she will leave the

plugged-in, wired-up world she has known thus far and enter one that still considers television an innovation.

(Fiske 1992)

There has been much talk about the technological backwaters of schools and the archaic nature of school curriculums across Australia that seem to be embedded in a past century of learning and education. The story of Emma does not seem quite so far-fetched when one considers that by the year 2000 intelligent agents of the digital world will be like well trained 'English butlers' and communicate directly with their human 'masters' or control the lighting, heating and air conditioning of our homes. Intelligent agents, AutoComputers, ViewPhone and InterNETional Colleges are already being trialed in America and Europe (Cropper 1997:48).

Information skill development must be taught in a context of study rather than as a separate activity. The learner needs to be activity involved and have an understanding of the purpose of the skill development. Initially, they may need to be supervised or provided with individual help in their early attempts to apply the skill and monitored in their development. Repeated opportunities need to be available for the student to learn and evaluate their success in using the skills. The skills need to be developed sequentially and with increasing levels of difficulty as the student moves from simple to more complex inquiry tasks. Many of the skills will be developed concurrently.

The inclusion of information skills in many of the strands in the national curriculum profiles is indicative of the importance being placed on an inquiry-based approach to learning and of students needing to become effective users of information and lifelong learners.

How? - Planning a Strategy
In January 1996, Education ministers of OECD countries met to consider the evolving global and information-based economy and to focus on lifelong learning in schools, the workplace and other locations that foster 'learning societies'. The challenge for the government is to develop policy to not only ensure that Australia advances in the economic world, but to ensure that all Australian citizens are able to participate effectively in Australia's economic growth; to be contributing citizens and benefactors of the same. Chapman (1996:26-27) indicates that the role of government can be characterised as that of:

- overseer of policy conception, development and implementation
- facilitator of policies among different sectors
- dismantler of barriers
- creator of community connections.

Alternatively, schools should consider developing a whole school approach to the development of policy and procedures for the realisation of lifelong learning for all students.

Schools need to be places where learning is enjoyable and relevant. Appropriate curriculum offerings, effective teaching and learning styles, supportive learning environments, adequate resources (human, material, physical) and appropriate methods of delivery need to be considered. Information literacy skills are an integral part of the learning process that will take place within such a learning organisation. Add to this, effective assessment, monitoring and reporting of learning to establish the school as a place where lifelong learning is valued and taken seriously.

Effective leadership from within schools with a vision for lifelong learning will be characterised by:

- considering the possibilities
- thinking in terms of process and balancing with content
- lateral and creative thinking
- effective communication
- consultation
- collaborative effort
- motivation
- commitment
- providing for professional development opportunities for staff
- participation
- sharing knowledge
- rewarding and productive learning relationships
- productive outcomes
- continuous improvement.

Classroom programs will be learner-centred, interactive, inquiry-based and resource based. The complexity of education will require teachers to work together, collaboratively and cooperatively, to maximise the potential for instruction for their students. Strong working relationships displaying characteristics of "extensive advanced planning, mutual concern and the ability to share ideas in a give and take situation" will need to occur within schools to generate active learning environments where students can engage in gathering and using information to construct new knowledge (Loertscher 1988:23).

Where? - Identifying the Curriculum Coverage
Information literacy skills are maintained through regular and repeated use.

There is a tendency for information skill development to be incorporated into the Humanities and Social Science curriculum areas only. The National Statements and Curriculum Profiles focus quite strongly on process and inquiry based learning. Information literacy has relevancy across all key learning areas where students interact with information learning technologies and resources.

Who? - Empowering the Teachers
Teachers will play an important role in helping students within an information rich world. The new technologies will enable students to do a lot of the information gathering and assessment. Teachers will be *learning technologists*. Lepani (1996:4) states that educators of this nature will have specialist skills in three main areas:

- learning diagnosis - the ability to diagnose a learner's individualised learning style
- learning strategy - the ability to design learning pathways for the student to achieve desired outcomes
- learning therapy - the ability to identify and 'repair' any failures in either diagnosis or the learning strategy chosen, in order to achieve the desired outcome.

As the curriculum becomes learner-centred, interactive and flexible, teachers will function in the role of facilitator, coach, collaborator, guide, friend, mentor and, sometimes, expert and learner. Even with the predicted arrival of Intelligent Agents by the year 2000, teachers will be the human intermediaries for learners.

There is a often-expressed fear that technology will replace teachers. I can say emphatically, IT WON'T. The information highway won't replace or devalue any of the human educational talent needed for the challenges ahead: committed teachers, creative administrators, involved parents, and, of course, diligent students. However, technology will be pivotal in the future role of teachers.

(Gates 1995:185)

Teachers will need to become creators and shapers of information, not just passive receivers of the information generated by the new technologies. This will require 'maintenance' of teacher professionalism through:

- exploring one's unique human endowments as an educator
- active professional networking (face-to-face, electronically)
- absorbing and digesting new knowledge
- establishing an educational focus
- establishing short, medium and long-term goals
- developing a 'self-employed' attitude
- becoming 'client' oriented
- adding 'value' to each educational experience
- being enthusiastic, optimistic and persistent
- becoming a lifelong learner.

Clearly the online world and the Net will not of its own accord help the students learn how to approach problem solving, the skills of debate, how to interact with fellow students, or how to address school social problems. Dedicated and caring teachers will continue to undertake the responsibility for all areas as well as teaching students how to find, assimilate and compile information.

(Petre & Harrington 1996:111)

References

Bonanno, K. (1997). Professional development: A multimedia experience. In *Information Online & On Disk97 Conference Proceedings*. Canberra: ALIA, Information Science Section.

Bonanno, K. (1996). *Information technology: Surviving the drive*. ASLA-ACT mini-conference (Planning for Information Technology), Binalong. [unpublished paper]

Chapman, J. (1996). *Leading the learning community: A keynote address*. National conference of the Australian College of Education and the Australian Council of Educational Administration, Perth.

Cropper, S. (1997). Home beautiful 2007. *Communique*, February.

Eisenberg, M.B. & Berkowitz, R.E. *The Eisenberg/Berkowitz Big Six skills - model on information problem-solving.* Norwood, NJ: Ablex. Available <http://ericir.syr.edu/big6/>. Accessed 22 March 1997.

Fisk, E. (1992). *Smart schools, smart kids: Why do some schools work?* New York: Simon and Schuster.

Follett information skills model. (1994). Illinois: Follett Software Company.

Gates, B. (1995). *The road ahead.* New York: Viking Penguin.

Herrigan, D. (1996). Time of change for Aust work practices. *The Courier Mail*, 22 Feb: 28.

Herrigan, D. (1996). World wants more 'temp' staff: survey. *The Courier Mail*, 22 Feb: 28.

Learning for the future: Developing information services in Australian schools. (1993). Carlton, Vic.: Curriculum Corporation.

Lepani, B. (1996). *Technology and learning: A catalyst for the re-design of teacher's work.* Keynote address, SLAQ conference, Brisbane, 26 June.

Loertscher, D. (1988). *Taxonomies of the school library media program.* Littleton, Colorado: Libraries Unlimited.

Petre, D. & Harrington, D. (1996). *The clever country? Australia's digital future.* Sydney: Landsdowne.

Spender, D. (1995). *Nattering on the Net: Women, power and cyberspace.* North Melbourne: Spinifex.

Teaching information skills. (1997). (CDROM) Belconnen, ACT: Australian School Library Association.

The Role of the Teacher Librarian in Meeting Student Needs in the New Millennium

A discussion paper of the importance of integration of higher order thinking, learning styles and information skills.

Lorraine Bruce[*]

Introduction

Rapid change in technology has determined a radical rethink of learning. The transient nature of information has led us to realise that to know *content* is not enough. Our students need to know how to be independent learners and to seek information in a variety of forms. Broadly, these skills fall into two groups of information skills. Those concerned with finding the information and those concerned with understanding and using information (NSW Department of School Education 1988). As teachers and teacher librarians we have a responsibility to assist in the development of skills and competencies that will prepare students to acquire new knowledge and adapt to changing circumstances.

Learning and Students

To prepare our students to deal with the growing bank of knowledge, we must encourage learners to take responsibility for their learning and to be able to make choices (Coil 1996). They need to make choices about where they locate information and they must be given flexibility about the type of assignment they are to investigate. As teachers we acknowledge that students learn in different ways, so we can't assume that the same research assignment will suit all learners. As teacher librarians we must look at the curriculum outcomes for the task investigated and assist the class teacher to create a research assignment that will reflect these outcomes, develop information skills and lead the student to be an independent learner. Teacher librarians and teachers should be seen as *knowledge navigators* (*Education 2010* 1996). This means that the teacher supports in the learning process by assessing and directing

---

[*] **Lorraine Bruce** is a teacher librarian at Pennant Hills High School and Cherrybrook Technology High School in Sydney, New South Wales, Australia. She works closely with teachers to integrate technology, higher order thinking and information skills into the curriculum. She has presented at many conferences and has worked as a part-time academic at University of Technology, Sydney. Lorraine may be contacted via email at <lobruce@zeta.org.au>.

students to suit their particular learning need. The partnership between the class teacher and the teacher librarian is crucial if we are going to empower our students as self-directed and committed learners (NSW Department of School Education 1995).

The changing nature of information and this changing role of the teacher and teacher librarian challenges the way we have performed our roles in previous years. We need to realise that we are learners too. The methods we use to locate information have changed dramatically in the past ten years. Internet, CDROMs and automated catalogues are common within schools. The discursive nature of the Internet gives us access to experts on all areas that we would never have had in the past. Students engage in collaborative research projects such as Streamwatch[†]. They need to be confident and flexible thinkers to make the best of this changing information environment (NSW Department of School Education 1988).

This means that we need to change our teaching styles to make the learners the centre of the curriculum. To help students to be independent learners, we have to be there to support them, not by giving them information but by guiding them through the information process and helping them develop critical thinking skills. These critical thinking skills were described by Bloom as a *Taxonomy of Educational Objectives*. Bloom's taxonomy acknowledges the importance of content but stresses a hierarchy of critical thinking skills. These skills are knowledge, comprehension, application, analysis, synthesis and evaluation (Coil 1996).

For the 1995 Higher School Certificate, a social science teacher at Pennant Hills High used independent student centred learning based on Bloom's Taxonomy with her class of Year 12 Legal Studies students (Plummer 1996). These students were given the syllabus and a choice about their topic area. The method for investigation was based on the information process. Students worked closely with the teacher librarians, while the teacher was the *knowledge navigator*.

[†] *Streamwatch* is a collaborative project of Local Governments and the Water Board to monitor the impact of man on the environment. Students from all parts of Australia use the Internet to record chemical and physical details of the local catchments and to report on biological and habitat details. At Pennant Hills this unit is a mandatory unit for Year 9 Science. The class teacher collects the information with their class and then books the teacher librarian to work with the class to enter these details onto a database, which is then converted to *Nexus* file and sent as an attached file through the Internet. At Cherrybrook Technology High School collection of data is done through the Streamwatch Club.

Students spent a great deal of time defining the issue. This was done on A3 paper and various aspects of the topic were identified for analysis. Because the students had choice, their interest was high. The location phase included resources within the library and the wider community. Students used the Internet, faxes to contact experts, newspapers and journals as well as traditional print based media. Students were encouraged to reflect on their learning and evaluate constantly.

Based on the Higher School Certificate results.... Of the seventeen legal studies students from our school, eight were placed in the 91-100% percentile; four in the 81-90%... The students who topped the group reflected on the independent learning process as the most valuable experience in developing skills for future tertiary study.

(Plummer 1996)

It is interesting to note, that these students were not a streamed class, yet 41% scored in the top 10% of the State and 76% of the class scored in the top 20%. The remaining students all performed beyond teachers' expectations. During the evaluation process when they were asked to respond to the type of method used, students claimed "being given the choice" made study more interesting. These students knew exactly what was required of them to cover the syllabus and were given choice and direction about how this was going to be achieved. This type of evaluation confirmed that we were on the right track. Since 1996 all assignments written in collaboration with the teacher librarian and class teacher have included choices about learning and student evaluation.

Another interesting observation is that classes that are working in this student centred mode are more on task than classes that have been given no choice about their research task. A mandatory unit in Year 7 is Myths and Legends. Students work with their English teacher and the teacher librarian to complete a series of tasks where all students get to choose the work samples they will do and the degree of difficulty. This allows students of lesser ability to achieve and students with more ability the opportunity to be challenged. Each activity accrues certain points depending on difficulty. Each student chooses which activities he/she will investigate. In these Year 7 classes students are on task and pose little or no behaviour problems. Students feel they have choice and can attain goals.

Conclusion

Curricula have changed and students need skills to cope with the changes. The teacher librarian is in the prime position to help students develop adequate information skills to cope with the rapidly changing technology. Although content and knowledge are valuable steps in the cognitive process, those students who can interpret and synthesis the knowledge who will be at the greatest advantage. The topic areas in 2 unit English are such an example. Students attempting this level of English need to do more than interpret the set text; they need to identify issues within the text and then read widely about them. They then need to analyse each issue based on a variety of media and formulate a synthesis. These skills were not required until tertiary level in the past or at least only in the top level of each subject. Students must be taught to be lifelong learners. The information process and Bloom's Taxonomy are the framework for achieving this outcome.

References

Booker, D. (ed.). (1993). *Information literacy the Australia agenda: Proceedings of a conference conducted by the University of South Australia.* Adelaide: Uni of S.A.

Coil, C. (1996). *Tools for teaching and learning in the integrated classroom.* Sydney: Hawker Brownlow Education Australia.

Education 2010: A preferred future for Victorian education. (1996). Melbourne: Victorian Association of State Secondary Principals.

Eisenberg, M. & Berkowitz, R. (1988). *Curriculum initiative: An agenda and strategy for library media programs.* NJ: Ablex.

Johnson, N.J. (1996). Reconceptualising schools as learning communities. *Reflect,* 2 (1), Jan.

NSW Department of Education. (1987). *Information skills in the school.* Sydney: NSW Dept. of Education, Library Services.

NSW Department of School Education. (1995). *Schools as learning communities: A discussion paper.* Sydney: NSW Dept. of School Education, Training and Development Unit.

Plummer, F. (1996). Independent learning? But what about the HSC? *Scan,* 15 (2), May: 15-16.

Todd, R. (1996). Independent learning and information literacy: An essential partnership for learning. In *Learning resourcefully: Challenges for teacher librarians in the information age.* Adelaide: Auslib Press.

Information Skills and Electronic Information Resources in Schools: the PLUS Approach

James Herring[*]

Introduction

The growth in the range of electronic information resources available in schools and particularly in school libraries in recent years has transformed the access which pupils[†] have to curriculum related information and ideas. The availability of CDROMs -- encyclopedias, newspapers and subject specific material; online information services such as Reuters; and the Internet, particularly the World Wide Web (WWW) has multiplied the *quantity* of information to pupils. Thus today's pupils have a much wider range of materials to work with than their predecessors and have access to much more up to date information than was previously available. This multiplicity of electronic information resources, in addition to existing print resources, is of great potential benefit to education but this benefit will only be fully realised if pupils have the requisite skills to exploit the value of *all* information resources. This paper will review the availability of electronic information resources in schools; examine the author's PLUS model of information skills; identify key issues in the exploitation of electronic information resources; and briefly examine future implications for school librarians and teachers.

Electronic Information Resources

CDROMs
CDROMs have been available to schools now for over 10 years but the past 5 years has seen a dramatic increase in the number of CDROMs available and a dramatic decrease in the cost of curriculum-related CDROMs. In the UK, a large number of national newspapers such as the *Times* and the *Guardian* as well as regional newspapers such as the *Scotsman* are now available and this trend is

---

[*] **James E. Herring** is Acting Head for the Department of Communication and Information Studies at Queen Margaret College, Edinburgh, Scotland. James may be contacted via email at <j.herring@mail.qmced.ac.uk>. His website can be accessed at <http://www.qmced.ac.uk/cis/ciherr>.

[†] The term 'pupils' is used in the paper to cover young people studying in secondary schools although it is recognised that in many countries (including parts of the UK) the term 'students' is often used instead.

reflected in countries such as the USA, Canada, Australia and New Zealand. Encyclopedias such as *World Book Multimedia Encyclopedia* and *Encarta'96* are used in schools across the world. In addition, subject specific CDROMs are available in all subjects taught in the school curriculum. For example, in Science, CDROMs such as *Redshift 2, Body Works 4.0, The Eyewitness Encyclopedia of Science, Forces and Effects,* and *Compact Questions: Science* are available at reasonable cost in the UK. CDROMs are now an integrated feature of most school libraries and are accessed either on stand-alone PCs in the library or computer workshops or via school networks. Pupils find CDROMs very easy to use and are able to find information easily. Whether pupils can find relevant information and effectively use that information is a key issue for school librarians and teachers.

Online Information Services
The use of online information services such as *DIALOG, Data Star* and *FT Profile* has been sporadic in the developed countries of the world. In many cases, the cost of using online information services has meant that most schools have not used such services or have used them only as part of research projects. In the UK, in the recently completed *Libraries of the future* (NCET 1997) project, a number of schools were given access to the *Reuters Advertising and Media Briefing* service and this service is now available to all schools in the UK at affordable rates (Reuters 1997). The Reuters product offers schools access to daily news from major national (ie. UK) and international newspapers updated each day; a global five year archive of stories from 2000 newspapers, newswires and business and general interest journals; news stories and articles in languages other than English such as French, German and Spanish; a picture library related to Reuters news and sports reports from around the world; and world economy and company information, including share prices, market indices and company information. Those schools using Reuters have found applications across the curriculum. As with CDROMs, pupils find Reuters very easy to use at a basic level but the need for search strategies related to a clearly identified purpose is vital if Reuters is to be used effectively.

The Internet
Johnson (1995) argues that the Internet has radically altered the use of information resources in schools, stating that, "In the past, the researcher's main challenge was to locate enough data to make meaningful use of it. The Internet researcher has the opposite

challenge: to select useful data from the glut of information on the networks of 11 million computers". The number of schools with access to the Internet increases daily and it will soon be difficult to find secondary schools in the UK which do *not* have Internet access. The WWW has been used a source of information by teachers and school librarians for every aspect of the curriculum and there is no doubt that the WWW provides a potentially vast increase in curriculum related material for schools. Problems of access (especially cost) and use (especially use of pornographic sites) have been highlighted in the press but the key problem for pupils is the sheer amount of information available which in some cases may threaten to overwhelm those searching the WWW for information.

Information skills: the PLUS model
There are a number of different models of information skills which have been proposed and implemented in the 1980s and 1990s (Herring 1996). The model advocated by this author is PLUS -- Purpose, Location, Use and Self-evaluation and it is proposed that school librarians, teachers and pupils can use this model in teaching and learning information skills in upper primary and in secondary schools. There are a wide range of skills included in the PLUS model and these skills are interrelated and should not be separated in information skills programmes in schools. For example, school librarians should not only be seen to teach the skills of locating information in the library but should be involved in the whole process which involves pupils effectively using information resources for curricular ends.

In identifying a clear purpose for information use (eg. completing an assignment) pupils will use cognitive skills identifying their existing knowledge and thinking skills such as brainstorming or concept mapping. In locating information and ideas, pupils will use locational skills as the ability to use a range of information sources including books, journals and electronic information resources and selection skills in assessing how relevant information resources are. The key aspect of location is that finding information -- from whatever source -- is related to an identified purpose. In using information resources, pupils will be expected to apply a wide range of skills such as reading skills such as skimming and scanning; interactive skills including the ability to understand the context of what is being read and relate this to existing knowledge; selective skills such as the ability to select relevant information and reject irrelevant information which does not meet the identified purpose; evaluation skills including the ability to evaluate the authority of the information or any bias in the text; recording skills such as note-taking which relates what is found to the identified purpose; synthesising skills such as the ability to bring together information and ideas from different sources; and writing skills such as the ability to present a logical, well structured argument in an assignment. Thus the skills included in using information are complex learning skills which pupils acquire and develop over a number of years. Self-evaluation includes the ability to reflect on what has been done in a particular assignment and to identify areas of improvement in the effective use of information resources in the future. If school librarians and teachers can teach pupils how to reflect not only on their work but on the process involved in producing that work, then the pupils are likely to benefit by improving their use of information skills.

Of the above list of skills, there is no doubt that it is the cognitive skills of thinking about purpose, reading, evaluating, synthesising, writing and reflecting which are the key learning skills. Location skills are necessary but school librarians have often been criticised for highlighting location skills at the expense of the other, more important skills.

Key Issues in Exploiting Electronic Information Resources
There are no new information skills needed by pupils who use electronic sources of information as opposed to print sources. There may be some new IT skills needed such as how to use Netscape to examine a WWW site but these are technical skills which pupils learn very quickly. The key issues lie in the use of electronic sources and these issues include the use of search strategies; the 'reading' of multimedia material and the evaluation of electronic information. Other issues not covered in this paper include note-taking from electronic sources and the use of electronic material in writing assignments.

Search strategies will be developed by pupils by identifying a clear purpose and this will result in the formation of keywords which can be used to search for information. Thus a pupil using *Reuters Advertising and Media Briefing* for a project on water pollution in science could be encouraged not merely to search for WATER POLLUTION but WATER POLLUTION AND RIVERS AND UK. Without a clear purpose, a pupil may use a simple keyword which will lead to information overload because the number of hits. This problem occurs with CDROMs and particularly with the Internet where a one keyword search will produce thousands of hits.

Electronic information sources have introduced a new element in schools in relation to reading and that is the use of multimedia. Print sources have challenged pupils by including graphics or photographs as well as text but multimedia resources require pupils to 'read' video clips. This form of 'reading' requires pupils to interact with the 'text' in different ways and involves visual skills and listening skills in addition to existing reading skills. School librarians and teachers need make pupils aware of the different skills needed when 'reading' electronic information resources and this can be done in discussions with pupils in the classroom and in the library.

Evaluating electronic information is similar to evaluating printed sources but pupils need to be made aware that information found on a website does not necessarily have the same authority as that found in an academic textbook or in a broadsheet newspaper and in many schools pupils are encouraged to examine carefully the source of any information located. In many cases, pupils may not have sufficient knowledge to do this and will need help from the teachers and/or the school librarian. Internet information which is regarded as 'political' by schools will need careful examination. Mediation of the Internet is now being examined by school librarians and this author is involved in a project with Linlithgow Academy in Scotland. The project aims to download websites, with copyright clearance from the owners, and place websites either on a CDROM or on the school's Intranet for use by pupils. Mediation of the Internet may be a partial solution to the problems of information overload and the need for evaluation of sources by pupils.

Future Implications
This author argues that, "The convergence of technologies in the future needs to be accompanied by a convergence of cognitive skills in the minds of pupils if they are to be effective learners in tomorrow's schools" (Herring 1996). Thus critical thinking skills outlined in the PLUS model will be even more necessary for pupils in the future as access to more (and more complex) multimedia information sources is available in schools and in the pupils' homes. If pupils are not able to cope with the sheer amount of information available, they will be unable to learn effectively from these sources.

The role of the school librarian in the future will partly be as the school's electronic information resource manager who works with teachers in identifying and where necessary mediating resources which can be used to support the curriculum of the school.

References

Herring, J. (1996). *Teaching information skills in schools.* London: Library Association Publishing.

Johnson, D. (1995). Student access to the Internet. *Emergency Librarian,* 22 (3), Jan-Feb: 8-12.

National Council for Educational Technology (NCET). (1997). *Libraries of the future* project and related Internet projects. Available <http://www.ncet.org.uk>.

Reuters. (1997). Information on Reuters services to education. Via email <education.uk@reuters.com>.

The Teacher, Teacher Librarian and Critical Thinking

Sandra Hughes[*]

Critical thinking is a foundation for success in the Electronic Age. Some provinces/states are identifying it as essential to their curriculum. Some boards/districts are emphasising it. Some schools are making it the focus of their program. Even if all of the levels of education proclaim critical thinking as a significant part of the curriculum, it is up to the teacher librarian and ultimately the teacher to find a way to develop students' critical thinking skills and processes. The teacher librarian might inspire, encourage, model, and support. Nevertheless, the teacher must take further what he or she has gleaned from this relationship and his or her own research. The teacher must set the development of critical thinking skills as a priority. Teachers must infuse their entire program with opportunities for students to learn, practice and apply these skills and processes, until they have internalised them. They must maintain this effort throughout the grades to build students' understanding and skills to the point where they can be effective, independent problem-solvers.

As teacher librarians we are in an ideal situation to help teachers make this development of essential skills and processes happen. We are already working toward the development of information literate students by helping teachers to integrate information skills and information problem-solving with their programs. If the teacher must make a shift to placing critical thinking or problem-solving at the heart of his or her program, then the teacher librarian must make a shift to taking more of a leadership role within the school, to introduce, model, monitor and support all teachers as they learn and apply the strategies needed to develop problem-solving in the information environment -- physical, print and electronic.

If students are to develop the critical thinking skills they need for the electronic age, they need teachers who are willing to refocus their teaching to a resource based approach that emphasises information problem-solving. They need teacher librarians who are willing to spend enough time becoming knowledgeable in the electronic environment that they can lead teachers and students to

---

[*] **Sandra Hughes** is a teacher librarian at Riverview School, Brantford in Ontario, Canada. Sandra can be contacted via email at **<sandhugh@hookup.net>**.

select and use resources appropriate to their learning tasks or problems. Students need teachers and teacher librarians who work in a partnership that recognises the importance of full teacher commitment to information literacy. That commitment is to teaching children how to learn, using information of all types, effectively and efficiently, to solve meaningful problems.

How must the roles change then?

The Teacher Librarian

The teacher librarian becomes more responsible from a school perspective for the implementation of the information literacy program. The role becomes one of:

- *Leadership*: information literacy program and technology introduction, training, support
- *Coordination*: information problem-solving skills and process collaborative planning, team-teaching to meet specific program needs, monitoring, tracking, ensuring intellectual access to all resources including electronic technology
- *Support*: ensuring physical access to all resources including electronic technology
- *Remediation*: one on one and small group mediation with students trying to build information literacy skills and understanding of the information problem-solving process.

In this role the teacher librarian must introduce, promote, train, support, model, remediate and coordinate the implementation of an information problem-solving model throughout the school. Eisenberg and Berkowitz suggest developing a matrix on a spreadsheet that plots teachers' long range plans, intentions to work with the teacher librarian and learning outcomes. This would be one at the beginning of the school year rather than the end. It would function as a planning and tracking tool rather than as a year end report, although it could also be used as such. The value of such a matrix, or curriculum map, is in its ability to clarify school progress toward information literacy skill development. Its complexity becomes easy to handle with the use of a spreadsheet and everyone can benefit from knowing what is being planned and done to develop student information problem-solving.

The School Program Curriculum Map identifies those units in which teachers are focusing on developing information problem-solving skills and process. It identifies the information needed for coordination and planning for the development of information problem-solving within the school. Samples of these charts can be found in Eisenberg and Berkowitz' books and articles on the Big Six, their information problem-solving model (1990). This school wide curriculum map makes the coordination and monitoring of the development of information problem-solving skills more manageable for the teacher librarian.

The Teacher
The teacher must make information literacy a priority in planning and implementing the day to day program. Long range plans must include information literacy outcomes. Integrated units of study must include problem-solving models such as the Big Six. Teachers should be constantly looking for opportunities to review and reinforce the information problem-solving model, if they wish to achieve information literacy outcomes.

The teacher uses a Classroom Program Curriculum Map to assist in long range planning, collaborative planning, monitoring and tracking the development of the grade level program, including the information problem-solving model. This assists him/her in identifying which units would best be done in collaboration with the teacher librarian and which would be most effective for developing particular parts of the process and skills. It also serves as a map to help the teacher monitor his or her progress toward his or her goals for student development of critical thinking/problem-solving.

The commitment must be deep on the part of the classroom teacher to enable students to internalise the information problem-solving process and learn the skills. This effort must be ongoing, every day, taking advantage of incidental opportunities to reinforce understandings and skills. It must not only be focused on in certain units planned collaboratively with the teacher librarian but developed in every unit. This is an essential part of the overall literacy that students must have for the Electronic Age and as such we cannot look at one unit, team taught per term, as enough to enable students to learn the process and the skills of information problem-solving.

A recent dialogue on the Big Six listserv reveals how essential this focus by teachers and teacher librarians throughout the grades, on the development of the critical thinking process and skills integrated with information skills. James Butler wrote of shock and frustration at the Grade 11 and 12 students who participated enthusiastically in his lesson on information problem-solving and then when given the opportunity to get to work on the research assignment that was the follow up, went back to their old ways of handling the information problem/research question (Butler 1997). In response to his cry of frustration on the listserv, several seasoned teacher librarians responded with thoughtful suggestions.

Among their responses emphasis was put on:

- the need for development through the grades before students were set in their approach to research tasks (Little 1997)
- making sure that the teacher understood, valued and collaborated in the planning and teaching of the skills (Symons 1997)
- including the process in the criteria and assessment of the assignment (Symons 1997)
- understanding that time is needed to change student and teacher attitudes (Scroggs 1997).

In this informal practitioner centred dialogue the importance of teacher commitment and teacher librarian leadership is clear.

So how can the teacher and teacher librarian begin?

Perhaps it is time for teacher librarians to help teachers make the connections between information problem solving and critical thinking; between critical thinking and success in this information rich electronic environment exploding around us; between research and the development of these skills. Perhaps it is time for teacher librarians to recognise the importance of teachers taking a deeper commitment to, or ownership of, developing information literate students who can think critically about a task or question or problem and access and use information effectively and efficiently to help complete, answer or solve it.

Perhaps it is time for teachers to listen to their students' pleas for help in deciding what's important in the sea of information they can now access through electronic technology and realise that building information problem-solving skills and process is essential to solving this learning/teaching problem. Perhaps it is time for teachers to take another look at the focus of their teaching and realise that they need to help students to find and use models for problem-solving, for critical thinking. Perhaps it is time for teachers to refocus their approach and connect with teacher librarians to take advantage of their support and ideas for developing student information problem-solving skills and processes.

Tips for Success

- Personalise and make the learning experiences relevant for the student.
- Infuse the information problem-solving process throughout the class, school and home program.
- Integrate electronic technology throughout the problem-solving process.
- Include the evaluation of the skills and process in the reporting to parents.
- Involve all of the members of the educational team: the parents, the administration, the support staff and the community in the learning so that they can reinforce and extend the critical thinking.
- Connect with the province/state and board/district expectations for critical thinking, electronic technology and information literacy.

Be aware that student learning of information literacy and the critical thinking process required by it demands greater commitment from the classroom teacher, greater understanding and support from the parents and greater leadership from the teacher librarian than may have been understood previously.

References

American Association of School Librarians. (1995). Information literacy: a position paper on information problem solving. *Emergency Librarian*, 23 (2), Nov: 20-23.

Brevik, P.S. and Senn, J.A. (1994). *Information literacy: educating children for the 21st century*. New York, NY: Scholastic.

Butler, J. (1997) 'Big six disappointment.' BIGSIX@LISTSERV. SYR.EDU [listserv] (17 April).

Eisenberg, M.B. and Berkowitz, R.E. (1988). *Curriculum initiative: an agenda and strategy for library media programs.* Norwood, NJ: Ablex.

Eisenberg, M.B. and Berkowitz, R.E. (1990). *Information problem-solving: the Big Six skills approach to library information skills instruction.* Norwood, NJ: Ablex.

Eisenberg, M.B. and Ely, D.P. (1993). Plugging into the 'Net'. *Emergency Librarian*, 21(2), Nov: 8-16.

Eisenberg, M.B. and Berkowitz, R.E. (1995). The six study habits of highly effective students: Using the Big Six to link parents, students and homework. *School Library Journal*, 41 (8), Aug: 22-25.

Eisenberg, M.B. and Berkowitz, R.E. (1996). *Helping with homework: a parent's guide to information problem-solving.* Syracuse, NY: ERIC/IT.

Eisenberg, M.B. and Spitzer, K.L. (1997). Skills and strategies for helping students become more effective information users. *Access*, 3 (2), Winter: 14-19.

Heide, A. and Stilborn, L. (1996). *The teacher's complete and easy guide to the Internet.* Toronto, Ontario: Trifolium Books.

Hughes, S.G. (1997). Information problem-solving: an approach to information literacy that is catching fire! *The Teaching Librarian*, 4 (3), Winter: 8-10.

Junion-Metz, G. (1996). *K-12 resources on the Internet: an instructional guide.* Berkeley, California: Library Solutions Press.

Little, T. 'Re: James and the trouble with Big Six.' BIGSIX@ LISTSERV.SYR.EDU [listserv] (18 April, 1997).

Mendrinos, R. (1994). *Building information literacy using high technology: a guide for schools and libraries.* Englewood, CO: Libraries Unlimited.

Probert, E. (1997). 'Re: Big Six Disappointment.' BIGSIX@LISTSERV. SYR.EDU [listserv] (18 April).

Stripling, B.K. (1997). School libraries: Catalysts for authentic learning. *School Library Media Quarterly*, 25 (2), Winter: 90-91.

Symons, A. (1997). 'Re: Big Six Disappointment.' BIGSIX@ LISTSERV.SYR.EDU [listserv] (19 April, 1997).

Learning and the Internet: From Promise to Positive Outcomes

Lyn Linning[*]

Reaching the stage where one can confidently use the Internet for communication, discussion, publication, information retrieval and integrated learning experiences is for most of us a bit like getting a driver's licence: uncomfortable to traumatic for a comparatively short time, then forgotten or at most dimly remembered. Yet there are people who try to learn to drive and admit defeat, and there are others for whom the licence does not bring all the benefits they had assumed would come with it. Similarly, initial experiences with the Internet can disappoint teachers and students at all levels (and even convince some to avoid further encounters) for a number of reasons:

- expectations based on reports of highly successful projects (from which most of the set-backs and problems encountered in the process have been omitted)

- expectations based on television documentaries or demonstrations featuring the most powerful, state of the art hardware (it is seldom the case that their hardware is comparable)

- local area network (LAN) problems which may arise because a school or institution's computer expert/s need (but may be unwilling) to ask for more technical assistance as the range of usage patterns and the number of users grows

- lack of on-site support and inservice opportunities

- computer 'labs' and access procedures which need reconsideration if they were set up for computer applications before the use of the Internet in education institutions was thought of

- time: lost time when technology-dependent in-class activities do not go according to plan (eg. server 'down'); 'wasted' time when students 'play around' instead of concentrating on their set tasks

---

[*] **Lyn Linning** is a lecturer with the School of Language and Literacy Education at the Queensland University of Technology, Kelvin Grove Campus in Brisbane, Queensland, Australia. Lyn may be contacted via email at <l.linning@qut.edu.au>.

- anxiety generated by mass media and community focus on access to inappropriate and/or illegal material and the possible legal consequences for schools and individuals

- pressure on teachers to be seen to be 'with IT' or admit to being 'past IT'

- pressure on students (based on unsubstantiated assertions that 'young people' take to the Internet like ducks to water and can manipulate it to their heart's content in no time at all) to be very successful very quickly

- lack of the metacognitive knowledge which would encourage them to see their frustrations and 'failures' as aspects of stages through which they will pass on the road to some degree of mastery.

Literature on Establishing Successful Electronic Communities
All causes of disappointment and frustration are worth investigating with a view to taking some constructive action. Most of them are addressed in print and online publications, and in discussions on supportive lists (once the new user is able to send and receive email messages). A recent research review "suggests how electronic communities can deliver and enhance...education, details successful and unsuccessful practices of these electronic communities, provides guidance on successful implementation of educational technology, and summarises advice to others from existing electronic communities" (Burgstahler and Swift 1996:1). Schools, universities and other organisations interested in enhancing learning through use of the Internet would find this document very helpful for identifying sources of disappointment and frustration or planning their programs to avoid them.

Metacognitive Insight: the Stages of Learning New Technologies
Russell (1995:173) found that "understanding the stages of learning to use the technology empowers the learner through the knowledge that feelings of tension and frustration will be overcome". She identified six stages which adult learners (few of whom were familiar with email or even computers initially) went through as they participated in an email activity in an introductory course for teacher librarians:

1. Awareness (of the technology and the fact that they are going to use it).

2. Learning the Process (frustration is common at this stage, constant support is essential).
3. Understanding and application of the process (the technology is less intrusive).
4. Familiarity and confidence.
5. Adaptation to other contexts (the technology is becoming invisible as learners see the possibilities for other activities and projects).
6. Creative application to new contexts (the learner uses the technology effectively for a range of purposes).

(Russell 1995:175)

Those teaching the use of new technologies and the learners themselves (children and adults) can benefit from knowing about these possible stages and viewing them as steps to mastery. As a consequence, outcomes should match expectations more closely and we should have fewer 'Internet drop-outs'. This approach also acknowledges realistically the time, effort and commitment required.

Learning to search and retrieve pertinent information from the World Wide Web (WWW) is qualitatively different from learning to use email effectively. Following carefully sequenced steps can contribute to 'learning the process' but learners will be unlikely to reach Stage 3 and beyond in searching the Web without some free exploration and 'play'.

Using 'Wasted' Time

Teachers and teacher librarians often express concern that students are getting the latest information on their favourite pop stars rather than becoming involved in more academic pursuits. Provided that the material is not offensive and the students have completed their curriculum-related tasks, these experiences can be used to advantage. Motivated and genuinely curious, students are most likely to develop higher level skills in relation to content attuned to their strong interests. They can be asked/encouraged to log the steps they used to find something they wanted and to generalise their process for transfer to other (curriculum-related) contexts. Students who have Internet access at home are at an inequitable advantage if there is no time at all for the others to have some opportunities for unstructured exploration at school.

Disabling Stereotypes

Most people understand that all learners bring different, though relevant, knowledge and experience to new tasks. However, both adults and children are disadvantaged by popular stereotypes: of young people naturally able to master new technologies quickly; of older people not being able to cope; and of people skilled in the use of print resources being superseded by masters of computing. Many young people are not noticeably quicker to master new technologies than adult novices, and feel that there is something wrong with them if they fail to become instant expert 'surfers'. People of all ages are highly successful, sophisticated users of new technologies: motivation, access opportunities and effort have more to do with this than age. Students quickly realise they need to master search strategies to get the most from the WWW, and often discover how helpful librarians and others who understand and have practised searching across the range of media can be.

Disappointments caused by LAN problems may be a by-product of disabling stereotypes of 'the librarian' and 'the information technology specialist/coordinator' in schools and universities. There are still instances (even in relatively small schools, let alone large schools and universities) of 'computing' and 'library' programs developing in isolation, even as hostile camps. Though they may approach the tasks from different angles, both librarians and information technology or computing specialists/coordinators:

- store, retrieve, and manage information
- deliver information
- establish and manage networks...
- train constituencies in aspects of computer and information literacy.

(Lipow and Creth 1995:vi)

Mutual understanding of roles/expertise and an integrated program produce the best results. This would seem too obvious to say except for the weight of anecdotal evidence to the contrary: frustration arising from different systems, incompatible programs and confusion about roles and responsibilities is rife.

All of the 'disabling stereotypes' which have developed around information technology, computing and libraries should be identified and examined - a collection of cartoons for deconstruction would be a good start. This could help learners feel more comfortable about their initial difficulties and contribute towards a better integrated approach to information access and services in educational institutions of all kinds.

Call for Comments

This discussion paper has focused on the frustrations and disappointments associated with the early learning of new technologies at the individual and institutional level. Comments are invited on:

- any of the sources of disappointment/frustration listed and helpful insights or strategies for improving the situation
- the metacognitive approach to supporting learners in this context
- planning for supportive, successful electronic learning communities.

The aim is to work towards positive outcomes for individuals and electronic learning communities.

References

Burstahler and Swift. (1996). *Enhanced learning through electronic communities: a research review.* [On-line]. Available <http://164.116.18.39/research_report.html>.

Lipow, A.G. and Creth, S.D. (1995). *Building partnerships: Computing and library professionals.* Berkeley and San Carlos, Ca: Library Solutions.

Russell, A.L. (1995). Stages in learning new technologies: Naive adult email users. *Computers Education*, 25 (4):173-178.

The Internet: a Bane or a Boon to Critical Thinking?[*]

Joy McGregor[†]

You have heard the outcry from both sides: "The Internet will ruin our children!", "The Internet is the answer to all educational problems!" We recognise the need to tame the hysteria in either direction, and search for truth (or truths) found somewhere in the middle. Certainly there may be dangers linked to Internet use, and it is easy to find a great deal of literature and rhetoric expounding on these. And yes, perhaps the Internet provides us with a tool that can improve education, maybe even dramatically so. The ways in which the Internet can be employed are many, but will be of little consequence if the use has no effect on improving education and thereby improving the lives of our students.

The Internet is often touted as a means to teach critical thinking. To determine whether this is a reasonable claim, we need to examine the idea carefully. One of the crucial needs of modern-day society is for people who are able to think critically. As societal problems become increasingly complex in a post-industrial world, those who are able to solve those problems will be highly valued. As more and more countries experiment with democracy, the need for informed thinkers increases. With available information and misinformation increasing exponentially, those able to evaluate and use appropriate information effectively to make decisions and solve problems will be in a position to improve society. As Glaser (1941:5) noted, "good citizenship calls for the attainment of a working understanding of our social, political, and economic arrangements and for the ability to think critically about issues concerning which there may be an honest difference of opinion".

Definitions of critical thinking abound in the literature, each one touching on different aspects of the concept. No one definition is agreed upon by those who study, discuss, or claim to teach critical thinking. Several definitions that include a number of important elements will be examined in this paper.

---

[*] Submitted and accepted as a refereed conference paper.

[†] **Joy McGregor** is Assistant Professor with School of Library and Information Studies at Texas Woman's University, Denton, Texas, USA. Joy's WWW homepage is available at <**http://venus.twu.edu/~F_MCGREGOR/**>. Joy may be contacted via email at <**f_mcgregor@twu.edu**>.

In 1971, Cohen (1971:5) stated that critical thinking is "using basic thinking processes to analyse arguments and generate insight into particular meanings and interpretations; develop cohesive, logical reasoning patterns and understand assumptions and biases underlying particular positions". Logic, reasoning, and in-depth analysis are important elements of this definition. Over a decade later, Ennis (1985:54) defined critical thinking as "reasonable, reflective thinking that is focused on deciding what to believe or do". He called this a "working definition," taking critical thinking a step beyond the evaluative element that he had earlier advocated and placing it into a decision-making or problem-solving context.

In 1996, Richard Paul described critical thinking as "thinking about your thinking while you're thinking in order to make your thinking better...[I]t is self-improvement (in thinking) through standards (that assess thinking)" (Paul and Elder 1996a:1). His description of it as "the art of taking charge of your own mind" (Paul and Elder 1996b:1) gives the notion a highly metacognitive aspect. Michael Scriven and Richard Paul (1995:1) formally define critical thinking as 'the intellectually disciplined process of actively and skilfully conceptualising, applying, analysing, synthesising, and/or evaluating information gathered from, or generated by, observation, experience, reflection, reasoning, or communication, as a guide to belief and action". Attempting to improve that thinking takes the concepts of logic, reasoning, analysis, evaluation, problem-solving, and decision-making to a higher level of self-awareness.

What does all this have to do with Internet use? Beginning with a premise that students' use of any resources should involve and ideally improve critical thinking, the Internet is a remarkable resource with potential to promote that improvement. But whether growth occurs depends greatly on how teachers expect the Internet to be used.

> No medium, in and of itself, is likely to improve learning in a significant way when it is used to deliver instruction. Nor is it realistic to expect the Web, when used as a tool, to develop in students any unique skills.

> (Owston 1997:29)

If the Internet is viewed as simply another source of information, roughly equivalent to the books in the library, students will treat it the same way they do those books. They will do no more and no less critical thinking than they have been encouraged to do with print materials.

The Internet's ease of use may be an advantage in many ways, but that ease may provide one of the biggest threats to critical thinking. Recent research shows that copying information directly from sources during research paper writing (which we have always been aware was a problem but have done little about except to preach against it on a moral basis) is not only rampant, but provides a clear indication that students are not constructing their own meaning about the topic they are studying (McGregor and Streitenberger 1997). An examination of the kinds of errors made while copying directly from sources shows that little basic comprehension occurs, let alone critical thinking. If this is true with information that must be laboriously handwritten or typed into a research paper, how much easier is it to download information and paste into a word processed paper? Earlier research by McGregor (1993) found evidence of exactly this downloading process in research papers. If teachers and librarians do not address the diseases shown by the symptom of copying -- non-involvement, non-critical thinking, non-learning -- the Internet, with its sheer volume of information, will only make the symptom harder to detect. As long as assignments do not require students to think critically about the information they encounter, giving them opportunities to apply this information to solving real problems or making decisions, information from the Internet will only make the standard behaviour of copying an even easier way out than it has been previously. Though not caused by Internet use, this problem will not be solved by simply introducing Internet use, and it and may well be exacerbated.

Assuming that students are motivated, however, to construct their own understanding based on the information they discover and that they are directing their energies toward problem-solving and decision-making with this information, the Internet provides an interactive, eclectic environment in which they can explore and make their own discoveries. But are they prepared to do that successfully? In what way does critical thinking impact this process?

For the most part, students assume that the information contained in their library is accurate, credible, and reliable. Why would the adults in charge order anything that was not? Where students have been encouraged to evaluate information, typical students apply whatever evaluative skills they have developed to assessing currency by looking at the copyright date and determining relevance to their topics (both of which are important critical thinking skills), but they probably appropriately assume accuracy, credibility, and reliability of that information. The same assumptions will be applied to information from the Internet unless students are taught specifically to do otherwise. Where those assumptions may have been largely valid with the encyclopedias and books in their library collection, they are much less valid with information that can be generated by absolutely anyone.

The very nature of information on the Internet provides a much more meaningful experience in evaluating information for accuracy, credibility, and reliability. Suddenly a need to evaluate can be demonstrated. No longer can students blindly accept information that has been screened for them by selection policies. They are like shoppers who move from an elegant jewellery store, where no one would question the genuineness of the jewels sold, to an open-air marketplace, at which anyone and everyone sells whatever they want to sell and the unsuspecting buyer might be fooled into believing a beautiful, worthless stone is real and valuable. Suddenly the shopper's ability to recognise real gems becomes necessary and important. With the open-air marketplace of the Internet, the teacher librarian has an unprecedented opportunity to prove the need for learning to evaluate information. The dangers of not doing that can be easily exposed. Critical thinking about the information they read -- using logic, reasoning, and analysis to go beneath the surface, reflecting on the ideas contained in what they find, determining their value in decision-making or problem-solving, and examining their own thinking about these ideas -- will be crucial as students encounter a variety of viewpoints, some of which will directly contradict others. Teacher librarians can "encourage students to explore the Web [or any part of the Internet] with the goal of having them weigh evidence, judge the authenticity of the data, compare different viewpoints on issues, analyse and synthesise diverse sources of information, and construct their own understanding of the topic or issue at hand" (Owston 1997:31).

To demonstrate graphically the ease of posting misinformation to the Internet, a teacher librarian could construct a simple web page providing information students know to be false -- a fire that destroyed their school last weekend, a football game lost instead of won, inaccurate names of teachers and principals, a fictitious student winning a prize that someone in the class concerned actually won -- and bring the file up within a web browser as if it were really a page on the web. When students see a page that looks just as official as other pages, but containing patently false information about their own lives, they will recognise that the information they see on a website cannot necessarily be taken at face value. The need for critical thinking will be made real.

The potential impact of the Internet on critical thinking goes far beyond the few factors mentioned here. Just as the Internet itself is almost limitless, so is the topic of critical thinking. The purpose of this paper was to address the reality that using electronic resources such as the Internet will not automatically trigger critical thinking. The individual user will make the difference. Those interested in the potential of the Internet will go beyond this point by reading further, exploring new avenues, and examining new ideas. That potential has only been alluded to, in terms of evaluative thinking, within the limits of this paper. You, the independent learner, will go away from this virtual conference with a germ of an idea, will investigate the subject further, and will take the risk of applying the ideas to your specific situation. Your students will be the beneficiaries, as you make learning real for them.

A variety of websites related to critical thinking exist. These can be used by teachers, librarians, and/or students for further investigation and for springboards to new ideas. Some are specific to Internet use; some are not.

Links to a few sites are provided below. Search engines will lead you to many more. Paul (1996a) makes the point that teachers cannot effectively teach students to think critically if the teachers themselves are not skilled at doing so. As you look at these sites, engage your own mind in some critical thinking -- do these sites really do what they claim to do?

The Just Think Foundation
<http://www.justthink.org/>

Salish Sea Expedition
<http://www.olympic.net/salish/>

Choose the Best Engine for Your Purpose
<http://www.nueva.pvt.k12.ca.us/~debbie/library/research/adviceengine.html>

Critical Evaluation Surveys
<http://www.capecod.net/schrockguide/eval.htm>

The New 'Homework'. Parents and Students Together on the Web: a Dozen Information Skills for the Home
<http://fromnowon.org/feb97/teach.html>

The Critical Thinking Community
<http://www.sonoma.edu/cthink>

Critical Thinking in an Online World
<http://www.library.ucsb.edu/untangle/jones.html>

How to Evaluate Information Sources
<http://www.santarosa.edu/library/lib.guide.qual.shtml>

Mission: Critical
<http://www.sjsu.edu/depts/itl/>

Critical Thinking
<http://www.fsl.orst.edu/cof/teach/for442/ct.htm>

Evaluating Information on the Internet
<http://www.infotoday.com/cilmag/may/techmans.htm>

Teaching Critical Evaluation Skills for World Wide Web Resources
<http://www.science.widener.edu/~withers/webeval.htm>

References

Cohen, Jozef. (1971). *Thinking*. Chicago: Rand McNally. Quoted in Barbara Z. Presseisen. 'Thinking skills: meanings and models.' In *Developing minds: a resource book for teaching thinking*, (ed.) by Arthur L. Costa, 45. Alexandria, VA: Association for Supervision and Curriculum Development, 1985.

Ennis, Robert. (1985). 'Goals for a critical thinking curriculum.' In *Developing minds: a resource book for teaching thinking*, (ed.) by Arthur L. Costa. Alexandria, VA: Association for Supervision and Curriculum Development.

Glaser, Edward. (1941). *An experiment in the development of critical thinking*. New York: Teachers College, Columbia University. Quoted in Jay McTighe and Jan Schollenberger. 'Why teach thinking: a statement of rationale.' In *Developing minds: a resource book for teaching thinking*, (ed.) by Arthur L. Costa, 3. Alexandria, VA: Association for Supervision and Curriculum Development, 1985.

McGregor, Joy. (1993). 'Cognitive processes and the use of information: A qualitative study of higher order thinking skills used in the research process by students in a gifted program.' PhD. diss., Florida State University.

McGregor, Joy and Streitenberger, Denise. (1997). 'Do scribes learn? Copying and information use.' Paper presented at Treasure Mountain Research Retreat 6, Portland, OR, 31 March-1 April.

Owston, Ronald D. (1997). The World Wide Web: a technology to enhance teaching and learning. *Educational Researcher*, 26, March: 27-33.

Paul, Richard and Elder, Linda. (1996). Critical thinking: Basic questions and answers. *The Critical Thinking Community*. [Online]. Available <http://www.sonoma.edu/cthink/K12/k12library/questions. nclk>. Accessed 22 March 1997.

Paul, Richard and Elder, Linda. (1996). Our concept of critical thinking. *The Critical Thinking Community*. [Online]. Available <http://www.sonoma.edu/cthink/K12/k12class/Oconcept.nclk>. Accessed 22 March 1997.

Scriven, Michael and Paul, Richard. (1995). Defining critical thinking. *The Critical Thinking Community*. [Online]. Available <http://www.sonoma.edu/cthink/fresource/faculty/defining.html>. Accessed 22 March 1997.

(Towards a Pedagogy of) Critical Learning in the Electronic Age.

Cameron Richards[*]

"When it was proclaimed that the Library contained all books, the first impression was one of extravagant happiness. All the men felt themselves to be the masters of an intact and secret treasure... As was usual, this inordinate hope was followed by an excessive depression..."
Jorge Borges, *The Library of Babel.*

Abstract
This work-in-progress paper discusses the challenge to 'critical' models of teaching and learning represented by the new electronic literacies of interactive multimedia, hypertext and virtual worlds. It provisionally considers ways of recognising that critical learning in the electronic age can be promoted in the very terms often denied or resisted by critical pedagogy theory - personal interest, popular culture, and the very process of learning.

The need for students to be actively critical thinkers in the new electronic age is most obvious in terms of how the Internet offers potential access to unlimited information. Many teachers and academics do tend to interpret the limitations and abuses of new electronic media in terms of what Roszak (1994) has called the 'cult of information'. However, just as the Internet is increasingly being developed in terms of global telecommunications, so too the new electronic literacies of multimedia, hypertext and virtual worlds represent, above all, opportunities for interactive modes of learning.

As well as challenging long-enduring models of education in terms of mere access to information and knowledge authorised by teachers, such developments also constitute an even more fundamental dilemma for models of critical pedagogy than the increasing encroachment of global popular culture into classrooms through the medium of television in particular (Giroux 1994, 1996; McLaren 1995). The similar versions of critical pedagogy developed

---

[*] **Dr Cameron Richards** is a lecturer with the School of Language and Literacy Education at Queensland University of Technology, Kelvin Grove Campus, Red Hill, Queensland, Australia. Cameron may be contacted via email at <**C.Richards@qut.edu.au**>. Cameron's WWW homepage is available at <**http://www.fed.qut.edu.au/staff/llit/richards/index.htm**>.

by Giroux and McLaren do tend to recognise that the interest of anybody in the seductive forces of popular media imagery is ever ambivalent. Yet, both critics conclude that the force of 'desire' ideally informing a critical pedagogy of resistance is somehow separate from that solicited for the passive mass consumption of stereotypical media images in contemporary popular culture (McLaren 1995:9). Hence, it may be argued (Richards 1996), this model of critical pedagogy tends to be not only inherently pessimistic, but also elitist in its implicit assumption that critically-aware students emerge from the mainstream to deny their own complicity in the 'disturbing pleasures' of false hopes and desires (Giroux 1994:ix-xi).

Contrasting with the 'passive spectator' model of media (especially television) consumption used in the version of critical pedagogy referred to above, the interactive nature of new electronic media provides a basis for describing teaching that models and facilitates 'critical learning' rather than 'critical pedagogy' per se. The following discussion will briefly consider several arguments for this perspective.

Hypermedia and Metaphor: Distinguishing Between Data, Information and Knowledge

The cultural studies model adapted by Giroux and McLaren's similar conceptions of critical pedagogy assumes that all forms of discursive and ideological representation can be simply visualised in the manner of a television program or magazine photo, and reduced to non-ambivalent oppositional images of Self versus the Other or sameness versus difference (Giroux 1994:82). The 'passive' modes of imagination which are sufficient to watch television or read magazines are inadequate for not only dealing with the new interactive electronic media, but also the sheer overload of information which increasingly confronts people and serves to collapse familiar concepts and categories of knowledge. An active imagination capable of making creative new associations is an important requirement for the effective use of World Wide Web search engines and hypertext links, and thus also for the critical thinking needed to selectively distinguish useful information in the electronic age.

In their discussions of how future libraries will need to cope with electronic information, Crawford and Gorman (1995:79-85) exemplify the general recognition of anyone substantially involved in the new applied uses of computer networks that the ability to recognise and use metaphor is a crucial aspect of electronic literacy. Developing the metaphor of scholars immersed in a 'sea of information', Crawford and Gorman make a distinction between 'drowning' in data, 'swimming' in information and people beginning to 'surf' in knowledge. Such a distinction emphasises how the ability to select and combine information in imaginative new ways is increasingly an everyday survival skill as well as a basis for knowledge in the electronic age.

These developments emphasise the increasing importance of preparing and supporting students in self-directed modes of learning. Teachers may no longer be seen as the authoritative mediators of fixed and stable knowledge. But students will increasingly need authoritative guides who model creative imagination and critical inquiry as they negotiate information in the electronic age and attempt to transform this into knowledge.

Self versus Social 'Knowledges' in the Electronic Age
A basic contradiction informs versions of critical pedagogy which recognise the importance of subjective interests and desires, yet concludes that the agency of self is inevitably manipulated and ultimately negated by the social and ideological determinations of a public sphere (McLaren 1995:74). Both Giroux and McLaren project a teaching situation in which students learn to escape their individual and collective subjectivities through intellectual resistance, through deconstructing the racial, gender, class, and other colonialist determinations of a dominant social order. This view of knowledge (and thus of self) as merely social construction leads to the conclusion that practical agency is a utopian hope.

Yet the kind of interactive media involved in the use of CDROM programs and computer networks does require a notion of self, which is a constitutive focus of learning. Influential conceptions of personal identity in the electronic age describe a model of self, which is a 'fluid' process reflecting diverse patterns and potentials, and not just a series of social constructions (Turkle 1995:177-192). In such a paradigm, learning can be approached as a process of communication. Many of the new educational CDROM programs, for instance, exemplify how any interaction with 'information' results in a transformative communication with self as well as potentially with others. Likewise, computer-mediated communication programs typically require participants to use anonymous nicknames; thus encouraging not only active participation in playful modes of interaction, but also dialogues among selves relatively freed from issues of conventional or traditional prejudices about race, gender or class differences. In such contexts, many classrooms are already taking the opportunity to dramatically open the personal and social horizons of students by interacting with other schools in other countries, and establishing new learning communities as well as collaborative learning projects.

With these opportunities for open networks of diverse learning groups and communities, collaborative learning may be increasingly recognised as a necessary precondition of knowledge in the electronic age, and not just the quaint, tacked-on idea it is often seen as in the traditional classroom. The relation between self-knowledge and social knowledges might therefore be reconciled in terms of a similar relation between self-directed and collaborative learning -- as different yet complementary stages of the learning process.

Critical Thinking in the Learning Process
For all their simplistic conclusions about popular culture as an instrument of social oppression, Giroux and McLaren freely admit their own personal ambivalence about this. In so doing, they themselves embody some of the tension in educational debates between opposing positions of naive enthusiasm for, and critical resistance to, the new electronic literacies and technologies (Kenner, Perelman and Postman 1992).

Such positions might be reconciled in terms of different stages of either an individual or collective learning process in which critical reflection is grounded in practical activity. As well as an open-minded and balanced approach, it seems to me -- from my own research in this area -- that a basic familiarity with the new kinds of media (and their exemplary uses and even abuses in actual educational contexts) is a necessary requirement to be able to talk about learning in the electronic age. Naive enthusiasts for new technologies may eventually become critical enthusiasts, but critical resistance per se can only result in self-fulfilling prophecy.

Given the fears and resistances many people experience towards computers, it is important that students (and, even more importantly, teachers) are supported in their initial efforts to explore and familiarise themselves with the skills and processes involved in new interactive electronic media. In other words, critical learning in the electronic age will not happen in a vacuum, but might be developed as a later stage in the process of learning -- especially if the initial stages allow a 'play' phase. This is reflected in how many parents and primary school teachers do make good use of recreational or educational games in not only familiarising young children with computers, but motivating them to develop further skills. Similarly, the various uses of the Internet for communication and accessing information generally reflects a trajectory from exploratory play towards practical applications; for example, there are obvious transitions in the use of synchronous computer-mediated communication for game-playing, for social chat and, very recently, also for conferencing applications.

Conclusion

Instead of talking about critical pedagogy in the electronic age, we might talk about a pedagogy of critical learning in the electronic age. The interactive nature of new electronic media invites educational uses of new literacies and technologies that especially emphasise self-directed and collaborative approaches to learning. There is an important pedagogical role in getting students to also become critically reflective and disciplined in their quest for knowledge (as well as encouraging actively imaginative modes of thinking) -- but it is to be seen in the wider context of guiding an overall learning process, and grounding student motivation to learn in both cultural interests and practical activities. I suspect that Borges anticipated the electronic age when he wrote *The Library of Babel*. In that short fable, Borges' narrator suggests that people need not ever 'drown' in information, since knowledge is an open-ended process of both creatively and critically attempting to recognise recurring patterns of meaning.

References

Borges, J. (1964). *The library of Babel.* Labyrinths, New York: New Directions.

Crawford, W. and Gorman, M. (1995). *Future libraries: Dreams, madness and reality.* Chicago: American Library Association.

Giroux, H. (1994). *Disturbing pleasures: Learning popular culture.* New York: Routledge.

Giroux, H. (1996). 'Is there a place for cultural studies in Colleges of Education?' In *Counternarratives: Cultural studies and critical pedagogies in postmodern spaces*. H. Giroux, C. Lankshear, P. McLaren and M. Peters, (eds.). New York: Routledge.

McLaren, P. (1995). *Critical pedagogy and predatory culture*. New York: Routledge .

Richards, C. (1996). A critical pedagogy of popular culture? *The Australian Educational Researcher*, 23 (1): 93-101.

Roszak, T. (1994). *The cult of information*. California: University of California Press.

Turkle, S. (1995). *Life on the screen*. New York: Simon & Schuster.

Topic D

Electronic Collection Development:

Selection and Management Issues

The Collection Devolution: Issues for Teacher Librarians in Managing the Changing School Library Collection[*]

Shelda Debowski[†]

It is predicted that by 1998, 80 percent of the world's information, which will be at least twice that available today, will be held electronically, in digital, voice or image formats. Of that amount, in excess of 50 percent will only be available by electronic access. This means there will be a need for a further merging of technologies and skills to ensure maximum access to the information needed...

(Cook 1995:2)

Traditionally, teacher librarians have managed a physical collection of resources which served to meet the majority of user needs. As the quote by Cook shows, the nature of information resources is changing, and leading to a different type of school library collection. Our future collections will assuredly comprise both locally held materials and access to electronic resources and services from other locations. The incorporation of external sources of information into our collection raises some important issues with which teacher librarians need to grapple.

Types of Electronic Resources

Most teacher librarians are now comfortable with the notion of CDROM technology and the way in which these resources may be purchased and loaded onto servers for access by users. The development of externalised electronic information services will reflect similar processes. It is likely that many more of our resourcing practices will be based on subscriptions to information services, such as database providers and document delivery services, and for the use of the Internet to locate additional materials (see Simeone 1996). These will be accessed and used at point of need, rather than holding materials in readiness for single usage

Submitted and accepted as a refereed conference paper.

[†] At the time of writing **Shelda Debowski** was a lecturer in teacher librarianship and library and information science with the Department of Library and Information Science at Edith Cowan University in Perth, Western Australia. Shelda may be contacted via email at **<debowski@commerce.murdoch.edu.au>**.

The Collection Devolution 119

during a year. In many ways, this is a practice which makes more sense, since the information is more current, better accessed simultaneously through the school network by students, and less prone to cluttering the shelves with unattractive materials.

With the increasing use of electronic resources, we will need to reconsider the ways in which we facilitate access to users, and the additional tasks which teacher librarians must incorporate to fully exploit these information sources. Furthermore, there are a range of issues which teacher librarians must also consider in the management of these materials.

User Support

The use of these external information sources demands additional methods of supporting users. Imagine, if you will, the teacher in your school. This person is overwhelmed by the demands of the job, and wants precise, pinpointed information and documents. There is no time to wade through extraneous material. Instead, the teacher requires accurate and timely guidance on new materials which are to be found through these services. Similarly, the student searching for information on a topic may wade through many search avenues unless there is guidance on the best sources of information. We should consider the development of 'closed reserve' electronic access: where users can fast-track the search process to reach the desired information quickly and accurately. These issues indicate that the teacher librarian needs to expand existing roles to include the functions of retrievalist and catalyst, while also helping users to develop their electronic search skills. The following includes new core activities the teacher librarian should consider.

Packaging of Information Sources

To avoid wasting time, the teacher librarian needs to create access points in which students (and teachers) can click on a range of information sources which have been vetted and approved. This leads to effective information investigation, and avoids people being lost in the Web, or accessing services for which the school is charged, but which are of little value. These packages for topics can be placed on the library home page, and users click on the topic of study. The choices which then emerge are of direct relevance to the user, and can be downloaded. The initial search is more efficiently conducted by the teacher librarian, and ensures effective use of class and teacher time.

Facilitating Initial Access to Services

It is likely that listservs, bulletin boards and document delivery services will be explored more extensively by schools. These often take time to find, and, in the case of document delivery services, like *UnCover*, profiles may need to be established for users, to make best use of the service. These are all worthwhile adjuncts to the support offered by teacher librarians (eg. Ellis, Garner and Rainford 1994; Dysart and Jones 1995).[†]

Creating Better Current Awareness Services

In addition, we need to use the emerging Intranets in our schools to create much stronger current awareness services. This facility opens up many possibilities for exploring the ways in which we can structure the sending of messages and information to individual users. We need to become quite innovative in the ways in which we employ new tools to create stronger links between our users and their required information.

Educating Users in Search Strategies

Furthermore, we have a whole new area of challenge in educating users to ultimately extend beyond the information we have packaged. Oliver (1996) demonstrates the complexity of search skills in CDROM encyclopedia searching. The Internet is even more complex as are large databases (see Debowski 1996). As we provide these sources for our users, we will need to amend our user education programs to create more appropriate user strategies in searching.[‡]

Electronic Resource Management

Teacher librarians will also need to review many of their collection management practices with the increased use of these information options. For example, the financial implications are quite substantial. It is probable that users will discover a wealth of new sources with the provision of these services. Many of these will become large cost considerations in the school library budget. A typical illustration is the development of teacher information profiles for use with services like *UnCover*. As teachers start to receive information about recently published articles in their areas of need, they will be likely to request copies. The teacher librarian will find that inter-library loan requests will escalate. Some would suggest that we just avoid establishing the service in the first place, but this is surely not in the best interest of our users... Instead, we need to anticipate the likely additional demands, and then need to become more flexible and anticipatory in our budgeting practices.

A second issue is that additional planning time needs to be set aside. Time will be required to search the Internet, and to identify likely information services which might be accessed. The need to then package access to these materials becomes a further demand. This all indicates a need to be well ahead of demand, since timely provision of information becomes more crucial. In addition, there needs to be a maintenance of the information sites, so that the created links remain viable and appropriate.

The increased range of electronic resources will obviously be an important issue in the coming years. The capacity of the service and servers to cater for the demand which will be placed on the systems is obviously of critical concern. This means that the teacher librarian should really consider developing a resource plan, so that the scope and nature of the collection are defined and planned for in the future. Great ideas are nothing without sufficient technology to drive the process.

Financial Implications
While the library should be prepared for reasonable jumps in electronic usage, and the subsequent impact on the budget, a major issue facing libraries is that the costs of electronic services are rapidly surpassing the budgetary allowance. An issue which will have to be faced by teacher librarians is the likelihood of needing to charge users for access to certain services. One practice used by some schools is to allow a certain budget amount for basic use, but to then pass on additional costs to the particular school sections. This enables management of the process to some extent. However, this type of radical change to the way we operate will need to be ratified by the school, and should be notified well in advance to users.

Conclusion
The increased incorporation of electronic resources will provide us with a better means of supporting the information needs of our users, and also enables more effective access to up-to-date and relevant resources. However, the increased provision of these materials also leads to much greater demands on the time of the teacher librarian, and requires a substantially greater funding commitment. To effectively integrate electronic services into our

collection base, we will therefore need to plan ahead, and be prepared for changes to the practices we follow.

References

Cook, B. (1995). 'Managing for effective delivery of information services in the 1990s: the integration of computing, educational and library services.' In *The Virtual Information Experience: Proceedings of the Seventh Australasian Information Online and On Disc Conference and Exhibition*. Sydney: Information Science Section, Australian Library and Information Science Association: 1-19.

Debowski, S. (1996). Preparing our users for the future: the training needs of end users. In *Reading the Future: 100 Centenary Conference*. Melbourne: Australian Library and Information Association.

Dysart, J.I. and Jones, R.J. (1995). Tools for the future: Recreating or 'renovating' information services using new technologies. *Computers in Libraries*, 15 (1): 16-19.

Ellis, A., Garner, L., and Rainford, A. (1994). Network document access: Planning an electronic document delivery service. A case study. *Australian Library Record*, 11 (1): 67-74.

Oliver, R. (1996). Information access and retrieval from electronic information systems: What do our students need to learn? *Access*, 10 (1): 20-22.

Simeone, P. (1996). The challenges of the Internet across the curriculum. *Access*, 10 (4): 27-29.

---

† For a more intensive exploration of these issues, contact ALIA about their continuing education program, through which a course entitled "Advances in Information Technology" is available.

‡ This issue is explored more fully in a paper published in the ASLA conference proceedings in July. (Debowski, S. (1997). 'School Libraries in a Learning Culture.' *Language and Learning*. Darwin: ASLA).

Electronic Resources: Selection Issues[*]

Shelda Debowski[†]

The notion of a virtual collection is now a well accepted basis for exploring the school library collection. This implies that the information will be provided from both physical and electronic resources, thus providing a current and viable collection to explore all subjects of concern to school library users.

Fundamental to this service is the inclusion of electronic resources. These resources require the use of hardware of some sort to interrogate the information. They include CDROMs, electronic journals and online services to which the library subscribes. Most school libraries are still focused on the exploration of the more physical forms of electronic resources, particularly CDROMs. This paper therefore explores this aspect most fully.

While we all recognise the value of CDROMs, their inclusion in the collection does offer some challenges to the teacher librarian. These relate to the selection and the ultimate management of the materials. This particular paper explores the selection of electronic materials while the previous paper (*The Collection Devolution*) examines the management issues which arise when online services and electronic resources are included in the collection.

Selection of electronic resources can be broken down into three concerns. First, there is the need to identify suitable resources from the range of materials which are present. Second, there is the need to establish suitable criteria for use in evaluating the selected electronic resources. And third, there is the issue of previewing the resources effectively. This paper explores these issues, and also considers some of the difficulties teacher librarians face in developing the most effective electronic collections possible.

Identifying Good Electronic Resources
Texts which explore collection management always indicate that the most professional means of selecting materials is to use reviewing

---

[*] Submitted and accepted as a refereed conference paper.

[†] At the time of writing **Shelda Debowski** was a lecturer in teacher librarianship and library and information science with the Department of Library and Information Science at Edith Cowan University in Perth, Western Australia. Shelda may be contacted via email at **<debowski@commerce.murdoch.edu.au>**.

124   *The Net Effect: School Library Media Centers and the Internet*

journals (eg. Evans 1995). Australia is poorly supported by non-fiction reviewing tools. *Primary Focus: Non-fiction* and *Resource Focus* (from the Education Department of W.A.) and *Scan* are the chief sources available. These include some reviews of electronic resources, and are perceptive in their critical evaluations. The difficulty is that many more resources are appearing on the market, and are not fully reviewed in these works. This is not singular to CDROMs, but is a problem for most non-fiction materials we try to identify. While we do have access to overseas reviews and publications, they often fail to fully explore the Australian materials we would like to examine and investigate. We really need an Australian based reviewing tool similar to *Children's Reference Plus*. This is an American school library selection tool, which enables searching by author, series, date, topic, format, publisher etc. In addition, it includes reviews of titles, so that the selector can gain a strong picture of the value of the item. Boolean logic can be used to create more sophisticated interrogations. *The Schools Cataloguing Information Service* (SCIS) has the capabilities to add such reviewing data to the cataloguing records, and this is regarded as one of the long-term plans.

Clearly, the inclusion of such reviewing data would entail extra cost. One of the issues teacher librarians need to consider, is how much they are willing to support developments of better services. *Bookscope* and *Children's Reference Plus*, for example, cost in the vicinity of $1,000 per annum. We need to be aware that additional support does come with a potential increase in charges. While selection support is not strong in Australia, there may be costs attached to gaining increased selection information.

Electronic Resource Criteria
The second issue which teacher librarians need to address is the area of selection criteria. Electronic resources differ from print materials in their style of interrogation and their presentation characteristics. The hierarchical nature of the knowledge structure means that the whole content and coverage of a resource can be difficult to determine. It is ironic that the resource which should be evaluated most intensively, because of its hidden facets, is also the most difficult to explore, precisely because the whole cannot be readily seen.

The best the teacher librarian can hope for, is to create some fundamental guidelines and to use these to explore the presentation as best possible. Some of the criteria which are of value to consider include:

- layout of the screen
- level of language and intellectual content
- degree of interactivity with the user
- conceptual framework depicted in the introductory screens
- ease of interpretation of the commands and underlying structure
- quality of information contained in sample segments
- existence of help devices, eg. indexes, glossaries, help screens
- ease with which information can be downloaded or copied onto disk or a work page
- proportion of content which is dynamic in nature, eg. music, film clips, animations
- quality of those inserts
- extent to which other publications are duplicated.

These criteria offer some basis for judging the worth of an electronic resource (see Debowski 1995, for a more detailed explanation of these criteria). Obviously, there are other criteria which could be employed also. However, these enable a quick preview of a resource to identify the major strengths and weaknesses inherent in the item.

Previewing Electronic Resources
Clearly, previewing is a necessary part of selecting electronic resources. This can be undertaken through three methods. The first is to obtain the item on preview, and to explore it with users and personally. This is obviously the preferred option, since it enables an effective trial of the resource with the particular users, and enables a comparison with other items in the context of specific topics and needs. However, this is not always possible. A second option may be the provision of a demonstration disk. These are not always fully representative of the whole product, and may need to be treated with caution. A third option is the exploration of the Internet, to see if sample elements of the work are provided on the Net. This is increasingly the case with print materials, and will not be long before we see the same offered for non-print. This is certainly a useful avenue as it grows.

Electronic Services
While this paper has examined the CDROM situation fairly specifically, many of the issues explored also relate to the

identification of suitable electronic services. In some ways, these are less difficult to evaluate, once the initial pre-selection of potential options has been made. The advantage of electronic online services is that most suppliers will provide a trial period in which the service may be tested. Promotions of the services are well-demonstrated online. This gives the teacher librarian a much better feel for how the resource will work. Increasingly, we may also be able to subscribe on a usage basis, where we are charged for real-access time, rather than on a subscription basis. Van Brakel (1995) offers further insights into electronic journals.

Selection Concerns for Teacher Librarians

The task of selecting electronic resources and services is not an easy one. This is primarily due to the primitive nature of our selection tool options. The absence of educational agency support is very evident in the dearth of tools we have at our disposal, other than the excellent guidance provided by N.S.W. and W.A. It is possible that other selection services are provided by other states, but they are little publicised outside their own vicinity. As professionals, we need to share the information we can find.

We do have one source of sharing already well established. For those of us subscribing to OZTL_NET, we have access to a forum for sharing insights into new resources we have located. Imagine the value of emailed reviews from colleagues who have located some good resources. These could be headed: REVIEW: [title] to distinguish them from other messages, and we could then download them into a separate reviews file. This would be a very efficient means of collecting good feedback from those with similar concerns.

The paper also points to the need for teacher librarians to ensure their needs are well recognised. We should, for example, be providing feedback to those agencies such as EDWA and NSW Department of Education, concerning the value their services offer. We have lost many supportive services over the years because we did not express satisfaction and support for their assistance. We need to be much more political about how our information support environment is structured. We need to express satisfaction with the good aspects of current services, and ensure our needs are understood by those who can improve support to teacher librarians. We also need to let others know of the good systems and services which are available.

Conclusion

The development of a virtual collection offers many opportunities for us to create a very strong and innovative collection for our users. In order to do so, we need to select new resources very carefully. As more electronic resources emerge, however, we are faced with the increasing difficulties of how to identify the widest range of materials, and how to then evaluate these effectively. We may need to become much more political in order to create better professional selection tools to suit our purposes.

References

Debowski, S. (1995). Forget the content: What does it do? Evaluating CD-ROM resources. *Access*, 9 (3), August: 16-18.

Evans, G.E. (1995). *Developing library and information centre collections*. Littleton, Colorado: Libraries Unlimited.

Van Brakel, P.A. (1995). Electronic journals: Publishing via Internet's World Wide Web. *The Electronic Library*, 13 (4): 389-395.

The Teacher Librarian as an Internet Information Provider

Julie Dow[*]

Introduction

The Internet, especially the World Wide Web, is an important information resource for school libraries as it extends the number and types of resources available to students in both the intellectual and geographical sense. The teacher librarian's links to external resources on the library Web site equate with the books on the shelves, while all of the non-linked Internet resources offer a vast selection of alternative and previously inaccessible materials. This new ease of access to a variety of sources is important to students who usually depend on adults to take them to libraries beyond their immediate neighbourhood. Thus Internet access gives unprecedented opportunities for students to develop and extend their independent learning within the formal curriculum. In addition, Marchionini and Maurer (1995:68) argue that the Internet is central to the self directed and opportunistic informal learning that continues throughout life as it facilitates access to other people, the environment and the mass media which we all use to continue our learning.

Any Internet user will testify that it is a vast, disorganised resource that is sometimes very difficult to use. Its unstructured nature can be a major problem for both novice and experienced users who may not be able retrieve relevant material in spite of extensive searching. Libraries on the other hand are organised collections of selected resources within which librarians try to ensure a close match between the resources and the specified information needs of an identified clientele. Librarians arrange and index these resources to facilitate user access and effective retrieval within that collection.

Teacher librarians who create links to external resources on their library web sites are performing a traditional collection development function within a new environment. They require Net surfing time to identify what is available, to develop suitable evaluation techniques and to learn how to write for the Web. With constant technological and educational change, teacher librarians

---

[*] **Julie Dow** is Senior Lecturer with the School of Communication and Information Studies at the University of South Australia. Julie may be contacted via email at <julie.dow@unisa.edu.au>.

have encountered and adapted to this learning process continuously as other new formats such as slides, videos, computer software, CDROMs and multi media have been integrated into library collections.

The library collection development policy should guide teacher librarians in shaping the site content links, and most will have wish lists of materials they want and need but cannot afford. In selecting Internet sites for links teacher librarians must maintain a central focus on identifying materials that relate directly to the curriculum and that are compatible with the age and intellectual levels of students. While new format principles must be integrated, the core evaluation principles that we apply to print materials remain. Mitchell (1996) gives an overview of these general selection criteria with pointers on how to relate them to the Web. Alexander and Tate <http://www.science.widener.edu/~withers/evalout.htm> also list ways to adapt traditional print criteria to Web resources. Tillman extends this discussion to examine Web publishing within the context of traditional publishing and the search tools that purport to evaluate Internet resources <http://www.tiac.net.users/hope/findqual.html>.

There are numerous tutorials on the Web to assist with learning HTML, the markup language of the World Wide Web. Some recommended HTML sources[†] are listed at the end of this paper. Many Web authors now opt to use one or more of the HTML editors that can be downloaded from the Web for both Windows and Mac platforms. These allow evaluative testing of the product for one month:

<http://sdg.ncsa.uiuc.edu/~mag/work/HTMLEditors/windowslist.html> or
<http://sdg.ncsa.uiuc.edu/~mag/work/HTMLEditors/maclist.html>.

Why be an Internet Information Provider?
A considered analysis of the collection in any school will reveal immediate needs for new or extended information in some if not most subjects. The Internet, in its present form, offers free materials and enhances opportunities for teacher librarians to deliver more resources within the budget. Of course schools must pay to connect to the Internet, though this is likely to be a cost irrespective of whether the library uses networked information.

The following are particular categories of materials are very accessible on the Internet and can supplement and complement the physical collection to enhance the school's information service:

- reference works to supplement those that date quickly and are expensive to replace annually;
- newspapers from many parts of the world that give different perspectives on daily events <http://www.webwombat.com.au/intercom/newsprs/>;
- experts in various fields who are prepared to share their knowledge and answer email questions, including the AskERIC site for teachers;
- electronic serials <http://ipl.sils.umich.edu/reading/serials/> to help the budget and eliminate the problems of storage, theft and vandalism. Some, such as *Scientific American*, will be available in both print and electronic format;
- interactive sites or multimedia sites based on museums, galleries, and geological phenomena, eg. *Nine Planets* which is mirrored in Australia <http://www.anu.edu.au/Physics/nineplanets/copyright.html>;
- sites sponsored by computer hardware and software vendors that offer files to update or extend the functionality of purchased software, beta versions of new software for downloading and trialing for a month, plus update information about products not supplied in their manuals <http://www.microsoft.com.au/>;
- databases of film and film information for media studies students;
- primary source material such as documents of American history found on the *American Memory* site <http://rs6.loc.gov/amhome.html>;
- sites that provide special links for children or that feature children's work are also popular with younger users; and
- government publications, and material about Australian law that is pertinent to legal studies.

Web sites often collate diverse materials and formats that normally would not be available in one library. Recently, for example, I searched the Web with a Year 10 student who wanted material on *Jack the Ripper*. One site <http://ripper.wildnet.co.uk/> gave an overview of the speculative nature of information about this serial killer. It then presented a wide range of material, including contemporary newspaper reports of the murders, official court documents of the case, thumbnail biographies of victims, and information about contemporary London.

Evaluation of this and similar Internet sources poses some problems, as material on most sites is not refereed and literally anyone can publish anything. This is both a strength and weakness of the Net. In this context we must help students develop their own evaluation methods for such materials. *Kathy Schrock's Guides for Educators* <http://www.capecod.net/schrockguide/eval.htm> with evaluation forms designed for teachers and for students at different levels will provide a good starting point. Web sites are probably one of the most challenging resources to evaluate as they do not go through any quality controls. Teacher librarians will find guidance from the links supplied in bibliographies such as Alastair Smith's *Evaluation of information sources* <http://www.vuw.ac.nz/~agsmith/evaln/evaln.htm> and Alexander and Tate's *Web evaluation techniques* <http://www.science.widener.edu/~withers/wbstrbib.htm>.

Providing links for students should not be the full extent of their access to Internet resources. Instead, the links should give a starting point similar to that provided by the material chosen for the shelves. It is useful to download a search engine onto your site to emphasise that there are many other resources available. This poses another set of questions about managing access to these resources that cannot be covered within the scope of this paper. Dillon (1996) gives a comprehensive overview of significant issues and Caywood's *Guiding children through cyberspace* <http://www.infi.net/~carolyn/guide.html> offers a series of links for information.

Define Goals for the Web Site
Before commencing a web development project, articulate and establish clear initial objectives, as building a web site is a challenging and time consuming task with a steep learning curve for the participants. It also needs commitment of school funds to ensure its success. The identified reasons for establishing the site will be central to its development, but a primary objective should be to provide better access to information. In this capacity teacher librarians should have a significant role in its initiation and planning.

Stated objectives may include some or all of the following:

- to link to resources to enhance curriculum delivery;

- to extend the bounds of the curriculum by enabling students to interact and cooperate with others in their learning;
- to extend the role of teachers and teacher librarians in developing the online information literacy and information access competence of users;
- to provide a place for authentic learning about electronic publishing and to facilitate the distribution of children's work;
- to promote the school within the community;
- to make available school curriculum, policies and other information in a form that is accessible to any interested person with computer access;
- to advertise services such as homepage production or computing classes for the public.

Mounting the Library Web Site

An early decision for teacher librarians is to determine how to deliver web-based information. The best approach may be to rent server space from the school's Internet service provider, who then has the responsibility to restore the system after a server crash, minimise server vandalism such as virus attacks, install firewalls to maintain the integrity of files and provide advice when the school encounters difficulties. Some agreements include a small amount of web space, but usually additional storage will be necessary to run a successful library site. Schools should explore the pricing and any maintenance costs very carefully before entering an agreement, for if the server space becomes prohibitively expensive there are some problems remounting the content elsewhere and in advising users of the new URL. *How the Web Was Won* at <http://www.wolfchild.com/htwww/step1.htm> offers plenty of good advice about these matters.

Another option is to explore local resources such as the public library or any higher education institution, particularly a School or Faculty of Education, which may be able to exchange server space for opportunities to research staff and student use of the Web. Some education system servers, like NEXUS, will host school homepages. See <http://www.nexus.edu.au/help/styleguide.html>.

If the school can afford a server and sees a need to own one, Powell's *Spinning the Web* <http://scholar.lib.vt.edu/reports/Servers-web.html> discusses the selection of platform, operating system, hardware and software, in addition to giving helpful information about how servers work. Before buying a server carefully consider whether you have the continuing funds, technical expertise, and staff to maintain it for 24 hour international access, as the 9 to 4 day does not exist in cyberspace. Online users expect that they can access resources at a time of their choosing including evenings, weekends and school holidays.

Planning the Site

Think long and hard about how to organise the site content into logical groupings. Time spent on this will be rewarded well. The links should be easily accessible and intelligible to users who need to develop a conceptual map of the content that lies behind each link. The page design and fonts should contribute to accessibility also. The *Internet Public Library* <http://ipl.sils.umich.edu> and the *University of South Australia Library* homepages <http://www.unisa. edu.au/library/libhome.htm> achieve these outcomes very effectively. In this context it is informative to view the homepage for the *University of South Australia* <http://www.unisa.edu.au>.

Be aware that fashions on the Web change as often as they do in designer shops and sites can look out of date very quickly. You will need to move with the times but not with every fashion trend. Initially most web pages used Netscape's default grey background with black text and few graphics. The tendency now is to use white backgrounds with darker text and discreet graphics, although the very up-market sites use frames and flashing icons which are not accepted universally as good practice. Some sites, particularly the search engines, are flooded with advertisements that blend in with the content so effectively that users may have difficulty identifying the content. This is an area for intensive information literacy education.

House Style

Try to develop a distinctive format for your web pages to give a sense of unity and predicability for users. They will need some visual clues about the navigation of your site. This is well illustrated on the *Australian Library and Information Association* site <http:// www.alia.org.au/> while the *Dynix Australia* <http://www.dynix. com.au/> and *Ameritech* sites <http://www.als.ameritech.com/> sites provide examples of achieving a corporate feel across separate parts of an organisation. Internal harmony on your site is best achieved by writing your own style guide for web page authors. It might include:

- general page layout requirements;
- page labels and the structure of heading through documents;
- the content of headers and of footers within documents;
- types of navigational tools to use;
- suggested maximum size and recommended file formats for graphics.

Possible models are available from ALIA <http://www.alia.org.au/alia/technical.notes.html> and Department of Education and Children's Services in South Australia <http://www.nexus.edu.au/help/styleguide.html>.

Bibliographic and Quality Considerations

Authors of web documents are the counterparts of book publishers and they need to supply the web equivalents of the publisher's imprint, blurb and dust jacket information. They should include the following:

- name of the document's author;
- the date of its creation;
- date of its addition to the Web;
- dates of revisions which equate to edition statements;
- the author's affiliation, to give some clues about the authenticity of the material;
- a navigation button to the homepage of the organisation sponsoring the site to orient users who come in directly to a specific document;
- the Web Manager's name and email address somewhere on the site for users who wish to comment on content; and
- the URL at the end of each document to assist users who may wish to cite it or return to your Web later, for it does not print automatically.

Site managers also need to assume the publisher's role in proof reading and checking the typographic accuracy of documents. Most importantly they need to check all links regularly to ensure that they are unbroken. Web sites, like periodicals, merge, disappear and change sponsorship or URL regularly.

User Access Courtesies

You may not have state of the art hardware, but neither will many of your visitors, so remember the lowest common denominator. Ensure that all browsers see an image of reasonable quality. Check this, if possible, by viewing your pages using each browser, on different machines and with varied configurations. Users will become impatient or disinterested if they have to wait too long to access your site. Kahn and Logan (1996:127) suggest that a page should take no more than 30 seconds to load when the viewer is using a 14.4 modem. This places severe restrictions on the size of graphics and on the overall Kbs for each page. Images need to be small in size and saved in the .gif or .jpeg format for greatest efficiency. There are various sites on the Net from which users may download suitable graphics.

Copyright
There is a myth that it is fair to copy anything on the Net. In fact all web resources are protected under the Australian Copyright Act <http://www.dse.vic.gov.au/copwrit.htm>, although users may make reproductions under the fair dealing section of the Act that permits single reproductions for personal private study or research. This does not allow schools to undertake wholesale copying of Internet resources to an Intranet, although individual authors like Werbach <http://werbach.com/barebones/> may authorise reproduction of their own texts, usually with the proviso that the purpose is non commercial or educational, the content is left intact and the footer notice of ownership stays attached to the document. Recognise that authors have a moral right to retain ownership of their material and that you should use it as they wrote it.

Meyer <http://www.cwru.edu/help/introHTML/tcopy.html> forbids reproductions of any part of his *HTML tutorial* without prior written permission and he requests that anyone who makes a publicly accessible link to it uses the form on his Copyright notice to register that link. This is also good Net practice, as it gives prior notice to sites that traffic may increase and the site owners may notify you if they change the URL.

Conclusion
In the early eighties when funds for resources were more plentiful, the challenge was to find time to order and process materials for users. More recently teacher librarians have struggled to fund sufficient library resources within static or reduced budgets to meet the demands of a more individualised curriculum and a wider cultural diversity among students. The library web site with well organised links and access to other resources may help to expand

the collection in new directions by providing access to resources rather than ownership.

There is a possible disadvantage in library web sites in that students may become so committed to web sources that they may not use the print resources well. Is this a major problem? Absolutely not, as the library will hold sufficient examples of paper formats to ensure that students to learn to use them well, and for some sources, particularly indexing tools, few users would opt for a hardcopy version when an electronic alternative is available. Our role in extending the collection to electronic resources is to offer more alternatives and to ensure that students learn how to operate effectively in the print and the electronic world of information.

References

Dillon, K. (1996). 'Management of student access to the Internet: Issues and responsibilities.' In *A Meeting of minds: ITEC Virtual Conference '96 Proceedings,* edited by Lyn Hay and James Henri. Belconnen: ASLA, 16-24.

Kahn, L. and Logan, L. (1996). *Build your own Web site.* Redmond, Washington: Microsoft.

Marchionini, G. and Maurer, H. (1995). The roles of digital libraries in teaching and learning. *Communications of the ACM,* 38 (4), April: 67-75.

Mitchell, P. (1996). 'The teacher librarian's role as evaluator of Internet evaluation services.' In *A Meeting of minds: ITEC Virtual Conference '96 Proceedings,* edited by Lyn Hay and James Henri. Belconnen: ASLA, 152-156.

[†] **Recommended HTML Tutorials:**

Meyer, Eric A. *HTML tutorial.*
Available: <http://www.cwru.edu/help/intro HTML/>.

National Center for Supercomputing Applications. *A beginner's guide to HTML.*
Available: <http://www.ncsa.uiuc.edu/General/Internet/WWW/HTMLPrimerAll. html#GS>.

Victoria. Department of School Education. *Publishing on the Web.*
Available: <http://www.dse.vic.gov.au/publish.htm#design>.

Werbach, K. *The bare bones guide to HTML.*
Available: <http://werbach.com/ barebones/>.

Integrating Information Technology with Information Literacy into Collection Building

Lynne Fletcher[*]

Forrest School's collection building unit based on the integration of Information Literacy and Information Technology for Grade 6 children arose out of a discussion between the Grade 6 teachers and myself. We all had specific literacy and technical educational outcomes that needed to be addressed. I wanted to ensure that all the children would understand the principles of collection building to analyse the collection and to consider the supply and purchase of appropriate titles for other grades, which would enable titles to be added to the collection and for the children to develop a variety of independent computer skills.

Together, we were looking for ways to encourage both boys and girls to read widely and to develop particular interest in Authors and the writing process. We aimed to establish a promotional peer group in which book selection and discussion of authors and their works was focal to their Library Resource Centre sessions. We aimed to provide the girls with skills involving risk taking and computer technology. What evolved was an innovative multimedia unit that did indeed incorporate Information Literacy and Information Technology skills being developed in the Grade 6 children at Forrest School and in keeping with the *Draft Plan for Information Technology in Learning and Teaching 1996-1998 for ACT Public Schools* (1995).

Forrest School has approximately 470 children from 32 cultures. There are composite and straight grade classes in the Kindergarten to Grade 6 spread of students. Specialist teachers include English as a Second Language, Languages other than English, (Indonesian and Spanish) Learning Advancement, Physical Education and Library Resource Centre manager.

In 1994 the school had taken part in the ACT Department of Education's Schools Program Review and Development (SPRAD) formal assessment. In 1995 in line with SPRAD recommendations

[*] **Lynne Fletcher** is the teacher librarian at Forrest Primary School in the Australian Capital Territory. Lynne may be contacted via email at <**Lynn.Fletcher@ForrestPS. act.edu.au**>.

the school had leased sixteen 580 Apple Macs and several Powerbooks to enable the acquisition of additional computing skills for all classes from Kindergarten to Grade 6.

In 1995 and 1996 teaching staff had engaged in professional development courses that enabled them to integrate use of computing skills into the Key Learning Areas. By 1996, children had access to ClarisWorks and graphics packages and were becoming familiar with their integration. In addition to the sixteen 580 Macs the school had leased a 630 Mac, a Quicktake 150 digital camera and a colour printer for the Library Resource Centre.

The Library Resource Centre had access to the Internet and a fledgling school web site was in place. The challenge was to integrate all of the hardware into the timetabled programs already in existence both in the Library Resource Centre and in the classroom.

School parliament, a system of child-oriented school management run by the children in Grade 6 and conducted along Parliamentary lines, raised $150.00 to purchase resources. The Library Resource Centre allocated $850.00 for the overall program. It was decided that I would take children selected by the school parliament to various bookshops around Canberra in my administration time. The children range the bookstores and asked for a mutually convenient time for browsing. The school parliament also sent representatives to each classroom to ask children for subject areas to buy in and individual authors and series. A discussion with the selected children ensued about the titles listed, a search was made of the school's database and new items for cataloguing and amendments made. A final list was them compiled and acted as the focus for our initial browsing search in the bookstores.

Once items were selected by all members of the group, including me, we had a discussion about cost versus quality and appropriateness for inclusion. It was amazing how rationally the children went about excluding titles that did not represent good reading value for money or would not stand the rigours of vigorous use. I was challenged on several occasions for considering expensive reference books that were not on the agreed list and asked to purchase them from my own funds! A calculator was taken and total cost determined. Reluctant pruning was needed on several excursions as boys and girls grappled with costings. Generous discounts were sought and in some cases given. Accounts were presented to the school's parliament and paid through the school's bursar.

On return to school, titles were taken to be viewed by the school's parliament and then by the classes that had asked for their purchase. Within a short time all children wanted to be selected for book buying duties. Adjustments had to be made to the method of preview and selection to speed up the process and to enable the whole Grade 6 class to be involved simultaneously. It was arranged with Jacaranda Educational that boxes of new titles be made available for viewing, reading and selecting. An extended 'On Approval' time enabled boys and girls to read the titles in Library Resource Centre time, their free time and their class silent reading time.

At whole class discussions children had to present a draft review, argue how the title would enhance or augment the collection and make links with other titles that their particular author had written. This task involved checking our database and taking a print of holdings. The children were then able to exchange bibliographies with their peers. Creating biographies was an off shoot of this task as children pored through blurbs and biographical reference books to support their chosen author and argue for purchase.

Formal written reviews were then presented on disk with overall suggestions about costings. A debate on paperback versus hardback was inevitable and resulted in more paperback editions being purchased. Children were taught the rudiments of cataloguing following the simplified process of author statement/illustrator statement, title statement, publisher, place and date as well as a collation note. Reference to subject headings were discussed. Drafts of cataloguing assisted on purchase of items and enabled speedy cataloguing. Children eagerly waited to see when their titles had been entered on the database and them took printouts to take home and show their parents. Books were covered using contact. Children made sure that spine labels and barcode numbers were in place.

We were then in a position to give instruction on the use of the Quicktake 150 digital camera. This proved to be a great success with an initial small group being instructed and them they further instructed others. Children posed with the book of their choice and this assisted the promotional activities of reviews and titles on display in the school foyer. As Children's Book Week was approaching we discussed the possibility of linking with the ACT

Library and Information Services, Griffith Branch. We had reviews, pictures of the titles and decided that we could videotape reviews to add a further dimension to our display. This activity generated a lot of excitement with the children who also had younger brothers and sisters attending Children's Book Week activities at the Griffith Branch as part of their week long celebrations.

Our final activity involved marking up our word processed reviews in HTML. Children were given rudimentary instructions as a whole class group on such conventions as <hr> horizontal rule, <br> break, <p> paragraph, <i> italics, <h> bold and how to end instruction given, eg. </i> close italics. Once again a core of children who felt confident to try taught their peers to mark up and put files up onto our web site. Parents were asked for written permission for children's work to appear on our web site. All conventions involving privacy issues were strictly adhered to in accordance to ACT Department of Education policy (Hinton 1996:66). (See Appendix A).

In all cases, the parents agreed to allow their children's work to be downloaded, marked up and uploaded onto our web site. We promoted our work through the school's weekly newsletter and made bookmarks that gave our URL. Parents seemed to be greatly interested, visiting our site and sending email advice and encouragement. The children wanted to continue adding to their reviews and repeated the activity in some cases up to five times throughout the year. Discussions occurred about authors and their titles. Boys were recommending additional titles that they had seen while browsing in book stores and held by the ACT Library and Information Services. Girls were asking to borrow the Quicktake camera to take photographs in the playground and to promote school activities.

Discussion with other teacher librarians exchanging ideas on how to integrate multimedia suggested that it would generate as much interest and excitement for reading as it had a Forrest School. I know of at least one school which has embarked on this activity with great success.

So where will we go to from here? We fully intend to continue to present this program to the older grade, perhaps taking it down to Grade 4 children and using Information Technology and Information Literacy skills in all levels of research. The initial outcomes and skills grid will be further developed from that indicated by Gwen Gawith (1991:13) and the Department's guidelines (1996). Visits by authors and illustrators will continue to be part of the Library Resource Centre's program with a special emphasis on videorecording. A writer's in residence workshop will be negotiated after discussion with the teaching staff, School Board and Parents & Citizens group.

An avenue of access to reviews written by children and any other interested persons would be canvassed. Possible sites for these reviews could be on the O'Connell Information and Resource Centre's homepage, EdNA or each State Branch of the Children's Book Council's homepage. Links between other organisations interested in promoting literature and literacy may also prove beneficial.

References

Plan for Information Technology in Learning and Teaching 1997-1999 for ACT Public Schools. (1996). Canberra: Department of Education & Training and Children's Youth and Family Services Bureau.

Draft Plan for Information Technology in Learning and Teaching 1996-1998 for ACT Public Schools. (1995). Canberra: Department of Education & Training and Children's Youth and Family Services Bureau.

Gawith, G. (1991). *Information skills: today's skills for today's schools a practical guide to introducing information skills across the primary and secondary curriculum.* Auckland: Information Studies and Teacher Librarianship Programme, Auckland College of Education, 13.

Hinton, F. (1996). *Plan for Information Technology in Learning and Teaching 1997-1999 for ACT Public Schools.* Canberra: Canberra: Department of Education & Training and Children's Youth and Family Services Bureau, 66.

---

† **Appendix A**

Throughout the process parents were kept informed of the program. Permission to travel in a private car was sought, reports were printed, sometimes weekly, in the School's Newsletter. Prior to marking up reviews in HTML permission was sought and no child's work was included on our web site until written permission was received.

The following note acted as an alerting device should parents not have been aware of the class work undertaken nor had followed the program through the School's Newsletter.

Dear Parents,

During Library Research time we have selected new books, read them, argued for their inclusion into the collection, costed them, reviewed them, presented the review, taken our photo with books using the Quicktake 150 digital camera, downloaded the images onto our 630 Mac, printed the picture in black and white and in colour. We have put our work on display in the school foyer and at Griffith Library. We now want to put our work on our web site on the Internet.

I give permission _____

I do not give permission _____

Signed Parent/Guardian _____

Date _____

School Library Front Ends: OPACs and Access Beyond Connectivity?

Kylie Hanson[*]

Teacher librarians have lead the evolution of schools as responsive information environments acknowledging the call for lifelong learners, establishing and reaffirming the school library as a principal environment for intellectual activity. Automation has been embraced as a pragmatic management solution to the burgeoning demands for increasingly sophisticated school library services, and at the same time teacher librarians are campaigning to influence opportunities for electronic access to information.

School libraries are shifting from being structured collections of publications to places for virtual browsing, exploration and navigation. As we move beyond automation to connectivity and electronic collection development it seems reasonable to expect that OPACs will provide static as well as dynamic customised access to collections.

However, in the scramble to automate and in the scramble to embrace electronic access the needs of users often become secondary as efforts are focused on learning to manage the 'computers' and learning to manage the 'access'. The intricacies of 'data entry' and the importance of standards and 'form of entry' within the powerful relational databases of the automated systems provide steep learning curves for many teacher librarians, let alone the complexity of document delivery and issues of equity of access to the electronic collection.

Wanding those first barcodes is a real joy, and there is nothing more professionally rewarding than building a school library service that is able to deliver those timely information items just when they are needed. But how much thought has been given to how school library collections will be accessed? How well are we using the current technology? Given the dynamics of school libraries, how feasible is it to expect intermediaries to be available to assist users to translate their information need into the language of the catalogue?

[*] **Kylie Hanson** is a lecturer in Teacher Librarianship with the School of Information Studies at Charles Sturt University, Wagga Wagga, New South Wales, Australia. Kylie can be contacted via email at <khanson@csu.edu.au>.

What are the fundamental needs of the user seeking information in any library? Aside from knowing what they are looking for, they need to be independent at interrogating the front end to the collection, the online public access catalogue or OPAC.

OPACs are, at this moment, the most important piece of software school libraries offer to their users. They are an essential aid for the user to access resources. Abbott (1997:115) marks a turning point in the Australian literature when she reports that 'circulation control and ease of cataloguing have become less significant than OPAC design and compatibility with other technology (such as multimedia, online databases, and the Internet)'.

The majority of school libraries in Australia provide access to collections via basic OPACs developed out of research carried out in the 1980s, displaying data according to AACR2 standards, providing in addition to the traditional entry points, keyword and Boolean search formulation and retrieval methods. Adequate enough when education was based on a passive input-output model where users were spoon fed and knew exactly what they were supposed to be looking for, but can we continue to claim that our OPACs are user friendly, providing efficient access to school library collections? Consideration must be given to maximising the potential of the OPAC, keeping in mind the identity of the client of the OPAC, not only from the point of view of user education but also from the point of view of OPAC extensions and interface design.

My recent paper (Hanson 1997:37-66) was developed to teach and explain the content and workings of the OPAC system being used in NSW government schools, OASIS Library, because current access to that system is not intuitive. Untrained and novice users require tuition to navigate the OASIS Library OPAC interface.

Emphasis, wherever possible, needs to be given to developing and delivering models of user education based on conceptual instruction that can then be transferred by the user to other information seeking situations. This becomes essential for children and student users as they articulate through education and the community, accessing a variety of OPACs, especially when one considers that there is no universal standards for the command language of second generation OPACs or for the icons driving GUIs (graphical user interfaces), the so called third generation OPACs.

Surely professional bodies such as ALIA and ASLA will initiate input into the development of a standard search interface for online catalogues, rather than allow vendors and educational authorities to impose what are swiftly developing as a myriad of default standards. Teacher librarians need to be aware of what works and what doesn't work. Observations need to be formalised through applied research in the area of search behaviour by children and student users of OPACs in school libraries, and communicated to vendors. If our students are going to be global problem solvers it is critical that the services provided, and information literacy skills nurtured by school libraries and teacher librarians are meaningful and can be applied in a global context.

There have been many papers calling for extensions to OPACs in school libraries, most notably in Australia, those by Freeman (1995 and 1997) debating SCIS data extensions to improve access to fiction collections. I suspect that a significant number of teacher librarians are already applying local solutions to enhance data with subject-rich and keyword-rich information. Given the rapidly changing nature of school library collections and the capability many libraries now have to identify remote information it is time that teacher librarians had input into developing the functionality of OPACs in order to provide one dynamic point of entry to the library collection, the veritable *user* friendly OPAC.

Allen (1993) makes some visionary recommendations, most notably the separation of the maintenance of bibliographic data from the mode of presentation of that data to the user. Hildreth (1995) advises us to beware of GUIs, saying they are so much fun to use the first time around, but behind the icons are the familiar lists of subject headings, titles and so on. It seems that until we reach that visionary OPAC contemplated by Allen (1993) information seekers will continue to need some form of user education teaching them how to make the most effective use of the library system, in order to breach the distance between data and information access.

References

Abbott, Rosemary. (1997). 'Factors influencing the selection of automated library systems in Victorian independent schools.' In Dillon, K. (ed.). *School library automation in Australia: Issues and results of the national surveys.* Wagga Wagga, NSW: Centre for Information

Studies, Charles Sturt University.

Allen, L. (1993). Towards a learning catalogue: Developing the next generation of library catalogues. *Cataloguing Australia*, 19 (3/4): 125-147.

Freeman, A. (1997). 'Providing access to fiction in school libraries: A time for change.' In Dillon, K. (ed.). *School library automation in Australia: Issues and results of the national surveys*. Wagga Wagga, NSW: Centre for Information Studies, Charles Sturt University.

Freeman, A. (1995). 'Providing access to fiction in school libraries: Some thoughts and observations.' In Dillon, K. (ed.). *School library automation in Australia: Issues and results of the first national survey*. Wagga Wagga, NSW: Centre for Information Studies, Charles Sturt University.

Hanson, K. (1997). 'Responsive information environments: Effective and affective user education strategies for school libraries.' In Dillon, K. (ed.). *School library automation in Australia: Issues and results of the national surveys*. Wagga Wagga, NSW: Centre for Information Studies, Charles Sturt University.

Hildreth, C.R. (1995). The GUI OPAC: Approach with caution. *The Public Access Computer Systems Review*, 6 (5). Available <http://info.lib.uh.edu/pr/v6/n5/hild6n5.html>.

Internet Sites: Finding Their Place in Collection Development Policies

Sandra Naude[*]

The Internet should be regarded as important as books, journals, audiovisual recordings or CDROMs when establishing a Collection Development Policy. Each format has its own peculiarities which impinge on the other formats and influence the Collection Development Policy as a whole.

The issues which should be considered when including the Internet in an Collection Development Policy are as follows:

- It is generally more time-consuming to search out suitable Internet sites and evaluate them than finding books or journals for your collection, as there is no organised publishing world, or comprehensive index for the Internet. There are however many useful aids to the Internet such as Internet journals; web pages listing useful sites; newspaper listings; and listservs, but as yet none of these are even remotely comprehensive.

- There is no easy, established method of listing these Internet references for student access such as the traditional library catalogue with its Dewey, SCIS or CIP for books, journals and audiovisual materials. However, organisations such as Informit are looking at producing a CDROM of Internet sites which can then be added to one's library catalogue so that Internet sites can be catalogued and listed just like any other resource. The biggest difficulty with Internet sites is that they change address and disappear.

- To counter the present lack of suitability of the traditional library catalogue for the Internet, it is necessary to ensure sites are accessible to students and staff by adding their URL to bookmarks, booklists or to a library homepage. Students should not be left entirely to their own resources. Just as you guide students by the choice of books and journals you stock in the library, likewise you need to guide students using the Internet with aids such as useful sites bookmarked or listed on a homepage. This does not mean they cannot search for

---

[*] **Sandra Naude** is Head of Library at St Hilda's Anglican School for Girls in Perth, Western Australia. Sandra may be contacted via email at <hildaswa@peg.apc.org>.

themselves, but they do need some guidance. Students can become involved and assist in the selection process by recommending useful sites they find themselves, just as they would by suggesting useful books or journals to be purchased for the library.

- The Internet will alter the way you allocate your budget in the library. Internet should have the advantage of enabling your budget to go further, provided the costs of establishing and maintaining the Internet are not taken from the acquisition budget. Less money is likely to be spent on areas such as reference books; journals; newspapers; books on countries; government publications and conference papers as the Internet adequately caters for these areas. The Internet may also replace the necessity to purchase some CDROMs and online information retrieval services.

- A difficulty with including the Internet in your Collection Development Policy is that unlike books and CDROMs the Internet is not static and continually updates itself. While this is a positive attribute and the one reason why the Internet is so useful, it does mean that you are never sure exactly what you have with an Internet site. There is no warning or control over updates, changes of address or removal of sites. If a site is updated, the previous version is lost unless one has saved it on disk or in hard copy. It can be very frustrating if a site is changed dramatically and whatever you found particularly relevant is removed.

- Modifications to sites can also be embarrassing. An 'innocuous' site used successfully with a primary school class one day can become totally unsuitable overnight because suspect links are added by the Webmaster. Sites can also become inaccessible because the server holding that site is down. This can destroy a carefully prepared lesson based around a particular site.

- Unlike your bookstock or journal collection which you can always be sure you have barring fire, earthquake, flood or similar catastrophe; access to the Internet can disappear with relatively minor disturbances such as power failure, computer failure, cable breaks, server failure or your Service Provider going down.

- If you do plan to include the Internet in your Collection Development Policy then you must ensure that students and staff can use it properly. As students and staff are taught to use the library catalogue and traditional library collection, so they need proper instruction in using the Internet. They need to understand features such as search engines to ensure they create the best possible search strategies. Issues such as relevance ranking, Boolean logic and the different methods search engines use to create their indexes must be understood if students are going to get the most out of the Internet.

- Students must also be taught to cope with the mass of information on the Internet. They must be able to sift through data, evaluate what they have and decide on the relevancy, authenticity and the reliability of the data. This skill which has always been considered important is far more critical with the Internet than was ever envisaged with the traditional library collection.

The Internet has the potential to broaden ones collection and eliminate the unwanted limitations imposed by lack of funding; location; space; inaccessibility and unavailability. All factors which have severely restricted our library collections. The Internet should enable library collections to reach standards considered unattainable and 'pure fantasy' in past years. However, to achieve these ideals will require a concerted effort by teacher librarians to pool their combined knowledge and experiences, to ensure that information is widely disseminated to eliminate the vacuum created by a lack of traditional publishing methods and indexes. Forums such as OZTL_NET should be congratulated as they are an important beginning.

Collection Development Policies, library collections and information skills teaching programmes need to be completely re-assessed and re-evaluated in the light of the above issues to ensure that schools get the most out of the Internet.

Topic E

More Hot Spots for Teacher Librarians

10 KidsConnect Hot Spots

*Blythe Bennett**

The following Web sites come highly recommended from KidsConnect, the question-answering and referral service on the Internet, provided by the American Association of School Librarians, a division of the American Library Association.

Chico High School Library Helpful Bookmarks
<http://www.chs.chico.k12.ca.us/libr/webres/helpful.html>

Well organised collection of secondary school resources, not only general subject areas but also includes special topics such as English as a Second Language, Sports, Minority Studies and Life Skills.

Kathy Schrock's Guide for Educators - Home Page
<http://www.capecod.net/schrockguide/>

Another favourite for general collections of curriculum related material as well as hobbies, news services, and education resources for teachers.

Children's Literature Web Guide
<http://www.ucalgary.ca/~dkbrown/>

The most complete collection of children's literature resources on the Web. Authors, publishers, stories, resources for educators, recommended books and Internet discussion groups.

The Math Forum's Ask Dr. Math
<http://forum.swarthmore.edu/dr.math/dr-math.html>
The first stop on the Web when looking for math-related questions and resources. Features Ask Dr. Math, archives of previous questions, and resources for all levels of K-12 math topics.

---

* **Blythe Bennett** is the KidsConnect Coordinator and works closely with the ERIC/IT Clearinghouse at Syracuse University, New York, USA. KidsConnect is a question-answering and referral service on the Internet, provided by the American Association of School Librarians, a division of the American Library Association. Blythe may be contacted via email at **<blythe@ericir.syr.edu>**. The KidsConnect web site can be located at **<http://www.ala.org/ICONN/kidsconnect.html/>**.

Animal Resources from the Electronic Zoo (NetVet)
<http://netvet.wustl.edu/ssi.htm>

The best collection of animal related resources on the Internet. Categorised by animal type, also includes veterinary topics. Collected by a practicing veterinarian.

SeaWorld/Busch Gardens Animal Information Database
<http://www.bev.net/education/SeaWorld/>

Excellent collection of marine animal related topics, careers in marine biology, and animal information database including land animals.

Nine Planets
<http://seds.lpl.arizona.edu/nineplanets/nineplanets/>

Multimedia tour of the solar system including planets and their satellites, comets and other small bodies.

VolcanoWorld
<http://volcano.und.nodak.edu/noframe_index.html>

Volcano related materials, Ask A Volcanologist, archives, and currently active volcanoes.

History/Social Studies Web Site for K-12 Teachers
<http://www.execpc.com/~dboals/boals.html>

One stop shopping for social studies related material on the Web... American History, World History, Social Issues, Genealogy, Ancient Civilisations and Diversity related resources.

Health Hotlist from the Franklin Institute
<http://sln.fi.edu/tfi/hotlists/health.html>

Collected health related resources on nutrition, diseases, fitness, drugs and alcohol, other ailments. Includes collections of images and fact sheets.

Chasing a Theme on the Internet

Karen Bonanno[*]

Australian Endangered Animals

<http://www.cyberdata.com.au/currumbin/eindex.html>
This site is attached to the home page of the Currumbin Sanctuary on the Gold Coast, Queensland. The index provides links to approximately 25 fact sheets that cover characteristics, habitat, status, detailed information and distribution of the specific animal. Has pictures and maps as well.

<http://www.schoolwolrd.asn.au/species/>
This gets you to the parent directory. From here you will have to browse through the list to pick out the Australian endangered animals, eg. wallaby, humpback, Tasmanian devil, wombat. The links provide access to student work on endangered species and are worth seeing. Each presentation covers the following headings: why study the topic?, what was already known?, search information, description, habitat, adaptation, reasons endangered, restoration action, what was learned?, conclusion.

<http://kaos.erin.gov.au/life/end_vuln/animals/>
Not quite as spectacular as the previous sites, but will provide detail on such animals as the tree frog and potoroo.

Famous Scientists and Inventors...

I picked up this listing from the *Australian Net Guide*, May 1997 issue. After a quick browse through the sites I found a feast of information.

Thomas Edison (Light)
<http://www.minot.com/~mps/edison/edison/edison.html>

Albert Einstein (Relativity)
<http://www.sofitec.lu/misc/einstein.htm>

---

[*] **Karen Bonanno** is Director of the library consultancy firm, Queensland Library and Information Services, and currently holds the position of National President for the Australian School Library Association (ASLA). Karen can be contacted via email at <kbonanno@bigpond.com>, or via snail mail at PO Box 255, Moranbah, Queensland 4744, Australia.

Isaac Newton (Physicist)
<http://www.hepth.cornell.edu/~leclair/Phys112/newton.html>

Marie Curie (Radioactivity)
<http://www.xray.hmc.psu.edu/rci/ss7/ss7_2.html>

Biographical dictionary of biologists (Biology)
<http://www.cshl.org/comfort/scientists/scientists.html>

Sigmund Freud (Psychoanalysis)
<http://laf.cioe.com/~jheinze/freud.html>

Charles Babbage (Computers)
<http://www.uta.fi/~majyho/guru/guru.html>

Louis Pasteur (Diseases)
<http://www.pasteur.fr/Pasteur/WLP.html>

Philo T. Farnsworth (Television)
<http://www.songs.com/philo>

History of Mathematics archive (Mathematics)
<http://www-groups.dcs.st-and.ac.uk/~history/index.html>

Inventors
<http://web.mit.edu/afs/athena.mit.edu/org/i/invent/www/archive.html>
and <http://www.invent.org/book/index.html>

Internet Hot Spots for Teacher Librarians: the IASL Web Site

*Laurel A. Clyde**

The mission of the International Association of School Librarianship (IASL) is to provide an international forum for people interested in promoting effective school library media programmes as viable instruments in the educational process. Membership is worldwide, and includes school librarians, teachers, librarians, library advisers, consultants, educational administrators, and others who are responsible for library and information services in schools. The membership also includes professors and instructors in universities and colleges where there are programmes for school librarians, and students who are undertaking such programmes.

The Association has a World Wide Web site <http://www.rhi.hi.is/~anne/iasl.html> that serves two main purposes:

1. providing information about the Association for members and non-members, and

2. helping members to explore the Internet, and particularly helping them to find resources and services that are relevant to library and information services in schools.

In keeping with these aims, the IASL Home Page site <http://www.rhi.hi.is/~anne/iasl.html> is organised according to the following scheme:

*   About the Association
*   The *IASL Newsletter* (with selected articles from the newsletter)
*   The IASL Journal: *School Libraries Worldwide* (with contents lists)
*   The Annual Conferences
*   Committees and Special Interest Groups
*   The IASL Noticeboard
*   IASL-LINK: The Association's Listserv

---

* **Dr Anne Clyde** is Professor with the Department of Library and Information Science, Faculty of Social Science at the University of Iceland, Reykjavik. An online version of this paper is available at **<http://www.rhi.hi.is/~anne/iaslweb.html>**. Anne may be contacted via email at **<anne@rhi.hi.is>**.

- Publications
- How to Join the Association
- Links to School Library Resources on the Internet.

It is the latter section, of *Links to School Library Resources on the Internet* <http://www.rhi.hi.is/~anne/linksiasl.html> that is particularly related to one of the themes of the ITEC Virtual Conference, 'More Hot Spots for TLs'. This section provides links to hundreds of Internet sites of interest to people who are involved in school librarianship, organised under the following headings:

- Library Associations
- School Library Associations
- School Libraries and School Librarians on the Internet
- Resources for School Librarians
- Educational Resources
- Information Skills Resources
- Children's Literature Resources
- Other Resources
- IASL Sponsors and Partners.

In keeping with the aim to help members of the Association (and others who are involved in school librarianship) to explore the resources that are available on the Internet, the site provides links to the best resources available. It is selective rather than comprehensive. The sites chosen tend to be those that lead to collections of resources, rather than those that lead to individual documents, though there are some links to important electronic books and other documents. In addition, 'authority' and 'recency' have been important considerations in the selection of links.

Another page on the IASL Web site (a page that was under development as this paper was being written) contains links to *Internet Resources that are Recommended by IASL Members* <http://www.rhi.hi.is/~anne/membersweb.html>. The idea behind this page was that it would be a place where members of the Association could share their interests and expertise with other members, and particularly with school librarians who are new to the Internet. Members were invited, through a notice posted to *IASL-LINK* (the IASL listserv on the Internet) <http://www.rhi.hi.is/~anne/iasl-link.html>, to contribute information about sites that they had found useful or interesting, sites that they wanted to recommend to others. This will be an ongoing project, with further invitations to contribute potential links being issued through IASL-LINK, and with a recommendation form available on the Web page as well.

Some IASL members have very limited access to the Internet; some, for instance, still have text-only access to the World Wide Web, while others are accessing the Internet through very slow or unreliable connections. For this reason, the IASL Web pages have been kept simple, with limited use of graphics. While this is necessary now, it may change in the future. The *Net-Trak* <http://www.superplex.com/net-trak> tracker program is being used to monitor 'visits' to the site; this program provides information about the countries from which users come, the machines through which they are accessing the site, and the browser software that they are using. It is clear from the *Net-Trak* statistics that usage of the site, and the hardware and software being used by those who are accessing the site, is changing rapidly. The *Net-Trak* statistics will be used as a basis for the ongoing development of IASL Web.

An article about the design and development of the IASL Web site will be published in the June 1997 issue of the North American school library journal *Emergency Librarian*, with the title 'IASL Web: a Home Base on the Internet for School Librarians'.

There are other Internet sites (in addition to the IASL Web site) that provide a basis for exploration by teacher librarians. The IASL page of *Links to School Library Resources on the Internet* <http://www.rhi.hi.is/~anne/linksiasl.html> has links to them. They include the following:

LION - Librarians Information Online Network
<http://www.libertynet.org/~lion/lion.html>
An "information resource for K-12 school librarians" from the Library Services of the School District of Philadelphia (USA).

School Librarians' Hotspots
<http://www.mbnet.mb.ca:80/~mstimson/text/hotspots.html>
From Assiniboine South School Division in Winnipeg, Manitoba, Canada.

Learning@Web.Sites
<http://www.ecnet.net/users/gdlevin/home.html>
A collection of resources for secondary school teachers and teacher librarians, maintained by David Levin in the United States.

Information Policy Issues: Curse or Cure?

Lyn Hay[*]

Why Information Policy for Schools?

I can see you now as you begin to read this paper -- cringing as you curse under your breath "Policy issues...yuk." Well you are not alone when it comes to an aversion towards tackling the development of policy in your school! Over the past 6 months I have had 64 postgraduate students complete a new subject in the Master of Applied Science (Teacher Librarianship) course at CSU -- *ETL523 Information Policy Issues.* Many of these students are practising teacher librarians in Australasian schools, and approximately 85% of these students claimed at the beginning of this subject that their school had no information policies in place. Sound familiar? Some students were not sure what information policy issues or problems actually existed within their schools.

In the Information Age, or 'information economy' as it also popularly referred, information has become a valuable commodity and currency, which individuals, organisations and businesses 'barter' or exchange to improve their knowledge base to assist in effective decision making, that is making 'informed choices'. Information policy development occurs at local, regional, state, national and international levels, and this can potentially (and in many cases does) impact upon the function and decision making of schools. Schools are 'information organisations' - organisations that store, use, disseminate and create information products everyday. The information products and information flows within a school must be managed effectively and efficiently to ensure the school is successful 'in business'. The integration of information technologies within the school as a learning community and workplace in the 1990s is literally forcing schools to develop policies to address problems and issues arising from the school community's increased access to the electronic information environment - the need for an Acceptable Use of the Internet policy is a good case in point.

---

[*] **Lyn Hay** is a lecturer in Teacher Librarianship with the School of Information Studies, Charles Sturt University, Wagga Wagga, N.S.W., Australia. Lyn's ETL523 subject is delivered to postgraduate distance education students online via the World Wide Web (WWW) as well as via traditional print-based mail package. Lyn may be contacted via email at <lhay@csu.edu.au>.

Traditionally, authors of works on information policy have focused specifically on policies governing the control of government information, however, in an information economy all organisations need to consider the impact of information. Mason (1983:93) defines information policy as:

...a set of interrelated laws and policies concerned with the creation, production, collection, management, distribution and retrieval of information. Their significance lies in the fact that they profoundly affect the manner in which an individual in a society, indeed a society itself, makes political, economic and social choices.

The teacher librarian as the school's information professional needs to consider information policy at both macro and micro levels. At the macro level, the teacher librarian must be aware of public policy issues from regional through to international policy processes and concerns -- these include legislative, regulatory, macroeconomic and social issues, such as intellectual property, copyright and fair use; freedom of and access to information; privacy and information literacy. At the micro level, the teacher librarian must examine information flows, and policy issues and policy development within their own information organisation -- the school, such as whole school technology planing; acceptable use of the Internet; and IT and information literacy integration across the curriculum.

Moore calls for a 'process of consciousness-raising' where policy makers and those in positions of leadership are: (1) made aware of the information problems and issues that exist; (2) contribute to debate and development of public policy in response to these problems and issues; and then (3) develop policy at the organisational level, where policy responses are:

...formulated on the basis of an understanding of the background to the issues, an appreciation of the need for flexibility in a rapidly-changing environment and an awareness of the inter-connections between the different issues.

(Moore 1991:5)

In the past much of the documentation outlining public information policy and calls for submissions and debate have been difficult to 'track down' in hard copy for the 'average teacher librarian'. We are all familiar with the phrase "Knowledge is power" – the WWW has become a powerful tool in making information policy documentation 'go public', and teacher librarians now have access to an incredible range of resources relating to information policy issues to assist with the development of 'in house' policy development in schools, as well as contribute to public policy debate. We, as a profession, must clearly harness this power and use it to advantage.

Legislative, Regulatory and Macroeconomic Issues

As developments in computer and communications technologies have expanded, so has our capacity to produce, transmit, store and retrieve information. It is therefore necessary to redefine, reinterpret and refine some legislation, such as copyright, so that it takes into account the new products and changes brought about by advances in technology. In some cases it has become necessary to draw new laws, eg. the *Data Protection Act*, to cope with problems which were not evident before. The commercialisation and popularity of the Internet has literally opened a 'Pandora's Box' of information policy issues to be addressed. While some of these questions may be resolved using existing legislation, many call for new legislation, particularly in the electronic information environment.

The Legal Issues Group on *Legal Issues* <http://www.nla.gov.au/archive/gov/pmc/nisc/aug95/legal.htm> for the National Information Services Council in Australia identifies those laws concerning the use of information that need to be reviewed within the electronic information environment. Here you will find links to legislative documentation such as the *Telecommunications Act*; *Radiocommunications Act*; *Broadcasting Services Act*; *Freedom of Information Act*; *Privacy Act*; *Archives Act*; *Copyright Act*; and *Classification (Publications, Films and Computer Games) Act*.

Key information policy issues currently affecting schools include:

- *Acceptable Use of the Internet* - see VC'97 papers presented Topic A by Georgia Phillips and Kerry Wellham.

- *Copyright and intellectual property rights* - the manipulation of data by machines raises questions of legal liability. For example, on the US-based listserv for library media specialists LM_NET (see *LM_NET Archives* at <http://ericir.syr.edu/lm_net/>) recently there was quite a 'heated discussion' on the legal, ethical and educational implications of schools using a caching software called *WebWhacker* which allows uploading, or caching whole web sites onto school fileservers. This has lead to the creation of school-based 'mini-Internets' for student use -- the main advantages being reduced online time (and costs) for student searches and minimising student access to 'unsavoury' material.

- *Technology planning* - management of whole school electronic information networks, including licensing agreements, eg. school's acquisition of electronic information and multiple licenses which can be prohibitive for schools.

- *Right to privacy* - schools with Internet access must now regulate the appropriate use of email, manage individual email accounts, and develop policy concerning publication of student information and photos on school Home Pages. An online version of *Child Safety on the Information Highway* is available <http://www.isa.net/empower/child.html>.

- *Access to information versus censorship* - schools, and whole education systems, employing filtering software to limit student access to potentially 'harmful' material on the Internet.

To effectively 'deal' with these issues, the teacher librarian must ensure that school decision makers are 'informed' regarding the nature and scope of each information policy issues; legislative, regulatory and macroeconomic factors affecting school-based decisions; and range of possible solutions and procedures available as inclusions in school-based policies. Here are some web sites to get you started.

Some WWW sites on legislative and macroeconomic issues

The ACLIS Web site <http://www.nla.gov.au/aclis/> includes information regarding the role of the Australian Council of Libraries and Information Services (ACLIS), statements and publications (ACLIS has developed a statement concerning the role of school library and information services within the electronic environment), and other documentation.

The Federal Libraries Information Network (FLIN) (Australia) <http://www.nla.gov.au/flin/>. This site includes submissions made by FLIN to government research and review committees heading inquiries into national information policy issues; copies of minutes and newsletters; and the work of various FLIN taskforces including those for copyright issues, collection development, lobbying/advocacy, and networks/databases.

Information Policy Notes <http://www.essential.org/listproc/info-policy-notes/>

Archives of *Info-Policy-Notes* newsletter which monitors public policy issues and trends including groups like the World Intellectual Property Organization (WIPO) and the public's rights to use information.

For Australian schools the *EdNA (Education Network Australia)* educational directory <http://www.edna.edu.au> provides links to sites that support educational initiatives on the Internet.

The EDUCOM Publications site <http://www.educom.edu/web/pubs/pubHomeFrame.html> includes back issues of the *Educom Review* on policy issues as well as the EDUCOM digest called *Edupage* which is a summary of news about information technology, providing regular snapshots of issues raised in the media relating to developments in information technology and education which can directly affect information policy. All *Edupage* digests are also archived at the site.

InterNIC News is a monthly bulletin which complements *Edupage* - for the latest issue go to <http://rs.internic.net/nic-support/nicnews/> and for back issues go to <http://rs.internic.net/nic-support/nicnews/archive/>.

A very useful journal *Internet Research: Electronic Networking Applications and Policy* is located at <http://www.mcb.co.uk/cgi-bin/journal3/intr>. This site features abstracts of articles on information policy issues. Some interesting articles include: 'Enter the Cyberpunk Librarian: Future Directions in Cyberspace'; 'Enforcement of Intellectual Property Rights on the Internet'; 'Networking for K-12 Education: The Federal Perspective'; 'Welcome to the Communication Age'; and 'Data Integrity and the Internet: Implications for Management'.

Copyright and Fair Use
Copyright has been an information policy issue in schools for decades now, however, the introduction of electronic information resources including multimedia CDROMs and the Internet has forced schools to seriously deal with this issue. From my experience with ETL523 students it seems that many schools have not developed school-based policy concerning copyright issues, however, copyright policy is secondary only to AUP development (the Number 1 priority in the majority of schools). There is an over-abundance of copyright-related material published on the Web. Here are some key sites to get you started:

The International Federation of Library Institutions and Associations (IFLA)
<http://www.nlc-bnc.ca/ifla/II/cpyright.htm>
Here you will find the general IFLA statement on copyright in the electronic environment and an excellent international bibliography on Copyright and Intellectual Property Resources which includes hyperlinks to WWW resources as well as books, journal articles and government publications.

LION: Copyright and Fair Use Information for School Librarians
<http://libertynet.org/~lion/copyright.html>.

Intellectual Property. a Pathfinder for Librarians and Educators
<http://home.ican.net/~pjnummi/alexa1.html>
You will find a Canadian-based pathfinder site currently under construction.

Libraries, Copyright and Document Delivery
<http://www.cc.emory.edu/WHSCL/libraries.html>
You will find a comprehensive field guide to sources including 11 pages of references.

The ILT guide to Copyright
<http://www.ilt.columbia.edu/projects/copyright/index.html>
This is a fantastic site comprehensively providing information and links of interest to educators and librarians.

Copyright Agency Limited's CAL Calender
<http://www.copytight.com.au/index.html>
A regular newsletter outlining how Australia is dealing with 'fair use'.

APRA, Australasian Performing Right Association
<http://www.apra.com.au/htm/index2.htm>

Library of Congress United States Copyright Office
<http://lcweb.loc.gov/copyright/>
Includes many links to information concerning copyright issues, legislation, organisations and resources.

10 Big Myths About Copyright Explained by Brad Templeton
<http://www.clari.net/brad/copymyths.html>
Attempts to answer common myths about copyright on the Internet, eg. Myth No.1 "If it doesn't have a copyright notice, it's not copyrighted."

C-net site - 'Tell it to the judge.'
<http://www.news.com/Quiz/Entry>

Special report on copyright law and includes a quiz that helps determine whether you follow legal procedure - try it, just for fun!

Social Issues: Information Access to All and Information Literacy

Organisations are placed under increasing pressure to develop local information policy in response to trends in public information policy and problems arising from new developments and initiatives in information use and the provision of new information sources and services.

Moore (1991:5) identifies a pressing social issue that schools and the public library sector are currently grappling with, when he states:

> *Information technology and the increased use of information within society can hold out the prospect of significant improvements in the quality of life. We must accept, however, that in the short term at least, we are facing the prospect of a growing division between the information rich and the information poor.*

At the macro level, because information has become such a powerful currency in the information economy, governments are coming under increasing pressure to ensure that individuals are given the opportunity to develop the skills required to effectively function within an information society - public policies have been developed to ensure a nation's workforce has the requisite literacy and numeracy to enable individuals to effectively participate in the world of work. In Australia the Mayer Committee's report *Putting general education to work* (1992) is one example of a national initiative used to highlight the importance of developing an information literate and numerate young Australia, and the responsibility of educational institutions in 'skilling up' students within the context of the competency-based education and training movement.

A variety of statements on information service provision exist in Australia to support the educational and information rights of children. School libraries play a pivotal role in supporting the intellectual, access and privacy rights of children. *Learning for the future* (1993) is a powerful support document which provides detailed guidelines and indicators for schools developing information policy. Professional library associations play an important part in developing national information policy to support the development of information services in school.

Australian Library and Information Association's (ALIA) national policy statements including 'Statement on Library and Info Services in Schools' and 'ALIA Statement on Freedom to Read' can be found at <http://www.alia.org.au/alia/policies.html>.

The American Library Association (ALA) web site <http://www.ala.org/> also has some powerful policy statements and support documents for teacher librarians to refer to when developing an information literacy policy. The 'Final Report by the American Library Association Presidential Committee on Information Literacy' is a good example of association leadership in developing national information policy aimed at addressing this important social issue.

An excellent site for teacher librarians to visit which deals with a range of issues under the banner of 'access to all' is The Internet Advocate: A Web-based Resource Guide for Librarians and Educators Interested in Providing Youth Access to the Net located at <http://recall.lib.indiana.edu/~webbook/netadv.htm>. Key issues addressed include: 'Inaccurate Perceptions of Porn on the Net'; promoting 'Positive Examples of Youth Internet Use'; developing an 'Acceptable Use Policy'; and understanding 'Software to Block Internet Sites and Related Safety/Censorship'.

An interesting site to visit dealing with freedom of access to information is The File Room Censorship Archive at <http://fileroom.aaup.uic.edu/FileRoom/documents/homepage.html>. This site includes information and updates on censorship cases worldwide - visitors can browse the illustrated archive of cases or submit their own 'tales of oppression'!

An informative essay on writing library policy Censorship in the Information Age by Debbie Abilock can be found at <http://www.nueva.pvt.k12.ca.us/~debbie/library/policies/censor96.html>. This also includes some useful links to other relevant sites.

Organisation Issues

Information is a key resource that needs to be managed and developed. The application of information technologies in schools has brought this to the fore. Principals and other school administrators now have the opportunity to use information to support school-based management decisions and 'market' their school's services -- it seems that 'successful schools', ie. those that have a 'competitive edge' as an educational provider within a community, are also innovative information managers. According to Moore (1991:4):

...Until now managers have had to develop coping mechanisms to enable them to overcome lack of information. Such coping mechanisms are no longer necessary.

That is not to say that all organisations have changed their way of operating or that managers have found it easy to adjust to an information-intensive way of working. Some organisations have used the technology simply to enable them to do more efficiently what they have always done before. There is growing evidence, however, to indicate that real benefits only arise when organisations radically rethink their style of operation to accommodate new opportunities which are opening up.

This calls for a recognition that information performs a different function at different levels within an organisation and that the information systems need to be planned accordingly...

...the collection and processing of information is a time-consuming task and already there are signs that specialist positions are being created for information analysts to work with groups of managers and policy-makers. This division of managerial labour itself calls for a reassessment of the management function within organisations.

In recent literature the concept of an Information Services Unit has emerged as an effective way of managing whole school information products and processes. The potential role(s) of the teacher librarian in supporting whole school information management has also been raised in the exploration of schools as information organisations.

The Central Computer and Telecommunications Agency (CCTA) (London) (1990:31) estimates that government departments devote "about half of their administrative budget on handling information so it obviously has a cost"! Managing information is a continuous process which requires a coordinated approach across an organisation. Hay and Kallenberger's (1996) 'The Role of the School Information Services Unit in the Teaching/Learning Process' <http://golum.riv.csu.edu.au/~lhay/isu.html> introduces the concept of the school as an information organisation and provides one potential model for schools to develop an Information Services Unit (ISU).

CCTA's document *Managing Information as a Resource* (1990:11-13) also illustrates how an ISU fits into an organisation. This document lists the responsibilities and tasks of an information management unit and suggests that the creation of such a unit 'does not necessarily imply a need to recruit any extra staff', in fact for most departments:

...the roles of the information manager and his/her team could most easily and logically be taken on by staff already working in either the information services area (eg. in the library, records management of information technology) or elsewhere (eg. management services or policy branches) who understand the issues. Each department should adopt the arrangement that best suits its own circumstances.

This approach reinforces the Hay and Kallenberger model. However, Lee (1996) contends that a radical organisational restructuring is required of schools if they are to effectively harness the power of information technologies and become successful information organisations. While *Learning for the future* (1993) can provide a blueprint for managing information services in schools, Caldwell and Spinks (1988:3-4) present a Collaborative School Management approach to policy development which has the following characteristics:

- It integrates goal-setting, policy-making, planning, budgeting, implementing and evaluation in a manner which contrasts with the often unsystematic, fragmented processes which have caused so much frustration and ineffectiveness in the past.

- It secures appropriate involvement of staff, students and the community, with clearly defined roles for governing bodies where such groups exist and have responsibility for policy-making.

- It focuses on the central functions of schools - learning and teaching - and, accordingly, organises the management of the school around 'programmes' which correspond to the preferred patterns of work in the school.

Caldwell and Spinks (1988) and Orna's *Practical information flows: How to manage information flow in organizations* (1990) are fundamental resources for schools developing information policy. Unfortunately there is no single policy planning and implementation process for schools to adopt in developing information policy. Individual schools must develop a process that suits its organisational culture, information flows, individual expertise of management personnel, and local school community's information policy needs.

Two other useful Web sites to visit for policy development include:

1. *Special K's Library Policies Page* (Karen Schneider) <http://www.intac.com/~kgs/freedom/policies.html>; and

2. Jamie McKenzie's *From Now On - The Educational Technology Journal* <http://fromnowon.org/>. A must visit site!! Jamie has written many useful articles concerning the integration of IT in schools and information policy issues, including copyright in his article 'Keeping It Legal'. The Bellingham Public Schools site at <http://www.bham.wednet.edu> also provides a range of online technology-related support documentation and courses.

Two major organisational policy issues affecting schools include: (1) the development of a whole school technology plan integrating IT into teaching and learning; and (2) an Acceptable Use Policy to assist in the management of student use of the Internet as an information source.

Technology Plans

The following sites will assist you in developing a whole school technology plan in your school:

Technology Connection's - The Impact of Technology
<http://www.mcrel.org/connect/tech/impact.html>
Provides an excellent annotated bibliography of research on the impact of IT on teaching and learning - bookmark this site now!

Gateways: Information Technology in the Learning Process
<http://learning.edna.edu.au/learnit/itlearn.html>
An Australian research paper (1996) based on case studies concerning the impact of IT in schools. Definitely check this out.

Plan for Information Technology in Learning and Teaching 1997-1999 for ACT Public Schools
<http://actein.edu.au/HLTP/plan.htm>
Outlines 3 year vision for IT integration in ACT schools in the learning/teaching process.

Pitsco's Launch to Technology Plans
<http://www.pitsco.inter.net/p/techplans.html>
Exactly what it claims to be - a great launching pad to WWW resources on technology plans for schools.

The National Center for Technology Planning (NCTP) Clearinghouse
<gopher://gopher.msstate.edu:70/11/Online_services/nctp>
This clearinghouse contains many documents related to technology planning, including school technology plans and technology planning aids, eg. checklists, brochures and sample planning forms.

The National Curriculum for Information Technology in the U.K.
<http://www.brixton-connections.org.uk/curric.html>
This site is still under construction, however, it is well on the way in extracting IT skills from UK national curriculum documents. Another good site to assist with identification of skills/grades in a continuum.

The Mountain Brook City Schools Computer Skills Scope & Sequence 1996-1997
<http://www.mtnbrook.k12.al.us/ss/bendset.htm>
An excellent document which charts skill development of students using word processing, spreadsheets, databases, and presentation software. Skills are displayed in grids that illustrate when each concept/skill should be introduced, reinforced, or at what point a student should become an independent user. These skills are also organised by grade level or subject and some sample activities are also provided. This site is a beauty!

The Jefferson County Public Schools Computer Applications Skills Continuum
<http://www.jefferson.k12.ky.us/continuum/continuum.html>
Includes skills continuum tables for Kindergarten to Year 12 -- a good place to start identification of computer skills with grade levels.

Integrating Technology in the Classroom
<http://www.sicc.k12.in.us/~west/slides/integrate.htm>
This slide presentation includes tips on how to manage 'computer centres' within classrooms.

Acceptable Use Policies
A variety of ways schools are currently dealing with information management issues resultant of student access to the Internet can be found in Spalding, Gilding and Patrick's (1996) report *Management of student access to controversial material on the Internet.* An online version of the Executive Summary of the final report is available at <http://teloz.latrobe.edu.au/circit/scexec01.html>.

You will find many web sites devoted to Acceptable Use Policies. An excellent place to start is *K-12 Acceptable Use Policies* located at <http://www.erehwon.com/k12aup/> by Nancy Willard, an Information Technology Consultant in Oregon, USA. Willard's site presents the educational and legal aspects and measures a school should consider in developing an Acceptable Use Policy. Other sites include:

Pitsco's Launch to Acceptable Use Policies
<http://www.pitsco.inter.net/p/accept.html>
Pitsco's is one of my favourite 'directory' sites. It is quite comprehensive -- definitely one to bookmark.

Dave Kinnaman's 'Critiquing Acceptable Use Policies.'
<http://spc.ccps.k12.fl.us/Teacher's.PowerPak/A_USE/aup.html>

Armadillo's WWW Server Acceptable Use Policies
<http://chico.rice.edu/armadillo/Rice/Resources/acceptable.html>

K-12 Acceptable Use Policies (AUPs) Frequently Asked Questions (FAQ)
<http://www.classroom.net/classroom/infobots/aup-faq.html>

Northwestern University's "What you need to know about Acceptable Use Policies"
<http://www.covis.nwu.edu/AUP-archive/CoVis_AUP.html>

Dillon's (1996) 'Management of student access to the Net: Issues and Responsibilities' also provides an overview of information policy issues relating to school information services and the Internet.

Conclusion: the teacher librarian and Information Policy

As evidenced above, a wealth of information concerning information policy issues is available on the WWW. Many peak bodies and associations dealing with national information policy development have quite sophisticated and up-to-date Web sites. The WWW has become an excellent medium for disseminating government policy information. Unfortunately for those people without Internet access, access to some of this current documentation in hard copy can be difficult locate and obtain (quite often for a fee). Much of this information can be retrieved from the Web for 'free' and is, therefore, an extremely valuable source of policy information for schools.

It is the responsibility of the teacher librarian to locate, collect and disseminate articles and documentation dealing with information policy issues. Let's take the issue of copyright as an example. The teacher librarian should regularly disseminate updates on copyright issues, potential problems and legislative changes to all members of staff. The school must then develop a (or revise their existing) local information policy which documents the school's procedures for information use within the guidelines of copyright legislation. A school's policy on copyright (or any other for that matter) is not to be written, then filed away in a filing cabinet and forgotten. Daily school practice must exhibit guidelines outlined in school policy, whether it deals with copyright, information literacy, acceptable use of the Internet or any other issue.

If you can't see 'policy in practice', your policy is not worth the paper it is written on!!

Schools as organisations need to understand how they use information to control management processes and make informed decisions. Many organisational issues must be considered throughout the policy process -- the introduction of an Information Services Unit is one management solution. However, armed with 'knowledge' and 'power' the teacher librarian can potentially play a key leadership role in the 'process of consciousness-raising' and initiating information policy development in schools.

.... Still cringing, or are you cured? :-)

References

Caldwell, B.J. and Spinks, J.M. (1988). *The self-managing school*. London: Falmer.

Dillon, K. (1996). 'Management of student access to the Internet: issues and responsibilities.' In *A Meeting of Minds: ITEC Virtual Conference '96 Proceedings*, edited by Lyn Hay and James Henri. Belconnen: ASLA, 16-24.

Hay, L. (1996). *ETL523 Information Policy Issues: Study Guide*. Wagga Wagga, NSW: Open Learning Institute, Charles Sturt University.

Hay, L. and Kallenberger, N. (1996). The Role of the School Information Services Unit in the Teaching/Learning Process. [Online] Available <http://golum.riv.csu.edu.au/~lhay/presentation/isu.html>.

Learning for the future: Developing information services in Australian Schools. (1993). Carlton: Curriculum Corporation.

Lee, M. (1996). Close the library: Open the Information Services Unit. *The Practising Administrator*, 2: 7.

Managing information as a resource. (1990). London: Central Computer and Telecommunications Agency (CCTA).

Mason, M.G. (1983). *The federal role in library and information services.* White Plains, NY: Knowledge Industry Publications.

Mayer Committee. (1992). *Putting general education to work: the Key Competencies Report.* Canberra: AEC/MOVEET.

Moore, N. (1991). 'Introduction'. In Rowlands, I. and Vogel, S. (eds.). *Information policies: a sourcebook.* London: Taylor Graham.

Orna, E. (1990). *Practical information flows: How to manage information flow in organizations.* Aldershot, Hants: Gower.

Spalding, B., Gilding, J. and Patrick, K. (1996). *Management of student access to controversial material on the Internet.* Canberra: AGPS.

10 Hot Spots Not To Be Missed

Sandra Naude[*]

OzeNews
<http://www.ozemail.com.au/~gillespi/>
A record of the news featured in the major newspapers around Australia.

Economics Charts of 40 Countries
<http://www.mexi.net/ECO/index.html>
Economic charts for 40 countries around the world detailing stockmarket rates, interest rates and monetary value.

Rulers
<http://www.geocities.com/Athens/1058/rulers.html>
Everything you have ever wanted to know about past and present rulers including those installed, deposed or deceased today.

Orbit
<http://www.pi.co/~orbit/>
An excellent site for finding information on remote areas of Australia.

Educational Current Awareness
<http://www.landmark-project.com/ca/>
An educational current awareness service which alerts one to the latest articles in all areas of education.

Educational Search Engine
<http://www.education-world.com/>
This is a search engine dedicated to education which means that educational searches are specific and relevant.

First World War
<http://www.pbs.org/greatwar/>
This site enables one to search specific events, battles, characters and dates during World War 1. There is an interactive timeline.

---

[*] **Sandra Naude** is Head of Library at St Hilda's Anglican School for Girls in Perth, Western Australia. Sandra may be contacted via email at <hildaswa@peg.apc.org>.

Anzwers Search Engine
<http://www.anzwers.com.au/>
An Australasian search engine that enables one to restrict a search by country. Its simplicity makes it an ideal starting point for primary school children

History Channel
<http://www.historychannel.com>
A very comprehensive site enabling one to find information on a wide range of historical topics.

Napoleon
<http://www.napoleon.org/>
Everything you have ever wanted to know about the First and Second French Empire. It is accessible in French or English.

Topic F

MOO Trek:

Using MOOs in Education

Internet Based Distance Education: From Dungeons and Dragons to Degrees

*William J. Gibbons, Michael B. Eisenberg, Robert L. Heckman and Adam Rubin**

Introduction
Multi User Dungeons (MUDs) and MUDs that are Object Oriented (MOOs), are widely used on the Internet as interactive role-playing games and social gathering places. Recently, however, MUDs and MOOs are being seen in a new light. These environments can become virtual 'places' on the network where people can meet and collaborate on business and learning. Adding graphics and sound to these traditionally text-based environments make them especially viable as mechanisms to improve the quality of non-traditional education delivered to students at a distance. It is hypothesised that these environments will enhance collaboration among students and provide a better learning experience.

Researchers in the Information Institute, School of Information Studies, at Syracuse University, directed by Mike Eisenberg, are engaged in harnessing the potential and studying the impact of these graphical MOOs to enhance collaboration among participants in graduate-level distance education degree programs. The goal is to enrich learning and increase participant satisfaction. This current development and research project provides an immediate, low cost, high impact, opportunity for examination of 'real time' collaboration and the impacts of visual images on learning.

A Variety of Distance Learning Models
A variety of distance education models attempt to properly link providers and recipients, in environments that include levels of interaction, specific learning objectives, and delivery systems that are affordable, manageable, and technologically efficient. Among them are:

---

* **Bill Gibbons** is a post-graduate student with the School of Information Studies, Syracuse University, Syracuse, New York, USA. Bill can be contacted via email at <wjgibbon@mailbox.syr.edu>. **Mike Eisenberg** is Professor and Head of the School of Information Studies at Syracuse University in New York, USA. Mike is also the Director of the ERIC Clearinghouse on Information & Technology. Mike can be contacted via email at <mike@ericir.syr.edu>.

- One to One: In this design one person has the information or knowledge sought by another. Almost any communication technology will support this one to one exchange with speed being a primary consideration. Land mail, electronic mail, and simple Internet chat modes, are commonly used in this model.

- One to Many: This is the more traditional classroom model where the instructor disseminates information to the class. Typical distance learning technologies in this model include ground mail, electronic mail, and listservs. The syllabus and assignments are sent or posted at the beginning of the course. Announcements throughout the course are made via listserv and assignments are submitted via ground or electronic mail. Since the primary objective is presenting information to a body of students and evaluating them as individuals, asynchronous technologies are quite sufficient.

- Many to Many: In this model the experience and contribution of the students is considered an important part of the learning process. The instructor adopts the role of facilitator rather than expert. Group activities and socialisation become major components of this collaborative learning environment. Technologies are being developed to support this model in both asynchronous and synchronous modes.

One common aspect of all of these designs is the displacement of participants in both time and space. As in any educational setting, the participants also possess different teaching and learning styles. Of interest and importance is the awareness and attention to these styles and the application of technologies and techniques which may in the distance setting be quite different from those most effective in the traditional classroom environment. The evolution of technology plays an important role in the success of distance learning programs.

The Importance of Collaboration (Required and Discretionary)
Another key determinant in successful distance education is the maintenance of interaction between students and faculty and among the students. According to Besser (1995), "distance independent learning imposes distance upon students, distance from their classmates and instructors. Such distance, both physical and psychic, makes it difficult to build collaborative relationships among students, and difficult to build strong mentoring relationships between students and faculty." Without mechanisms to support

these relationships, distance learning can become lonely learning resulting in decreased participant satisfaction and increased drop-out rates.

Badger (1996), of the University of Phoenix, describes an online collaboration sequence that includes getting acquainted activities, classroom activities (lecture, brainstorming, class discussion, and role playing), and ongoing interpersonal activities. Many of these are created and carried out by the class facilitator or moderator. Of greater importance in the building of relationships are the discretionary activities initiated by the students themselves.

Palace and the *AskERIC Classroom*
At Syracuse University, School of Information Studies, the Independent Study Degree Program (ISDP) follows the 'many to many' model with ongoing experimentation and evaluation of available technologies. *HyperNews*, an asynchronous enhanced email technology, enables the exchange of information among the participants. However, *HyperNews* does not support "real time" brainstorming and fails to provide a desired emulation of a face-to-face collaborative environment.

One alternative or supplement to enhanced email technologies is to use synchronous chat technologies available on the Internet (IRC, ICQ, and *PowWow* as examples) which permit "real time" interpersonal communications among individuals or groups. An innovative extension of these text-only domains is the animated graphically enhanced MOO known as the *Palace*. Our hypothesis is that use of this technology, with its "real time", spatial, and personalisation attributes, will provide more satisfaction and better ease of use than its text-only, asynchronous counterparts.

The *Palace* is a virtual world chat software program that allows people to communicate interactively via the Internet with the added value of pictures and sounds. *Palace* software is a development of The Palace, Inc., which is owned jointly by Time Warner, Intel, and Softbank Holdings. Palace, made available in September 1995, allows people and organisations to participate in a virtual community where they talk (via typed text), interact, and share experiences in a graphical world on the Internet. The program was created to be as user-friendly as possible. Installation and operation are easy and the software may be used on various platforms (eg. Macintosh and Windows-based PCs). The software provides a variety of meeting rooms and graphical outdoor settings and also includes extensive artwork and tools for the creation of customised virtual environments known as 'user Palaces'. The *Palace* environment has grown to more than 300,000 users in well over 1000 Palace sites (<http://www.thepalace.com>, Jan 97).

Researchers at Syracuse University, led by Mike Eisenberg, Director of the AskERIC Project, began looking at the possible application of this animated graphical software for "real time" collaboration in distance learning in early 1996. Adam Rubin, an Information Technology undergraduate student, designed a Palace classroom environment called the *AskERIC Virtual Classroom* suite. Researchers are actively engaged in preparing and documenting procedures for faculty and student use of this environment along with evaluation techniques for assessment of the technology and its usefulness across a range of distance learning tasks.

The evolving classroom suite presently consists of eight rooms; Homeroom, Main Classroom, three Discussion Rooms, Student Lounge, Schedule Room, and Prop Room. Each of these settings is a colourful visual simulation of its real world equivalent.

In the *AskERIC Virtual Classroom*, each participant, student and teacher, represents him/herself with a small digitised self-image, complete with name tag, as their avatar or Palace prop. These avatars can be moved freely within the rooms.

Communication is by keyboarding short messages which are displayed in 'balloon' clouds emanating from the avatar. On some PCs, these messages can be announced or 'spoken' in addition to being displayed. The on-screen displays are variable in duration, font, and color at the discretion of the user. A log function allows display of a scrollable conversation history which can also be saved in computer memory for future reference.

These graphical animated settings provide meeting places for required or discretionary work. They can be used for classroom discussions either moderated or free-for-all style. They also provide a place for participants to meet and collaborate for social purposes.

Using the *AskERIC* Classrooms
First attempts to use and evaluate the classrooms were implemented in November and December 1996. The participants were generally unfamiliar with computers and online communication. They were

fascinated by the graphics and learned quickly how to communicate with each other. It was encouraging to see that the technology's use of images appeared to make its acceptance easier. There was no sign of intimidation in this 'game like' atmosphere.

Positive comments about the experience included "personalisation provided by the avatars," "immediate interaction among participants," and "a short learning curve due to the product's simple design." Areas of concern included proposed use, class size, and the need for protocols or rules for class behaviour. "Slow typers are at a disadvantage and it is difficult to read and type simultaneously," "multiple conversations are distracting," and "instructor control is mandatory but difficult."

The first large scale application of this technology in distance education is occurring at Syracuse University in Professor Robert Heckman's, Information Technology Industry course in the Spring 1997 semester. Eighteen students received Palace training during a four day residency period at the University and are completing course requirements using both *Palace* and *HyperNews* over the Internet during the 15 week course. The Internet experience levels vary widely in this geographically dispersed group.

Data collected during this course will be used to help answer research questions concerning the user's acceptance of technologies in distance education, learning and socialisation aspects of asynchronous and synchronous communications, a comparison of text-only and graphical systems, and the impact of collaboration among participants, both discretionary and required, on participant satisfaction.

Early indications of user acceptance and satisfaction with the *Palace* classrooms obtained during the residency period include positive student comments on ease of use, significance of graphic and spatial designs, and the advantages of 'real time' conversation.

Typical student comments include: "The ability to see a picture of the person I am talking to and my ability to move closer to that person on the screen definitely enhances the communication," "I am familiar with text chat, the addition of the avatars adds reality and personality to an otherwise dull process," "Doing work in this setting is like playing a game, the novelty may wear off but I like it," "Trying to hold a conversation here is much easier than in *HyperNews* as the responses are immediate."

Conclusions and Future Research

Throughout the Information Technology Industry course, lecture, assignments, and discussion activities are being performed using a combination of *HyperNews* and Palace technologies. Student writing and conversation logs in each technology will be analysed to better understand the relationships and benefits associated with asynchronous and synchronous communication, the relative amounts of required and discretionary collaboration, and the perceived benefits of graphical enhancements to the traditional text-only models. Attention will be given to both affective and effective parameters of the learning model. The affective or 'personal touch' impact of the synchronous technology may be "glue that holds the class together" in an otherwise impersonal and distant environment.

The use of the *Palace* as representative software is convenient. It is inexpensive, readily available through Internet downloads, and works across a wide variety of user platforms. It provides a low cost, high impact opportunity. Other synchronous software systems will also be examined. Of particular interest are those systems, like the *Palace*, that supplement traditional text-only chats with graphical designs adding animation and spatial representations.

This field is evolving rapidly. It is likely that animated videos will be available as replacements for the static digital images used today. If desired, audio may replace text. In each case trade-offs involving cost, ease of use, attainment of objectives, and user satisfaction must be considered. It is the intent of the Syracuse University research team to conduct a comprehensive investigation of a full range of asynchronous and synchronous technologies for distance education and group conferencing and develop fundamental guidelines for data collection and future research.

References

Badger, A. (1996). *University of Phoenix online faculty training module,* Phoenix, AZ: University of Phoenix Press: 23.

Barron, D.D. (1996). 'Distance education in North American library and information science education: application of technology and commitment.' *Journal of the American Society for Information Science,* 47 (11): 805-810.

Besser, H. (1996). School of library and information science: Asynchronous distant independent learning project. Presentation at the meeting of the Association for Library and Information Science Education, San Antonio, TX, January.

Busey, A. (1995). *Secrets of the MUD wizards.* Indianapolis, IN: Sams.net Publishing.

Grenquist, S. (1997). *Broadcasting over the Internet.* Rolla, MO: University of Missouri-Rolla.

Holland, M P. (1996). 'Collaborative technologies in inter-university instruction.' *Journal of the American Society for Information Science.* 47 (11), November: 857-863.

Roberts, J. M. (1996). 'The story of distance education: a practitioner's perspective.' *Journal of the American Society for Information Science.* 47 (11), November: 811-816.

Web Sites:

Palace Homepage
<http://www.thepalace.com>.

Topic G

Multiple Personalities?:

Teacher Librarian, Cybrarian, Director of Information Services

What's in a Name?

Trisha Benson[*]

Introduction

If you are reading this, then I am writing to those of you who have decided to not stagnate! You have chosen/accepted CHANGE as something that has happened to your life as a librarian. Good! What comes next? Well, that is up to you -- on how much reading, talking and thinking you do on this topic. This is one of the reasons for this VC, to help you think about what you do as a librarian, how you do it and how do you want to change? Are you undergoing evolution or a revolution in your role as a Librarian in your school?

Yes, I am using the word 'Librarian'. I feel there is nothing wrong with this word. I know that several other titles have been bandied around. An examination of the *Concise Oxford Dictionary* shows the following:

Librarian: *custodian of library*
Library: *a room or collection of books for use by some class of persons; similar collection of films, records, computer routines, etc.*
Custodian: *guardian, keeper*
Director: *superintendent, manager*
Manager: *person controlling activities of person or team*
Coordinator: *bringer of parts, movements, etc into proper relation.*

Saying that we are Information Specialists or Manager of the Resource Centre can mean lots of different things. Well, Librarian can too! Do we change the name of the post office because it now sells posters, toys, gifts and books? No, it is still the Post Office. Newsagents haven't changed their name either, although they no longer deal only with news items. At least, in libraries, you know that the service available is directed towards providing information. We have always been, and still are, one-stop shops for information. It is our products that have diversified, and our skills as well. Has our role changed -- well, read on!

---

[*] **Trisha Benson** holds the position of Librarian at Caroline Chisholm High School in Chisholm, Australian Capital Territory (ACT), Australia. Trisha may be contacted via email on <Trisha.Benson@CarolineChisholmHS.act.edu.au>.

What the Past Situation Has Been

In ancient times, librarians were the custodians of information for posterity. Just to make sure, scrolls and books were chained to the shelves! Even 400 years beyond Gutenberg, our information materials came as books and paper records. In this century, though, we have seen the development of video tape, posters, CDROM and computer disks as information materials. Not just paper-based information.

What has been our role? The school Librarian has been seen as separate from the classroom, often from the school community and not part of the main curriculum decisions. Our professional association was mainly for the dissemination of information on new resources and for technical assistance.

As well...

- From the student perspective, the Librarian was seen as a bespectacled old bag, with twin-set and pearls, admonishing anyone who spoke above a whisper -- and not a teacher.

- From the classroom teacher perspective, the Librarian had a really easy job -- no reports and she got to read books or the newspaper all day -- not a REAL teacher.

- From the Principal's perspective, the Librarian was handy for getting hold of journal articles, recreational reading and the library took a large slice of the budget -- not a real teacher though.

- From the Parents &Citizens' (P&C) perspective, the Librarian was the keeper of books, seen much from the students' point of view and good for supplying books for their children to read -- not a real teacher.

What the Current Situation is

There have been some name changes, eg. information resource centre managers, information specialists and a lot more emphasis on that word 'information'. Some Librarians feel that they have become more like chooks without heads, or their minds are expanding exponentially -- fit to burst or, alternatively, NOTHING HAS CHANGED!

Books, paper, CDROMs, Internet, Enquiry stations, photocopiers -- information can be borrowed, reproduced, downloaded, accessed, uploaded, and so on!

The role of the school library may be seen as a break from the classroom, for work that is an extension of classroom activity. For some Librarians, there is involvement in curriculum decision-making, maybe even some involvement in computer technology decision-making. Our professional associations have changed, taking on the role of alerting Librarians to new developments and organising professional development courses.

As well...

- From the student perspective, the Librarian may still be the same as above or may be seen as someone who knows how to help find the material needed for an assignment -- may or may not realise librarian is also a teacher.

- From the classroom teacher perspective, the Librarian may still be the same as above or seen as a servant, to fetch things and organise their classes, a minder. A third scenario is that of colleague, who can advise or suggest ways of using the library and its resources, working collaboratively.

- From the Principal's perspective, may still be the same as above or seen as a 'mover and shaker' -- the library a centre for the exciting developments occurring in information technology, a centre where change might originate from -- still takes a good slice of the budget, but this might not be such a bad thing with these changes happening!

- From the P&C perspective -- may still be the same as above or may invite parents to become library members and/or helpers, provides informative material for their use, occasionally asks for assistance with funding of resources.

What the Future Expectation will be...
Well, I think we will still be custodians of information, and more in the way of technical wizards (but not technicians -- there is a distinction here!).

There will still be books... and computers, terminals, CDROMs, Internet, and whatever else we're into then!

The centre of the universe!? The role of the library will be to not only act as the centre for curriculum needs and organisation, but also to be the hub of the technology in the school. The Information Technology (IT) and Library departments have merged into one, with a computer technician as well as two or more library assistants on staff. The Librarian is involved in consultations with executive on hardware, software and other items that meet the need of school curriculum requirements. Will be automatic member of IT and Curriculum committees.

The professional association will be very involved with professional development and continue to disseminate latest trends in job delivery. Very big on public relations of the Librarian's role in school, working closely with unions and universities delivering librarianship training.

As well...

- From the student perspective, the library is a cool place to be in. The Librarian can show you how to find the answer to any question; helpful; a teacher that works with their classroom teacher.

- From the classroom teacher perspective, a colleague who can be partnered for team-teaching, provides professional development in the new information technologies, contributes to curriculum planning, one of the executive teachers on staff.

- From the Principal's perspective, a valued executive teacher who provides support to staff with their expertise in information acquisition, provides professional development, is a key person in the development of the school within the community and its surrounds, deserves every bit of the budget that is allocated -- where can we find some more!

- From the P&C's perspective, one of the important teachers in the school, gets on well with their child, has provided some very useful information for the parents and even some training nights in all this new technology (can't let the kids get too far ahead!).

Is this Future Expectation Realistic?
Why not? It has been said that the future is anything you want to make of it, but I am well aware of those school Librarians (have been one myself in the past) who get no support from the Executive in

their school and the library is considered more of a hindrance than an asset.

So, some of this future is possible, if you consider what you want to be! Will you concentrate on your collection management and bibliographic organisation, so that the library is known to contain a lot of useful and easily located resources? Will you concentrate on working with one or a few teachers, increasing in number each year, to establish a network of supporters, who can spread the word around within their faculties and executive, of how helpful you have been with classes? Will you hold information sessions with the Executive teachers, or invite staff from key learning areas to afternoon tea in the library, to promote the information technology resources you can incorporate into their assignments? Will you go to as many professional development sessions as you can fit into your life, so as to be able to understand and use new technologies? Will you open the library after school for professional development sessions for the staff on how to operate the IT resources you have, so that the knowledge becomes shared? Will you be a 'mover and shaker'? Is your role as Librarian in the school one in evolution or is it a complete revolution? Will you be a Librarian, a Cybrarian or a Director of Information Services? *WHAT DO YOU WANT TO BE?*

Conclusion

I think that you will still be a Librarian, because, after all, you are still the custodian of information. It is the way we do our jobs, and the way that those we work with get to know us, that will count, rather than any fancy title. Why not educate those we work with to think 'Librarian' is to think 'Teacher' and 'Information Technology'. This way, we don't go changing our name every few decades to try and raise our status or make us look professional. We already are! We remain as 'Librarians', and the public relations campaign we wage -- by what we do and how we do it -- within and without our school communities, is what will support our status and promote our profession.

References

Bonanno, K. (1996). *'A point of view.'* The Internet and TL's Role in the School: Possible, Probable and Preferred Futures. ITEC Virtual Conference TL Strand, April 1996.

Bonanno, K. (1996). 'IT - *Planning for change.*' Planning for Information Technology. Paper presented at ASLA ACT Conference, Binalong, November 1-3.

Borgmeyer, V. (1996). Priorities and balance in the role of an R-12 Teacher Librarian. *Access,* 10 (2), May: 33.

Eisenberg, M. (1996). *'The Internet challenge: Using technology in context to meet educational goals.'* The Internet and TL's Role in the School: Possible, Probable and Preferred Futures, ITEC Virtual Conference TL Strand, April 1996.

Feuerriegel, C. (1996). If it's high-tech, it can't possibly be a 'library'... *Orana,* 32 (1), Feb: 24-25.

Franklin, A. (1996). The teacher-librarian as a member of the school's executive staff. *Scan,* 15 (4), Nov: 30-31.

Hanson, K. (1996). Change or be changed. *Scan,* 15 (2), May: 41-42.

Henri, J. (1996). A Director in Information Services? Flying a kite or pie in the sky? *Orana,* 32 (3), Aug: 199-201.

Henri, J. (1996). *'Teacher librarians: the best of times and the worst of times.'* The Internet and TL's Role in the School: Possible, Probable and Preferred Futures, ITEC Virtual Conference TL Strand, April 1996.

Hughes, S. (1996). *'Revisioning.'* The Internet and TL's Role in the School: Possible, Probable and Preferred Futures, ITEC Virtual Conference TL Strand, April 1996.

Lee, M. (1996). Into the Information Age: a Director of Information Services for your school? *Scan,* 15 (1), Feb: 38-40.

Mitchell, P. (1996). *'A Point of View.'* The Internet and TL's Role in the School: Possible, Probable and Preferred Futures, ITEC Virtual Conference TL Strand, April 1996.

Rowan, L. (1996). Time to end the disparagement. *Orana,* 32 (3), Aug: 202-207.

White, S. (1996). 'ITEC - Director Info Serv.' <OZTL_NET@listserv. csu.edu.au> [Online]. 1 May.

Alone in the School... Wearing Many Caps: Library Media Specialists Taking an Internet Leadership Role

Peter Genco[*]

Whenever discussion leads to the role of the Library Media Specialist, I immediately think of the salesman in the children's book *Caps for Sale* by Esphyr Slobodkina. He stacks 17 caps upon his head and goes about his business, encounters roadblocks, demonstrates leadership, overcomes adversity, and makes his way along his successful path.

Library Media Specialists could easily label those 17 caps with the variety of roles one must embrace. Media Specialist, Teacher Librarian, Cybrarian, Technology Team Leader, Media Librarian, Information Educator, Information Specialist, AV Coordinator, and so on. These labels are indications of our ever evolving process where definitive roles of the Library Media Specialist cannot be limited. The School Librarian of two decades ago could not have imagined the possibilities we face today. One's ability to adapt to the perpetual changes in the profession lies in the leadership role each Library Media Specialist should play in the education process. No matter what labels one wears, the one that is most imperative should be Educational Leader.

Regarding the usage of Internet in schools, the Library Media Specialist has many opportunities to become an educational leader. It provides a new dimension in resources that allow for student inquiry to expand beyond the limits of any library. Many aspects of the Internet need to be taught to students as well as staff. Library Media Specialists can be responsible for teaching a variety of topics, including copyright, curriculum integration, critical evaluation, Boolean logic and the mechanics of using the Internet. It is imperative that the Library Media Specialist be involved in the process of education within a school and/or school district. Internet is an excellent catalyst for the Library Media Specialist to wear the Educational Leader cap.

---

[*] **Peter Genco** is Library Media Specialist and Technology Team Leader at Fairview High School in Fairview, Pennsylvania, USA. He has held the position of Editor for the *IASL Newsletter* for the International Association of School Librarianship, and is PSLA Technology Committee Chair for the Pennsylvania School Librarians Association. Peter may be contacted via email at <pgenco@iu05trc.trinet.k12.pa.us>.

Library Media Specialists in northwestern Pennsylvania were given the opportunity to take a leadership role in Internet usage. The initiative involved secondary schools in Crawford, Erie and Warren counties.

Internet Access in NW Pennsylvania
In 1993, the Pennsylvania Department of Education offered a statewide grant for educational institutions. The Northwest Tri-County Intermediate Unit <http://www.trinet.k12.pa.us> applied jointly with twenty-nine secondary schools and was successful in receiving funding. This allowed the IU to expand their existing services. They set up as an Internet service provider, developed Internet training and got schools connected to the Internet. Each of the twenty-nine secondary schools identified a facilitator; most schools selected a Library Media Specialist. After a week of intensive training at the IU, each facilitator and school was prepared to access the Internet through a SLIP connection. Connect NW, a consortium of trained building level Internet facilitators, was developed. Commitments of the grant will continue until 1999 and include two full days of additional training for each facilitator annually, turnkey training of teachers at a minimum of 10 per year, and documenting curricular usage/integration of the Internet.

The initial intensive training was instructed by Carrie Gardner, a PhD student from the University of Pittsburgh. It covered all the basics and empowered the NW PA Library Media Specialists to take a leadership role in Internet training. Since the grant required turnkey training of teachers, the Library Media Specialists immediately began to plan and take initiatives in their respective schools. After school and staff development days became the time best utilised for the training.

The IU was able to expand services by offering SLIP connections to educators in the area and network connections to schools. SLIP connections are now upgraded to PPP connections and network connections provide dedicated access <http://www.trinet.k12.pa.us/cnctinfo.html>. Many school districts bought into network connections as a way of obtaining low cost dedicated access using either a 56K or a 128K frame relay connection.

Connect NW continues to provide support to keep the Internet facilitators up to date and has addressed issues including curriculum integration, copyright, staff training, browsers, censorship, site evaluations and technology planning. In addition to the biannual meeting, a mail list has been established to facilitate discussion and sharing among the Internet facilitators.

As educators continue to become more aware of the Internet, the need for staff development and training continues to grow. Based on the NW Pennsylvania Model, the Library Media Specialists remain in place to hold the leadership role. While individual Library Media Specialists continue to develop training sessions in individual schools, some of the Connect NW Library Media Specialists developed training courses for area educators. Both scenarios allow the building level Library Media Specialist the opportunity to teach other educators, including administrators, how to become connected to the Internet, what benefits are available to curricular areas and how to evaluate what is found.

Internet applications for K-12 Educators

This 12 hour course was planned as part of the IU's Summer Staff Development Institute for Summer 1996. It was cooperatively developed by four NW PA Educators: Priscilla Breese, Library Media Specialist at Youngsville Jr. Sr. High School; Dr. Ann Noonen, IMTS Director at the IU; Cheryl Tunno, Library Media Specialist at Meadville Jr. High School and myself. Each of us then taught various sections of the course at locations in Erie and Warren Counties.

This beginners course included a history and introduction to the Internet curriculum connections. It was divided into four sessions:

1. Introduction to the Internet;
2. Surfing and Searching on the WWW;
3. Netscape Bookmarks; and
4. Electronic Mail.

Over 140 educators completed this hands-on course. Due to the great demand other courses have been developed to focus on specific curricular areas. The 1997 Summer Staff Development Institute will offer sections of the basic course again as well as ones geared to math, science, elementary, language arts, social studies, guidance or the arts.

Recommended Resources for Developing Training

The following list is by no means exhaustive. It includes some of the many print, non-print and Web sites which have been and are being used by Library Media Specialists in NW PA.

Print and Non-print Resources

Baule, S.M. (1997). *Technology planning*. Worthington, OH: Linworth Publishing.

Classroom Connect. (1996). *Internet curriculum integration video series*. Lancaster, PA: Classroom Connect.

Fitzgerald, M.A. (1997). Misinformation on the Internet: Applying evaluation skills to online information. *Emergency Librarian*, 24, Jan-Feb: 9-14.

Hay, L. and Henri, J. (eds.). (1996). *A meeting of the minds: ITEC Virtual Conference 1996 proceedings*. Belconnen, ACT: ASLA Press.

LeBaron, J.F., Collier, C., and de Lyon Friel, L. (1995). Building bridges to the Internet: Opportunities for Media/Librarians in self-renewing schools. *School Library Media Annual*, 13: 73-77.

LeBaron, J.F., Collier, C., and de Lyon Friel, L. (1997). *A travel agent in cyber school: the Internet and the library media program*. Englewood, CO: Libraries Unlimited.

Pappas, M.L. and Tepe, A.E. (1995). Preparing the information educator for the future. *School Library Media Annual*, 13: 37-44.

Simpson, C. and McElmeel, S.L. (1997). *Internet for schools*. 2nd ed. Worthington, OH: Linworth Publishing. (Revised edition of *Internet for Library Media Specialists*).

Tate, M. and Alexander, J. (1996). Teaching critical evaluation skills for World Wide Web resources. *Computers in Libraries*, Nov-Dec: 49-55.

WWW Sites

1997 Users and Hosts of the Internet and the Matrix.
<http://www.mids.org/press/pr9701.html>
Includes statistics on Internet usage world wide, including future projections.

Copyright, Citing Web Sources, Netiquette
<http://sehplib.ucsd.edu/aboutnet/cr.html>
Although the copyright section is based on US copyright law, the other sections are more global.

ICONnect:HomePage
<http://www.ala.org/ICONN/index.html>
Offers a great variety of online courses via email, including I-Basics (Internet Basics), CurriWeb (Curriculum Integration Using the Web), SLMS21st (The School Library Media Specialist in the Twenty-first Century).

The Internet Guide - Welcome - Demo
<http://www.fis.utoronto.ca/conted/TIG/Demo/>
From the University of Toronto, an online Internet training for a fee.

Internet Help
<http://www.albany.edu/library/internet/index.html>
Site of links about the Internet, Netscape Navigator, research guide and software training.

LION Internet Forum for School Librarians
<http://www.libertynet.org/~llon/forum-inter.html>
This extensive site has a variety of links appropriate to Internet, libraries and schools.

Sarah Byrd Askew Library - Citing Electronic Resources
<http://www.wilpaterson.edu/wpcpages/library/citing.htm>
Provides specific examples of how to cite the Internet.

Teaching Critical Evaluation Skills for World Wide Web Resources
<http://www.science.widener.edu/~withers/webeval.htm>
Site provides a very nice PowerPoint presentation.

Technology Connections | The Impact of Technology
<http://www.mcrel.org/connect/tech/impact.html>
Links to a variety of resources about Internet/technology and education.

Walt Howe's Internet Learning Center
<http://world.std.com/~walthowe/index.html>
Training site for individuals or groups.

Welcome to AskERIC
<http://ericir.syr.edu/>
Access to the expansive ERIC database.

Naming Rights and TL Worlds[*]

James Henri[†]

In some circles they call it naval gazing and it could be argued that teacher librarians, notwithstanding all of the outstanding things that they have achieved and their high level of professionalism, are the best naval gazers of them all.

The teacher librarian world is certainly a mixed bag with a very significant variation in practice (and a growing variation in nomenclature) across Australian schools. But whose world is it and who has the naming rights in this world? It can be readily accepted that in 1997 a teacher librarian's day looks rather different from what it did in 1987, 1977 or 1967, and among schools there may be little consistency in practice. But does this mean that the teacher librarian's role should change (or has changed) for the better? And who should make this judgement? Is the title 'teacher librarian' beyond its use-by-date, and who should decide that? Should teacher librarians expect that teachers joining their ranks have a specialist university qualification? And should there be an insistence that a teacher appointed as teacher librarian, but not so qualified, be referred to as something else -- teacher in charge of library resource centre -- for example? Does anybody other than a few teacher librarians and the odd interested spectator actually care?

The role of teacher librarian has been a topic of conversation among teacher librarians since their inception and perhaps even in earlier times when class teachers looked after 'the library' as an extra. In Australia there has been an ongoing struggle to define just what teacher librarians should be and what they should do. In this country this struggle goes back to the 1960's when Australian governments and educational bureaucrats first 'discovered' the need for school libraries. The struggle has, however, not been limited to Australia. The same or similar debate has a history in New Zealand, England, Canada, and the USA (Hamilton 1982; Haycock 1981; Henri 1988, 1991, 1992; *Learning for the future* 1993; Valentine and Nelson 1988).

---

[*] Submitted and accepted as a refereed conference paper.

[†] **James Henri** is Senior Lecturer in Teacher Librarianship at the School of Information Studies, Charles Sturt University in Wagga Wagga, New South Wales, Australia. James may be contacted via email at <jhenri@csu.edu.au>.

In recent time the debate in Australia has become more complex (Hay and Kallenberger 1996; Henri 1996; Rowan 1996; Todd 1996). One might suggest a number of possible reasons for this. The advent of the invasion of schools by the new technologies has, some would suggest, radically altered the work that teacher librarians actually do. The economic rationalist policies of successive governments at the federal and state levels has tended to move educational funding away from anything that is not seen as core. (What happens in classrooms is usually the benchmark for what is regarded as core. What happens outside the classroom is more likely to be identified as available for rationalisation.) In this climate funding for libraries and the staff that underpin them has been identified as 'non-core'. (On the other hand funding to maintain class size, to meet the needs of special education, and to test outcomes has remained core.)

The advent of the electronic world and the economic rationalist vision are colliding to form a twin danger for teacher librarians who may well be perceived by some as wedded to a print based world that is seen to be fading fast. In this world funding (read 'large buckets of funding') will be found for bells and whistles that are smaller, faster, easier, more complete, and less expensive than ever before. The concentration on funding information technology infrastructure as well as on the latest bells and whistles in a world of limited budgets means that less funding will be available at the system level for traditional information resources. Schools have some discretion over the disbursement of their own funding but even here many schools are finding it difficult to maintain traditional information products and services.

The fact that educational decision makers often see information technology as distinct from other forms of information and hand the control of that technology to those who are good at maintaining it provides another angle on the challenge faced by teacher librarians. Teacher librarians certainly have a role as custodians of information, but if that is perceived as their major role then they are likely to have a limited life span. On the other hand, many teacher librarians are at the cutting edge of the application of all forms of information technology to the instructional program. Schools that recognise the leading role taken by teacher librarians often appoint them as information technology coordinators. Likewise a number of teacher librarians have been seconded to lead the Technology in Learning and Teaching (TILT) initiatives.

The distinction drawn above, provides a hint at the reason for the existing teacher requirement in teacher librarian. In a school setting the search for information should follow the posing of interesting yet serious questions that require solution. In this environment information is a tool, it is clay in the potter's hand. As the learner works with that information in a way that is characteristic of effective learning then s/he learns from that information (including for example that s/he has the wrong information!). The learner becomes informed. Specific information is only the answer if the potential recipient of that information has asked the right question(s). In this way the informing process has value.

It is in this difficult, messy, and largely unexplored area that the teacher librarian has a significant teacher role; a role that differs from those played out by other teachers. Many teachers themselves do not have especially sharp information literacy skills (O'Connell 1997). These teachers may find that working with a teacher librarian is part of the solution. The teacher librarian's tool kit of information skills should not be limited by the colour of the box in which information resides, nor with the sophistication of the wrapping paper and ribbon. Whether the information is audio, visual or kinaesthetic should make little difference to the teacher librarian's value. Of course this assumes that the teacher librarian has the professional competence, and ongoing inclination and opportunity to keep abreast of developments that affect his/her skill level. Which leads me to some more thoughts.

We talk about teacher librarians as though every school has one. We assume that there is a common bond among teacher librarians: that they are all competent, alive and well, and respected by their teaching colleagues. We assume that there are sufficient opportunities for aspiring teacher librarians to take a professional qualification, and for experienced teacher librarians there are ample professional development opportunities. These assumptions clearly exaggerate reality.

Many schools do not have a teacher librarian. Many small schools have a weekly teacher librarian allocation of a few hours. The likelihood of such allocations being taken seriously or filled by a qualified applicant are remote. Many schools that appear to have a teacher librarian, don't!! This is because a percentage of those who are titled 'teacher librarian' have no specialist qualification in the field. Some employers accept short inservice programs as an acceptable measure of competency. Such situations would not be tolerated in other areas of education, nor would they be accepted in other professions. Can you imagine the local medical practitioner, not having undertaken further specialist study, hanging out a shingle with the words 'brain surgeon' inscribed, expecting to stay in business. We expect specialists to have specialist qualifications. We want more than a name change to prove that new skills have been acquired.

The universities that offer education for teacher librarianship are not overrun with applications and far too few graduate from these programs to make any significant impact on Australia's 10,000 schools. In-school funding, and employer wide funding for the professional development of teachers is at an all time low which means that the maintenance of skill levels will soon become problematic.

In times past each state had a significant professional teacher librarianship unit that was able to lobby on behalf of teacher librarians and for school library services. These are now distant memories ASLA and ALIA (Schools Section) are the profession's major hope, but they cannot expect to be overly influential unless they form key alliances with other significant interest groups. The point is that while we debate the role and appropriate name for the tribe, we may miss the genocide at the doorway.

My conclusion is that while naval gazing has value as a sensitising exercise it is more essential that teacher librarians get on with what they do best -- performing as outstanding, leading edge practitioners. And in their spare time (qualified) teacher librarians can make a difference if they:

- continue to encourage the best teachers to take a university course in teacher librarianship
- continue to encourage under-qualified teacher librarians to upgrade their qualifications
- inform principals about the need to advertise a teacher librarian position when it is vacant
- write about teacher librarianship possibilities for newspapers and teacher journals
- give joint presentations with principals to principal gatherings
- lobby within the teacher unions for better industrial outcomes for teacher librarians (including career paths)

- provide professional development for teachers with respect to information literacy issues, and
- continue to engage in professional development initiatives at the cutting edge. (See for example Henri and Hay 1996).

Claiming the territory is important but so to is being aware of the insights offered by those outside the field. Sometimes those who are closest to the action are blinded by the niceties of current theory and practice. Often a paradigm shift is brought about by an outsider when the current way of doing things is at a peak. Teacher librarians should not ignore the ideas of 'outsiders' on the questions of role and nomenclature but they should not jump on bandwagons without serious thought to the consequences (See Lee 1996).

References

Hamilton, D. (1982). The principal and the school library. *Education Canada*, 23 (3): 31-38.

Hay, L. and Kallenberger, N. (1996). 'The future role of the information services unit in the teaching/learning process.' Paper presented at the Electronic networking and Australia's schools conference. 12-13 April, Sydney.

Haycock, K. (1981). The role of the school librarian as a professional teacher: a position paper. *Emergency Librarian*, 8 (5): 4-11.

Henri, J. (1996). A director of information services? Flying a kite or pie in the sky? *Orana*, 32 (3): 199-201.

Henri, J. (1992). Teacher/Librarian: Concept, role, function, and possible future. *Orana*, 19 (2), May: 53-57.

Henri, J. (1991). Libraries in crisis: Teacher librarians and survival of the species. United we stand, divided we fall! *Access*, 5 (3), Aug: 14-15.

Henri, J. (1988). Teacher Librarians into the 1990's: Demise, survival or power?' In *Forging links - strengthening bonds: SLAQ '88 State Conference proceedings*. Mackay, Qld.: SLAQ.

Henri, J. and Hay, L. (1996). Principals are leaders. Teacher librarians can be too! *Access*, 10 (2): 8-10 & 41.

Learning for the future: Developing information services in Australian schools. (1993). Carlton, Vic.: Curriculum Corporation.

Lee, M. (1996). Close the library: Open the information services unit. *The Practising Administrator*, 18 (2): 7.

Rowan, L. (1996). Time to end the disparagement. *Orana*, 32 (3): 202-207.

Todd, R. (1996). The case for a director of information services. *Orana*, 32 (3): 196-198.

Valentine, P. and Nelson, B. (1988). *Sneaky teaching: the role of the school librarian.* London: British Library.

Don't Be Left Behind!: Redefining the Role and Title of the Teacher Librarian in a Digital School

Grace Kinch[*]

We live in an Information Age where computing technologies have changed the way we store, exchange and access information. This has had an impact on the nature of information services provided by the traditional school library. No longer do we need to rely on the provision of static information sources as the basis of a collection. Dynamic services utilising CDROMs, online sources and the Internet have transformed the nature of information services. In schools where networking forms the basis for access to these computing technologies, teacher librarians must realise that they have a key (and essential) role to play in the school team which determines the direction of, and access to, learning and information technologies. Information is the basis of the service we offer! This is why teacher librarians need to re-examine their role and title within such a networked school.

Networking in a digital school requires a whole-school approach where learning environments such as these can exist:

> *Computing technology is a key to the most powerful knowledge bank and multimedia the world has ever known.*

(Fleming 1996:19)

and

> *Information and opportunities for immediate access should pervade the learning environment, not be an attachment to it.*

(Todd 1996:197)

Teacher librarians as information experts are in a strategic position to assist with this implementation. Their major concern is with information access and the ease of such. They are also always planning ahead to ensure that the services they offer are those that are required. (I think it's known as crystal ball gazing!!) Implementing networking in an Information Age requires people with this skill of looking to the future. Their value is further

---

[*] **Grace Kinch** holds the position of Director: Information Services Centre at Kilvington Baptist Girls' Grammar in Ormond, Victoria, Australia. Grace may be contacted via email at <gkinch@kilvington.schnet.edu.au>.

enhanced by the fact that they have a 'whole of school' perspective due to the nature of their role. They are not faculty-aligned. Judy Douglas recently summed up this position in reflecting on her former role as a teacher librarian.

In retrospect, being the teacher-librarian in a school also gave me the opportunity to see the organisation I worked in as a whole. I couldn't get too caught up in the politics of the school as I had to be able to get on with all departments and staff. Individuals would tell me things in passing and, as I moved around the school planning with teachers and working with all the students, I could see a complete picture of the culture and climate within the school which is rarely available to others.

(Douglas 1997:6)

Creating networked learning environments where the model of learning has changed, brings with it a change in our vocabulary to describe such learning environments. Di Fleming, Principal of Kilvington has identified these fundamental shifts which should occur in a school which is using the computer as a learning tool:

FROM	TO
Industrial revolution model	Knowledge Age
Teaching	Learning
Organisation of learning	Learning organisation
Pen and pencil	Computing tools
Reactive	Future makers
Subject-centred	Interdisciplinary/action learning
Isolation	Open learning
Classroom	World Wide Web
IT Lab	Networked world
Instruction	Construction
Lower order questions	Higher order questions
Hours open	Open all hours
Inertia	Creativity
Computer labs	Transparent technologies

(Fleming 1996:1)

Engaging students in this learning environment has had an impact on the traditional library project. The move to project based learning where students are asking the questions impacts on the way students "race to the library to collect everything you've got on such and such a topic". Project based learning usually involves learning of a constructive nature; where students can use the information they access to evaluate, ask further questions and exhibit their learning as part of a team of learners. The Internet adds a dynamic aspect to the search for information in a project based learning environment.

This change should be reflected in the roles and titles of key personnel in the school who are leading the changes in learning and the resourcing of that learning. The teacher librarian is one of these people. The term 'teacher librarian' is jaded. It does not reflect or say anything about what or how the teacher librarian is 'doing' to meet information needs in a digital school. It does not reflect the dynamic part we play in providing access to online and CDROM information services. The word 'librarian' is traditional and says to those hearing it: custodian, static, etc. In learning environments where skilling our students in key competencies is a focus, we in these schools are educators or leading by example rather than 'teachers', working with students to facilitate skill development; learning together. So even the 'teacher' in 'teacher librarian' can seem inappropriate as part of the title of the 'new' person being the teacher librarian. (Obviously, though the person must have education qualifications. I am not suggesting that we take the educational/teacher aspect out of the role.)

A name change obviously has an impact on the name of the unit that this person is responsible for. I agree with Mal Lee (1996:7) when he states that we need to close down the library and open up the 'information services unit' or whatever is chosen to reflect the new 'resources' unit in a networked school. The word 'library' reflects an outmoded institution. I have been the Director of the Information Services Centre since the start of 1995. I came up with the new name for my title and 'unit' I would lead after discussion with the Principal about the nature of the information services we wanted to provide for our students in a computing and networked learning organisation. Our concept of 'library' is more dynamic than what a traditional library offers.

Information services are dynamic when one has CDROM and Internet available via a network. Our definition of an information service is far-reaching when one considers the range of multimedia and online communication features of the Internet. Di Fleming describes the computer as "a think pad; a key to access data – from *Encarta* to *Reuters*; a tool to store, organise and manipulate information; a doorway to the most powerful multimedia formats; a construction site for learning; a gallery to exhibit knowledge and understanding; a multi-dimensional tool in a multi-media age and a communication tool to express feelings share ideas and to develop powerful relationships" (Fleming 1996:2). Information services is part of this and the Centre needs to reflect and be a user of these technologies if it is not to be left behind as the school immerses itself in the new technologies.

The ASLA document, *Learning for the future* (1993:4) states:

> *The richness of the school's library resource services will influence and may even determine whether or not teachers and students are empowered to be independent learners both today and for the rest of their lives.*

In a school implementing fundamental changes to the learning environment, the 'library' must move with it and be able to enhance what is being stated above: another reason for the title of the 'teacher librarian' to be changed. It needs to reflect the fundamental changes in learning taking place, as a major support to this learning style.

What about the role of the 'teacher librarian' in such a place? As Director of the Information Services Centre there has been a change in the nature of my role. Much of this has to do with:

- implementing the Internet as an information source as a part of my 'library' — not looking at the 'library' then the Internet, but the concept of 'library' as being a total information service;

- in supporting and enhancing the integration of the laptop computer by students when they use information services in the Information Services Centre (ISC); and

- in confronting the issue of information literacy in an environment where the ability to access online and networked information sources has become a 'necessity'.

My role has changed and support for this change has come from the Principal. The way your role can be perceived in your school may have much to do with the Principal's understanding of information technologies. Is this your Principal?

> *Information technology is not an option for educational leaders. The learner-principal must become immersed in the use of computing technology because it is an area of literacy, a learning tool, a key to accessing information and it is a construction site for knowledge and*

understanding...technology is not an end in itself but has always been a part of learning.

(Fleming 1996:19)

Even if this is not your Principal, I believe that 'teacher librarians' can take up the challenge and be part of the educational vision by confronting the future by being a user of emerging technologies.

The world of the Internet is not a panacea but a communication and information tool.

(Bonanno 1996:1)

As an 'information expert', the 'Director of the Information Services Centre' has a key role to play in putting the Internet into a context for students and staff. We have a key role to play in advising about the most appropriate information source for the purpose at hand. The 'Director' can act as the intermediary between what is on the Internet and how it can assist the learning programs and information needs in the school. The fact that information on the World Wide Web is not necessarily as structured or as concise in books -- and educators realise this -- provides the 'Director' with an opportunity to lead in the area of navigation and making effective use of class time. Colleagues appreciate the fact that you can support them in their use of the Internet. You need to be pro-active and lead the way. It can be done.

In an Information/Knowledge Age where the ability to access information is vital in order to support enquiry-based/ knowledge construction learning styles, the ability to use that information effectively is even more vital. Information literacy is about enabling learning. The new 'Director of Information Services' must be at the forefront of ensuring that an integrated approach is developed to information literacy. One need only refer to the Mayer Report (1992) where reference is made to the Key Competencies which need to be developed in our students to prepare them for the transition to the world of work and further study:

It is also important that young people understand that the ability to access and organise information is crucial to their ongoing education and training and development of competence. Competence in collecting, analysing and organising information is central to all acquisition of knowledge and skills.

(Mayer Committee 1992)

So the 'Director of Information Services' needs to be pro-active in leading the way here. Again I refer to Judy Douglas who has described a feature of the role of the 'teacher librarian' which is relevant here:

> ...being a teacher librarian is not unlike being a consultant. You have expertise to offer in a situation where you can see the whole picture. You have to deal with all students and teachers as your customers, assisting them to identify their needs and then meeting them. You can be pro-active while still keeping the customer happy as you sell them the benefits of what you can do for them.
>
> (Douglas 1997:6)

Closing comments

I think there is a chance that teacher librarians can be 'left out of the total school picture' if they do not reassess their role in a networked school utilising information and learning technologies. In a learning organisation where the focus is on project/enquiry based learning the traditional library project has gone. Directors of Information Services Centres need to reassess their 'consultancy' role in order to ensure that they are part of the team that plays a key role in the 'project building' and 'action learning' occurring as they work with staff and students to make the most effective use of information services.

The change in your title and emphasis in your role will provide a much clearer image of who you are and what you do because as you discuss this with your Principal and other key players you will be 'selling yourself' and what you have to offer in the digital and networked school.

References

Learning for the future: Developing information services in Australian Schools. (1993). Carlton, Vic.: Curriculum Corporation.

Bonanno, K. (1996). 'The Internet and TL's role in the School: possible, probable & preferred futures: a point of view.' ITEC Virtual Conference, 5 June 1996.

Douglas, J. (1997). From books to business. *SLAV Newsbulletin*, Summer: 6-7.

Fleming, D. (1996). Learning in a Knowledge Age. *TISP Online*, 1 (1): 1-2.

Fleming, D. (1996). Of Principals and computers. *EQ Australia*, Autumn: 19-21.

Lee, M. (1996). Close the library: Open the information services unit. *The Practising Administrator*, 18 (2): 7.

Mayer Committee. (1992). *Putting general education to work: the Key Competencies Report.* Canberra: AEC/MOVEET.

Todd, R.J. (1996). The case for a Director of Information Services. *Orana*, 32 (3), Aug: 196-198.

What Title the Teacher Librarian in the Digital Age?

Mal Lee[*]

What nomenclature should be used to describe teacher librarians in the Digital Age?

It is becoming increasingly clear that this is not a simple academic question, but rather one that relates to the continued existence of teacher librarians.

I suspect teacher librarians are the group of teachers that best understand the power of Don Tapscott's observation that:

> *In the 1990s there is no status quo. The velocity of change in information technology has seen to that. Products are becoming digital. Markets are becoming electronic. Industries are in upheaval. Organisations are having to go far beyond reengineering to fundamentally rethink everything about themselves and their future.*
> Tapscott (1995:11)

Let's recognise the Digital is as dramatic as the Industrial Revolution. It is already occasioning fundamental societal change, and will continue to bring about the end of time honoured practices.

Michael Hammer (1996:257) makes the profound observation that:

> *Past results are not a guarantee for future performance.*

Many vocations are already undergoing dramatic change or fast disappearing.

Already educational administrators across Australasia are questioning the need for teacher librarians.

I happen to believe that teacher librarians can and should play a central role in future schooling, but that role needs to be proclaimed loudly and clearly, hopefully with the help of a simple title.

Over the last year I have been advocating in my presentations and writings the importance of:

---

[*] Mal Lee is Managing Director of ITEC Pty Ltd, an information technology in education consultancy firm based in Canberra, ACT, Australia. For more information on the work of ITEC visit their website at <http://www.itec.com.au>, as well as their new online service for educators called *EdDirect* at <http://www.eddirect.com>. Mal can be contacted via email at <mlee@pop.cc.adfa.oz.au>.

- schools adopting a whole of school community approach to the development of information literacy
- schools creating information services units to support that quest
- creating a 'director of information services'
- dropping the name 'library', and the connotations that that name still carries.

Those observations are based on the belief if schools want to move away from the present Industrial Age model and adopt an approach that educates the young for the Information Age and beyond they need to make a number of key structural changes.

Amongst those changes is the creation of a whole of school information services unit that can provide the staff, students, parents, and possibly the wider local community, the assistance they require to thrive in these rapidly changing times.

I have also argued that:

1. the term 'library', based as it is upon the Latin for books, has been archaic for some time; that quality school libraries have been far more than book collections for many years; and
2. while many teacher librarians are to the fore in the movement of schooling into the Information Age the term 'teacher librarian' still conjures up a very staid, conservative image amongst educational administrators, and school principals.

In recent workshops and discussions with senior bureaucrats I have encountered a strong move to get rid of the teacher librarian, and to employ librarians and to make the commensurate savings.

It was very apparent that 'teacher librarians' had a very real image and marketing problem; a problem that could bring about your demise.

I would suggest it is vital that teacher librarians address this image problem now, and in so doing give careful consideration to:

1. clarifying the role you should play; and
2. identifying a title that reflects that role.

Most importantly recognise the magnitude and seriousness of the problem.

The immediate challenge is to clarify the role to be played by the teacher librarian.

Once that role is clarified effort can then be more effectively directed towards repositioning the profession.

In time the new position and the work being done will not only shape the nomenclature used, but more importantly will determine the future of teacher librarians in Australia's schools.

The Changing Role

In the discussions on OZTL_NET late last year, it was apparent that all of the group which contributed to the discussion on the future nomenclature for teacher librarians not only recognised the role of the teacher librarian needed to change, but more importantly that it was essential that the issue be addressed.

This latter recognition places the teacher librarians probably eighteen months ahead of any other teacher or principal grouping, as most of the latter are only now tentatively beginning to consider their future role. Of note is that at the time of writing there is still no 'OZTL_NET' or chat groups for Australia's principals or educational administrators nor, as far as I can ascertain, any other teacher groupings that are discussing their role in future schooling.

While James Henri is quite correct that the OZTL_NET group is not representative of all the nation's teacher librarians, one can validly argue that it is does reflect the thinking of the teacher librarian leadership, and as such can be compared to the pathfinding groups in the other parts of the teaching profession.

Clarifying the Position

The nomenclature discussion reinforces my belief that now is the time for the teacher librarians to reposition.

The same discussion also suggests that the profession does need to clarify what role it wants to play. While virtually all writers spoke of the importance of contributing to the school wide development of information literacy and the other key process skills, and appreciated the importance of all teachers operating as facilitators few commented on teacher librarians:

- building on their 'whole of school' perspective and playing a leading role in the development of an integrated, networked, learning community;

- working as 'infoliteracy' (Drucker) coaches, and providing ongoing support and direction for staff, the students and indeed the wider parent community; or
- harnessing their understanding of information technology, and in particularly those elements that relate to internetworking and the acquisition, analysis and storage of information.

While one should ask whether teacher librarians ought play the latter roles those functions, and probably many others, the questions need to be addressed.

Repositioning

In these crazy, rapidly changing times where the future is being shaped by the proactive, who are prepared to take control, the ball is clearly with Australia's teacher librarians.

They have a marked strategic advantage. They, for example:

- are aware of the need to reposition
- have a significant proportion of their number who have repositioned, and are aware of what is required to make the move
- understand the importance of knowledge in the Digital Age
- are imbued with a service culture; a commitment to supporting their clients and colleagues
- possess the 'whole of organisation' perspective required to create a networked school community.

One could continue at length: suffice it to say, once again, now is the time for teacher librarians nationally to take control.

Don't wait for the systems. Most are light years behind.

Act as a total group; determine the position you want to fill and set about filling that role.

I appreciate the magnitude of the impediments facing many. The anachronistic New South Wales Department of School Education staffing formula that links the number of teacher librarians with the number of classes is an immense blockage, particularly in the primary sector, but one already sees NSW teacher librarians who have found ways to overcome those 'challenges'.

Let the Position Determine the Title

In time, in the not too distant future, the position adopted will determine the nomenclature used to describe teacher librarians.

Evidence of this development is already apparent across the nation in the naming of those executive positions that have significant responsibility for the provision of information services. One sees, particularly in the independent schools and in the Victorian government schools, terms like 'Information Services Coordinator'; 'Manager Information Services' and 'Director of Information Services'. One also encounters terms like 'Head Library Services', but even there, efforts are being made to shift away from the 'older title'.

Take Charge

The networked world, and situations on it like this virtual conference and OZTL_NET provide a rare opportunity for teacher librarians as a whole to take charge of their fate and to use the new high speed, low cost communications to shape the way forward.

My suggestion is that the leadership use the new medium, as well as the existing modes, to both clarify the desired role of the teacher librarian and to provide the requisite support and direction.

References

Hammer, M. (1996). *Beyond reengineering*. New York: Harvard Business.

Tapscott, D. (1995). *The digital economy*. New York: John Wiley.

Identity Crisis: Roles of the Teacher Librarian in the Information Age

Victoria Pennell[*]

"I need to find today's stock market report"; "Where can I find a map of Europe after World War I?"; "I need help formatting a table for my statistics assignment."; "How can my students find information on small business?"; "I need help constructing my home page."; "Can you fix the overhead projector?"; "How can my students connect with another school to share information about Canadian issues?"; "I need help using an electronic index."; "I need a new network password"; "How do I cite a Web page in my research paper?"; "Do we have any books about eating disorders?"; "The printer is not working, can you help me?"; "I need a new workstation linked to the school network."; "How do I post assignments for my students to the Mathematics home page?"; "Can we purchase these materials to support the new biology program?"; "Can we plan a research activity for my Social Studies class?"; "When can we meet to plan for the technology professional development session?"; "How do I send an email message?"; "I need help with a Power Point presentation." These are all requests which a typical teacher librarian would hear in the course of a day's work in a typical school library in today's educational environment. There are demands to be an information specialist, a teacher, a technician, a network administrator, an instructional consultant, a technology coordinator and the list goes on. These demands are constantly changing as new technologies evolve and as new instructional strategies are employed. No wonder there is an 'identity crisis'!

The role of the teacher librarian has been under scrutiny for many years, but probably never before have we found ourselves in such a paradoxical situation. At a time when the exponential growth of information is presenting an opportunity for students to access more information than ever before, we are faced with the dilemma of how to provide equitable access so that all students have an equal opportunity to develop their information literacy skills. At a time

---

[*] **Victoria Pennell** is Teacher Librarian at Mt. Pearl Senior High School in Mt. Pearl, New Foundland Canada. Vicki can be contacted via email at <vpennell@calvin.stemnet.nf.ca>.

when educational reform is focusing on the needs of the individual learner, varied instructional strategies and resources and lifelong learning, economic restraints are affecting the staffing of schools and in particular the position of teacher librarian which is so essential to all these areas. To add more confusion there are debates about what the position should be called, many people feel that teacher librarian no longer adequately describes the role.

While there have been many documents and policies written, for example, *Partners in Action: the Library Resource Centre in the School Curriculum* (Ontario, 1982); *Information Power: Guidelines for School Library Media Programs* (AASL & AECT, 1988); *Learning for the future: Developing Information Services in Australian Schools* (1993), which have attempted to outline the critical role of the teacher librarian in the learning environment of the late 20th century, there still appears to be difficulty in convincing the educational decision makers of the importance of having such a person in every school. In the trends towards educational restructuring and reform, the position of teacher librarian has not received much attention and in the downsizing which has been affecting education worldwide, many teacher librarian positions have been downsized or eliminated altogether.

For many years there was very little in the way of research to support the impact of teacher librarians, however in recent years there have been many studies which have strongly supported the role. One of the most significant pieces of school library media research to be published in recent times was done by Keith Curry Lance during the 1988-89 school year. This study, entitled *The Impact of School Library Media Centers on Academic Achievement*, involved 221 Colorado public schools. Some of the major findings from this study were:

1. The size of a library media staff and collection is the best school predictor of academic achievement;
2. Library media expenditures affect LMC staff and collection size, and in turn, academic achievement;
3. The instructional role of the library media specialist shapes the collection and, in turn, academic achievement; and
4. Students who score higher on standardized tests tend to come from schools with more SLMC staff and more books, periodicals, and videos - regardless of other factors, including economic ones.

Stephen Krashen, in his book *The Power of Reading* reviewed hundreds of research studies done in the 19th and 20th centuries that explored the power of free voluntary reading. Some of his major findings were:

1. Voluntary free reading is the best predictor of success in reading comprehension, vocabulary growth, spelling ability, grammatical usage and writing style;
2. Access to school library media centres results in more voluntary reading by students;
3. Having a school library media specialist makes a difference in the amount of voluntary reading done; and
4. Larger school library collections and longer hours increase both circulation and amount read.

In his book *What Works: Research About Teaching and Learning Through the School's Library Resource Centre*, and in his *What Works* column in each issue of *Emergency Librarian*, Ken Haycock has drawn together relevant doctoral research about the effectiveness of the teacher librarian and the school library. These research findings need to be more widely publicized, they need to be shared with the decision makers if they are going to have any impact on maintaining the position of teacher librarian in the schools of the 21st century.

In today's educational milieu there is extensive emphasis being place on students becoming information literate and lifelong learners. *Information Literacy: a Position Paper on Information Problem-Solving* (American Association of School Libraries, 1996) states that "by mastering information problem-solving skills students will be ready for an information-based society and a technological workplace". It goes on to say "Information literacy... equips individuals to take advantage of the opportunities inherent in the global information society. Information literacy should be part of every student's educational experience." These information problem-solving skills are ones which teacher librarians have been emphasizing for years, yet very rarely are teacher librarians mentioned as being critical to the development of these competencies except within the school library domain. The main emphasis being placed on these skills by the majority is one of physical access -- having the technology to access the information. Little attention is being paid to what happens to the information once it is accessed. Information in and of itself, does not make information literate students. Being information literate involves enabling learners to create meaning, to get understanding from the information they access. It puts the emphasis on connecting students to information, guiding them in accessing, evaluating, analyzing, synthesizing and presenting it in a meaningful way to meet their information needs. This cannot be done in isolation, it must be integrated into the everyday learning experiences. There is a need for teacher librarians who can build bridges between the information and the specific curriculum outcomes to ensure that students become effective users of information to prepare them for the workplace and the societal demands of the 21st century.

How are we as teacher librarians to meet the critical challenges we are presently encountering? The demands we are facing call for many new skills which for many of us were not part of our original training and our positions are under constant scrutiny as to the necessity of the position in the restructuring and downsizing of education. What are our choices? Do we maintain the status quo and turn our backs on the emerging technology and the curricular demands or do we continue to learn and evolve and firmly establish our status as the information leader in the school?

I contend that we must continue to evolve, to broaden the concept of the position of teacher librarian. During the 1970s and 1980s the traditional concept of the teacher librarian as the 'keeper of the books' (one who selected, catalogued, circulated and shelved and taught 'library skills' in isolation) evolved into much more of a teaching role. Through the work of people like Ken Haycock, teacher librarians took on a much higher profile in the school through their involvement with cooperative program planning and teaching and resource based learning. Teacher librarians were seen as more of a teaching partner with a variety of expertise to support teachers in their instruction and students in their learning. During this time also, teacher librarians began to take on broader initiatives. Many became more involved in curriculum development, in professional development activities and in technological development. However, not all have evolved to this extent. Some are still 'stuck' in the era of CPPT and are expending all their energies there without embracing some of the change which has taken place. While planning and instructing with teachers is a very important part of the role, the focus has shifted somewhat and there is a need to go beyond this kind of activity as we move into the 21st century.

If we are going to maintain our positions as teacher librarians, we must be perceived as being valuable to the entire school system, not just the resource centre. We must be part of the change process. Teacher librarians must become involved in local planning teams -- strategic planning, curriculum committees, technology planning, assessment, school accreditation, instructional improvement. There is a need for people who can 'see the big picture' and be able to integrate the emerging changes to most effectively impact on student's learning. There is a role here for teacher librarians. These people, through working with all staff members, usually know the strengths and weaknesses of the school. They are accustomed to effective planning and implementation strategies and have good interpersonal skills. They have a broad knowledge of the curriculum, of learning styles, of instructional strategies, of information problem-solving needs and skills. Many have technological expertise and have been involved with a variety of professional development activities. Teacher librarians must become part of the leadership team where they can ensure that the goals of information literacy permeate the entire school program.

According to John Crowley (1995:9) "since times of crisis are usually days of opportunity, the teacher librarian can become an integral part of the future by helping invent the school system of tomorrow". Teacher librarians can only do this if they are prepared to practise the 'lifelong learning' motto which they promote. Teacher librarians must become the professionals in the school responsible for the effective integration of change into the school curriculum. Much of that change is currently being driven by technology. Teacher librarians must renew themselves by learning about the new technologies and take their place as the natural leaders for this area in the school. There is a need for people who can design and maintain schools which are electronically networked to information sources, and administration, faculty and student needs. Teacher librarians must become proficient in this area and assume a leadership role if they are going to survive. Society is demanding that students become technologically and information literate -- we must be at the forefront in ensuring that the 'literacy' is one that enables students to access and use information effectively to meet their needs as citizens and members of the workforce in the Information Age.

There is much controversy among the profession today over the designation of teacher librarian. Many claim the name no longer adequately defines the role. Some of the proposals for a name change include such titles as information specialist, information director, learning resource specialist, instructional consultant, information professional. I contend that it is not the name attached to the position which defines the role (we have had different designations in different areas for many years), but how the person in the position accepts the challenges of the changing times to reconstruct their vision and continue to assist teachers and students in their quest to become information literate. As stated by Richard Worzel (1996:14),

> ...if you learn to use the new technologies... then they can be the tools to assist you in what you have always done: help students move upwards towards understanding, confidence and self-esteem. But if you do not master the technologies, you risk becoming irrelevant. The choice is yours.

References

American Association of School Librarians and Association for Educational Communications and Technology. (1988). *Information power: Guidelines for school library media programs*. Chicago: American Library Association.

American Association of School Librarians. (1996). *Information literacy: a position paper on information problem-solving*. Chicago: American Library Association.

Learning for the future: Developing information services in Australian schools. (1993). Carlton, Vic.: Curriculum Corporation.

Baron, D.D. (1995). May the force be with you: School library media specialists and technology. *School Library Activities Monthly*, May: 48-50.

Crowley, J. (1995). A leadership role for teacher librarians. *Emergency Librarian*, May-June: 8-13.

Haycock, K. (1993). *What works: Research about teaching and learning through the school's library resource centre*. Vancouver, BC: Rockland Press.

Henri, J. (1996). Information-literate schools without a TL? I'd like to see that! *School Libraries in Canada*, Spring: 31-32.

Krashen, S.D. (1993). *The power of reading: Insights from the research.* Englewood, CO: Libraries Unlimited.

Lance, K. Curry, Welborn, L. and Hamilton-Pennell, C. (1993). *The impact of school library media centers on academic achievement.* Castle Rock, CO: Hi Willow Research and Publishing.

Ontario Ministry of Education. (1982). *Partners in action: the library resource centre in the school curriculum.* Toronto: Ontario Ministry of Education.

Worzel, R. (1996). Does tomorrow's library have room for librarians? *School Libraries in Canada*, Spring: 13-14.

Why Am I Here?

Chris Skrzeczynski[*]

The profession of teacher librarianship has undergone dramatic change since its conception to the present time. Some view the future with gloom and they can be excused for this as budget and staffing cuts, use of teacher librarians for release from face-to-face (RFF) and a myriad of other depressing factors block the fulfilment of our role. In response to this negativity it is not silly to ask, "Why am I here?", "What is my role?" To face the next century positively I gain encouragement from reviewing the development of the role of school libraries in Australian primary schools. School libraries stand as honest testimony to the knowledge and expertise, skills and strength of teacher librarians who have led their development throughout this country. In response to the question, "Why am I here?" I see that if teacher librarians had not been there during the rise of school libraries that these structures would not have been anything more than a storehouse for resources. I foresee that, while the nature of the learning tools is changing, teacher librarians will remain the driving force in keeping the education factor as the foremost purpose of school libraries into the next millennium as Teacher Librarian, Cybrarian, Director of Information Services -- all of the above.

WHY AM I HERE?

1. To Establish

Put in historical perspective, since the commencement of formal schooling, the role of school libraries, and more recently, the role of the teacher librarian, have evolved quite rapidly and in relatively recent times. Few 'baby boomers' would recall a primary school education which involved interactive research-based learning activities or experiences aimed at highlighting the information process. Few primary schools boasted libraries.

As a primary teacher in the early seventies it was my annual challenge to create a class 'library' collection. Finally I was appointed to a primary school WITH A LIBRARY! This was remote (way down

---

[*] **Chris Skrzeczynski** is Teacher Librarian at Our Lady of the Rosary P-7 School in Kenmore, Queensland, Australia. Chris may be contacted via email at <cxyz@gil. com.au>.

the paddock), unstaffed (run by volunteers) and tiny (only half my class of forty students could fit in at a time) but IT WAS A LIBRARY! There was funding put aside by the Parents & Citizens' (P&C) Association for the purchase of books. A collection of both fiction and non-fiction books began. This collection was used for two purposes:

a. Students borrowed fiction books for home reading.
b. Teachers took 'bulk' loans to the classroom to provide information for projects. (A 'bulk' loan constituted more than one book a time - stock was limited).

Why was I there?
a. To provide students with 'real books' which were beneficial to both their reading skill development and their enjoyment of literature.
b. To help children use books as an information source.

My next appointment took me to a two-teacher school where no such luxury existed. Inspired by my previous experience I set about fund raising exercises (amongst the very few families), winning over the P&C (of four), collecting donations from the Postmistress, the Storekeeper and the Station Master and soon we were able to purchase a skeleton collection of new and exciting titles ranging in interest from K-6. This collection was housed on a shelf with wheels. This was wheeled onto the verandah by day so it could be accessed by both classes in the school. At night it was wheeled inside to ensure it would be there tomorrow. Another library was launched. It's function was similar to the 'library down the paddock'.

Why was I there?
a. To develop a school-wide resource collection which students and teachers could access to assist in learning programs.
b. To help students in my class use these books in their learning programs.

Throughout Australia similar rudimentary school libraries were being established and used by teachers who saw the need for 'real' reading and for information sources. These schools ranged from 'big-smoke' establishments to remote one-teacher schools. Teachers committed to making the most out of nothing scrounged and battled and made an impact on student learning by developing these humble resource collections. To country students these collections were often their only access to non-textbook style learning.

My next appointment introduced me to my first teacher librarian. Still in the seventies, there I was in a school with a library which housed a school-wide collection of fiction and non-fiction books and a part-time teacher librarian. The procedure was for the teacher librarian to 'teach library skills' to classes in the absence of the teacher. Since my Year 2 class was considered 'too young' for 'library skills' they heard stories in their 'library time'. Older students filled in worksheets about Dewey numbers. We may scoff at this now but look at it in historical perspective. Examine from where we had come. This was progressive stuff in those days.

Why was I there?
To see the potential of a program of instruction in library usage and to wonder why Year 2 students were too young for this.

In the mid-seventies a dramatic change occurred in relation to school libraries. Those who had fought so hard to show the need for resources in educational programs had a giant breakthrough. 'Disadvantaged Schools Grants' were made available by governments. Much of this money was spend on bricks and mortar to build structures to house school libraries. These structures led to the acquisition of collections and provision of staff to manage these collections and teach students how to use them. Suddenly 'The School Library' existed. Suddenly 'Teacher Librarians' were needed.

Equally as suddenly I found myself in a school with many government dollars to spend on the establishment of a library collection. This was one of the most exciting experiences I have ever had in teacher librarianship. It is not common nowadays to be presented with a magnificently refurbished room and $10 000 to stock it.

Why was I there?
To establish a school-wide resource collection and a system of access to it.

WHY AM I HERE?

2. To Use
Enter the Teacher Librarian... Having established this magnificent entity, the responsibility shifted to how it was to be used. As a teacher I could see that many skills were required by students to use these resources. These skills had to be taught. I could not teach them to all students myself as I had a class of my own half of each day. In

order for students to use this wonderful collection in their learning programs an educational program had to be developed. This was done in conjunction with the teachers as they were to be involved in the implementation... enter cooperative planning and teaching (CPT).

Why was I there?
To develop a program which facilitated students using the resources in the library collection to develop their reading and information skills... enter literature based reading programs... enter the information skills continuum.

The eighties came - a dynamic period for teacher librarianship. During this decade huge steps were taken. School libraries continued to appear throughout Australia. Teacher librarians were trained. Cooperative Planning and Teaching became the recommended modus operandum. Resource based learning was examined and promoted. The emphasis moved from product to process. Information skills were developed in context of curriculum studies. School-based information skills continuums were developed to ensure this happened. Some schools adopted flexible timetabling to better address the needs of students and teachers. Professional associations focused on providing support and training for teacher librarians. Local networks flourished. In some instances these were the ideals. In others these were reality. Not every school achieved all. Many strove towards these goals, against many odds in some cases. Against some odds in many cases. These goals and patterns of development are well documented in literature published in the eighties by such gurus as Gawith (1978), Haycock, C.A. (1985), Haycock, K. (1985), Henri (1988), Lundin (1983), Marland (1987) to name but a few.

Why was I there?
To establish these patterns in my schools. Each school needed to adopt a particularly individual structure to allow these ideals to become reality. I was there to find, by experimentation, the framework which would work for us.

I was there to motivate teachers to participate in resource based learning programs, to work with me as an equal teaching partner and use my knowledge and experience in the information process to guide teachers and students in their teaching and learning. I was there to help teachers dissect the information process into its component skills and teach these in the context of relevant projects. I was there to work with teachers to develop a whole school literature-based reading programs that followed a continuum of exposure for students to a wide range of genre, authors, illustrators, themes, characters and literary styles.

I was there to draw together the learning programs in the school. The position of teacher librarian is often unique in that this is the only position from where one can be involved at the grass roots level of implementation with all teachers in all year levels (Skrzeczynski, 1993). The principal has involvement in an overarching way. Specialist teachers have involvement with particular groups of students. Subject coordinators and key teachers focus on particular subject areas. Only the teacher librarian works with all levels of mainstream students across all curriculum areas. Yes Maths! Yes PE! (The theoretical aspects of these subjects benefit from a dose of resource based learning). This sets us in the ideal position to view school programs vertically. This is of major benefit in structuring skills continuums and deciding upon topics of study through which these skills can be developed. I was there to structure the library collection to facilitate its use by teachers and students; to establish systems that allowed equitable use of resources, equipment and facilities and to lead the development of a collection development policy that reflected the mission of the school.

I was there to submit budget proposals to increase funding to allow all this to happen. This required me to convince the administration team and funding bodies that what was happening was beneficial and would be more beneficial given more dollars.

WHY AM I HERE?

3. To Develop

If the growth and development of school libraries in the eighties was a challenge, it prepared us well to tackle the technology push of the nineties. During this period the face of the role has undergone a multiplicity of changes. Technology has been the most significant force in this metamorphosis. This push began with library automation which allowed us to efficiently implement central resource location within schools.

Why am I here?

I am here as a highly proficient database manager whose role it is to establish systems to facilitate resource access and use.

In many schools, the establishment of computer-based information management systems introduced the first sophisticated computers to the school. Little wonder that when other computers were acquired it was presumed that teacher librarians knew all there was to know about them because they had computers in the library. Coupled with the evolution of data base software, information CDROMs and now the Internet, the teacher librarian is seen as the key player in managing and utilising these systems.

Technology is part of every facet of Resource Centre operations today. Cameras, television, videos, computers, printers, scanners, digital cameras, the world wide web and email facilities all provide unprecedented scope for information gathering and presenting.

Why am I here?

I am here to organise the acquisition of these tools, their organisation, management, training, equity of access, trouble shooting and maintenance. This is a little more complex than maintaining the bookshelves in working order but, like the shelves, this 'techno-role' is a sideline. The real goal is to use these tools in learning programs. This is where the established principles of CPT and resource based learning are maintained and the new technologies worked into the planning.

Many schools are renovating and replacing their libraries. At my school an ambitious building program resulted in the opening of the Resource Centre. This houses the library, computer centre, AV centre, teacher-reference library, small and large meeting rooms and student work areas. The unification of these centres under the one roof has led to greater integration of resource use. Technology blends with traditional and the two are used interchangeably.

Why am I here?

I am here to make it all work -- to translate it into student learning experiences. The whole concept needs a manager. It also needs an educator, an information specialist, a literature expert, a cybrarian, an accountant, a trainer, a technician, a diplomat, a cleaner -- it needs a teacher librarian.

References

Gawith, G. (1987). *Information alive!* Auckland: Longman Paul.

Haycock, C.A. (1985). Information skills in the curriculum: Developing a school-based continuum. *Emergency Librarian*, 13 (1): 11-17.

Haycock, K. (1985). Strengthening the foundations for teacher librarianship. *School Library Media Quarterly*, 13 (2): 102-109.

Henri, J (1988). *The school curriculum: A collaborative approach to learning.* Wagga Wagga, NSW: Riverina-Murray Institute of Higher Education.

Lundin, R. (1983). The teacher librarian and information skills: an across the curriculum approach. *Emergency Librarian*, 11 (1): 8-12.

Marland, M. (1987). Libraries, learning and the whole school. *Emergency Librarian*, 15 (2): 9-14.

Skrzeczynski, C. (1993). *Linking literacy: The role of the teacher librarian in literacy education.* Unpublished Master of Applied Science thesis, Charles Sturt University.

Topic H

Process and Product:

How Do We Assess Students Work?

Real Teachers Do Assessment[*]

James Henri[†]

This paper explores the literature that investigates the changing nature of student assessment and analyses the involvement that might be undertaken by a teacher librarian. It is suggested that since assessment of learning is a critical component of teaching and learning it must be given significant attention. Teacher librarians are teachers and therefore they have a professional responsibility to assess learning and a specialist responsibility to articulate the need for assessment of the learning process in addition to the assessment of the results of the process. A range of teacher librarian entry points into the assessment swamp are noted and explored.

In his VC'96 paper Lupton (1996:112) argued that assessment is an integral part of learning. It would be equally true to say that assessment is an integral part of teaching. Both the teacher and the learner need to know whether or not the teaching/learning process associated with any particular planned learning agenda provides a new experience. It is after all new experiences that provide the opportunity for new understanding, new meaning, new knowledge.

The process of assessment provides the opportunity to verify (both for students and teachers) that learning has occurred. Assessment of learning might occur at the conclusion of a teaching/learning program. It may occur during the learning process and it may occur prior to the learning task. A combination of the three moments will provide the richest and most accurate picture of the impact of the program upon the learner and will provide the best evidence of the impact of the teaching process.

Assessment might be learner driven or teacher driven or it could be a combination of the two. Assessment might seek evidence in a range of learning strands. The subject-matter, life-skills, information-seeking-and-use, and production strands were identified by Pitts (1994) as crucial. It might also consider evidence of how the program has affected motivation and student self worth. Assessment that is integrated into the learning program will create

---

[*] Submitted and accepted as a refereed conference paper.

[†] **James Henri** is Senior Lecturer in Teacher Librarianship at the School of Information Studies, Charles Sturt University in Wagga Wagga, N.S.W., Australia. James may be contacted via email at <jhenri@csu.edu.au>.

meaning in its own right. Such assessment is likely to be enjoyable (presenting a realistic challenge) and rewarding. This is not likely to occur unless it is first made clear what it is that students are expected to know (Diez and Moon 1992).

Henri (1996) argued that the process of assessment must not be an after thought. He claimed that:

> *Authentic assessment is designed to provide a reliable measure of a students understanding and may encompass a range of techniques including testing of key concepts, observations, ratings, interviews, questionnaires, and performances. Within this paradigm students become much more involved in the assessment process. They contribute to decisions about what is important and what part of their achievement should be measured. Because of its emphasis on real-life learning and reflection on that learning, authentic assessment changes content and teaching strategies. Teachers become more reflective about how their instructional practice is facilitating learning, and about how well their assessment instruments are measuring that learning and motivating students to want to learn. In the best situations teachers give up their role as a 'director of traffic' and become involved in the learning process. This blurring of the distinction between teaching and learning provides the teacher with a powerful window into the learning milieu.*

(Henri 1996:110)

Lupton (1996:114) took the view that "While teachers are essentially responsible for their students' learning outcomes, there continues to be an important role for teacher librarians..." A stronger position would suggest that since assessment is an integral component of learning and since part of the teaching process is to design and deliver learning programs all teachers must be involved in assessment. Going further, it could be argued that one of the ways that teacher librarians demonstrate that they are teachers is by their involvement in the assessment of learning. Another way of looking at the issue is to consider the extent to which teacher librarians are involved in the instructional program. The greater the collegiality in the teaching program between teacher and teacher librarian the more obvious to the observer that the teacher librarian is a teacher. The more distant that teacher librarians are from the teaching coal-face the less obvious that the teacher librarian is a teacher (and the less the need for this to be the case). Real teachers do assessment!

Callison (1994a:53) takes up this issue in stating that: the critical evaluation process of student performance is within the role of both teacher and [teacher librarian]. He elaborates:

New methods of evaluation should be explored because students may be judged on questioning techniques, search and location strategies, listening skills, organization skills, scripting and editing skills, and presentation methods. Just as a house is appraised and valued at several stages of construction, so too is the process by which students and teachers construct knowledge and intelligence from the information surrounding them. Foundation, framework, and finished product each have need for new appraisal instruments and new collaborative appraisers who have an inquiry method orientation.
(Callison 1994a:54-55)

Stripling (1994) identified three levels of involvement for teacher librarians with respect to assessment. Stripling suggests that at the initial level of involvement in assessment the teacher librarian is able to raise awareness among school staff about the need for and value of authentic assessment. To this end the teacher librarian would identify appropriate resources for inclusion in a teacher reference collection. The teacher librarian might circulate appropriate articles, and identify useful URLs as a precursor to discussion on the merits of authentic assessment and the implications from that for school policy and practice. Since authentic learning is linked to in-depth collections the teacher librarian should seek to identify those topics that will trial the process and build in-depth school based collection in those areas, and also ensure that access is available to external sources of information.

Lupton (1996) extends Stripling's scenario. He states:

As information literacy specialists, teacher librarians input to student learning will necessarily be related to advocacy for and support of the implementation of a model of the information process which is consistently developed across the curriculum and year levels. Part of this approach should also involve the inclusion of check points in assessment tasks to monitor mastery of the steps in the information process, a process [in which] skills continue to expand as the modes of information delivery expand.

Lupton identifies the need for an information specialist to identify the appropriate checkpoints and to monitor mastery of process. These checkpoints should cover the three learning domains: actions, thoughts, and feelings (Kuhlthau 1993). Lupton makes the important assumption that the teacher librarian is an information specialist and by implication suggests that teachers are not. Both assumptions need testing. To what extent are teacher librarians experts in the information process? How many teacher librarians have undertaken action research to test the authenticity of a number of information skill models? (Eisenberg and Brown 1992). How many teacher librarians are personally acquainted with the messiness of the information process from their own learning? Recent research certainly indicates that teachers expectations for their own learning do not generally match what they expect from their students (McGregor 1994, O'Connell 1997). It could be argued that teachers ought to be much more expert in their understanding of the information process through personal experience and this lack of expertise may be a roadblock to the introduction of authentic assessment. There is a professional development role for teacher librarians here.

Stripling (1994) suggests that at the moderate level, the teacher librarian is more actively involved in the design and assessment of a unit of work. At this level the partnership is identified as one of shared responsibility. Stripling states:

> *If the assessment will be in writing, the [teacher librarian] offers use of library computers and instruction in word processing for those students who are not experienced. If the assessment is to involve production of audiovisual materials, the [teacher librarian] assumes responsibility for teaching students production techniques and for helping students produce quality work. If the assessment is to be performance-based, the [teacher librarian] offers to teach certain performance techniques such as how to make an oral presentation or how to present oneself on camera. The [teacher librarian] also monitors preparations and rehearsals for certain performance groups while the teacher is involved in assessing the performance of other groups. The support of the [teacher librarian] frees a teacher to try alternative assessment forms.*

(Stripling 1994:90)

Stripling's scenarios certainly involve the teacher librarian in the teaching of a unit. In my view it is essential that the division of labour struck between the partners reflects the professional expertise of the teacher librarian and does not place the teacher librarian in the unit as a general help-mate. The partnership among teacher and teacher librarian should reflect differences of role that would not be evident in a partnership between two teachers.

Stripling's third level of involvement is dubbed the in-depth level. At this level the teacher librarian works with the class teacher to design assessment tasks. These tasks follow from the goals of the unit and reflect the teacher librarian's whole school perspective of student accomplishment. Likewise the teacher librarian evaluates student work. Stripling suggests:

> Because performance-based assessments should be evaluated by someone without a vested interest, the [teacher librarian] helps the students and classroom teachers by filling that role whenever possible. [Teacher librarians] also evaluate written student products, especially those based on research in the library.

The teacher librarian is well placed to make judgements about students' questions, the sources pursued, and the evidence that was gathered.

Biases need to be reconsidered as well as ethical standards stemming from temptations to cloud or shade evidence through editing and lifting out of context... Process assessment should include examination of the merits of resources identified and used and considerations for seeking access to resources initially beyond reach. Did the student make the extra effort to obtain what was previously off limits? (Callison 1996a:54).

Since authentic assessment is intended to gauge 'real' rather than 'plastic' learning it makes sense to place emphasis on the way that learning occurred rather than on the evidence of learning per se. It is evidence of the learner's ability to add value to his/her existing knowledge that is critical. This means that students and teachers alike have to experiment with a range of process tools such as, note taking templates, process diaries, thinking logs, data charts, and think-aloud-protocols. These tools being information based provide ideal areas for teacher librarian assessment. And not simply as a learning destination but also as part of the learning journey.

Creativity with forms of assessment does not come easily to all teachers but there is nothing worse than the application of repetitive and boring assessment tasks. As teacher librarians experiment with a range of process tools in their own learning they are better able to appreciate the value of these for assessing student learning. Callison (1994:128) reinforces this point:

In order for educators to establish meaningful information literacy exercises that challenge the student, assessment is best undertaken by means of a progressive portfolio of student's work. Both the teacher and the [teacher librarian] must think in terms of assignments that establish a broad range of sources the student will need to investigate and that are developed in recognition of the equally broad range of responses the student might produce.

Of major importance are the techniques of modelling information literacy skills developed by the teacher and the [teacher librarian] and the establishment of inquiry environments in which students work together in order to explore and share the challenges of information search and selection... The time is ripe to go beyond the simple tests of the past in our explorations of what can be observed, what can be discussed, and what abilities can be enhanced.

Callison is in essence putting a strong case for the use of a range of qualitative tools, as well as traditional quantitative ones, that will facilitate the identification of the value adding that occurs in school. In this environment it is likely that the traditional distinctions between learners and teachers will blur as teachers and students learn together (students often taking on the role of teacher). The fact that teacher librarians as a professional group are constantly testing the cutting edge in educational practice and in the exploration of new technology ideally equips them to take a much more proactive role in this brave new world.

References

Callison, D. (1994). 'The potential for portfolio assessment.' In Kuhlthau, C.C. (ed.). *Assessment and the school library media center.* Englewood, CO: Libraries Unlimited: 121-130.

Callison, D. (1994a). 'Expanding the evaluation role in the critical-thinking curriculum.' In Kuhlthau, C.C. (ed.). *Assessment and the school library media center.* Englewood, CO: Libraries Unlimited: 43-57.

Diez, M.E. and Moon, C.J. (1992). What do we want students to know?... and other important questions. *Educational Leadership,* 49 (8): 22-23.

Eisenberg, M. and Brown, M. (1992). Current themes regarding library and information skills instruction: Research supporting and research lacking. *School Library Media Quarterly*, 20 (2): 103-109.

Henri, J. (1996). Students on the Net: Enhancing learning through authentic assessment. In Hay, L. and Henri, J. (eds.). *A meeting of the minds: ITEC Virtual Conference'96 proceedings*. Belconnen, ACT: ASLA: 109-111.

Kuhlthau, C.C. (1983). The library research process: Case studies and interventions with high school seniors in advanced placement English classes using Kelly's Theory of Constructs. Unpublished Ed.D. dissertation. Rutgers University.

Kuhlthau, C.C. (1993). *Seeking meaning*. Norwood, NJ: Ablex.

Lupton, P. (1996). 'Assessing students' work from the Net: An impossible dream?' In Hay, L. and Henri, J. (1996). *A meeting of the minds: ITEC Virtual Conference'96 proceedings*. Belconnen, ACT: ASLA: 112-114.

McGregor, J.H. (1993). 'Cognitive processes and the use of information.' Unpublished PhD dissertation, Florida State University.

O'Connell, J and Henri, J. (1997). 'Information literacy: Teacher's perspectives of the information process.' Paper presented at IASL-ATLC conference. Vancouver, July 8.

Pitts, J. M. (1994). 'Personal understandings and mental models of information.' Unpublished PhD dissertation, Florida State University.

Stripling, B. (1994). 'Assessment of student performance: the fourth step in the instructional design process.' In Kuhlthau, C.C. (ed.). *Assessment and the school library media center*. Englewood, CO: Libraries Unlimited: 77-93.

Assessment of Information Processes and Products: Matching Strategy and Purpose

*Jean Donham van Deusen**

Introduction

The term 'assessment' has recently challenged the term 'evaluation' in much of the education literature. Examining the etymology of the two words gives some insight into why. The word 'assessment' derives from the past participle of the Latin verb 'assidere' - 'assess(us)', meaning literally to sit down beside. Over time it has come to mean the careful judgment from close observation that results from sitting down beside someone. The visual image of assessment is collegial. 'Evaluate', on the other hand, lacks that collegiality in its etymology and instead means literally to place value. The visual image is quite different. As mental models like collaborating and facilitating have become favoured paradigms for teaching, new models for assessment have followed.

Why is assessment changing? Cognitive theory has generated some critical perspectives on learning. Among these is the emergence of constructivism. This perspective on learning describes learning as a process of creating personal meaning by relating new information to prior knowledge (Pitts 1992:14-24). Such a perspective on learning emphasises the individual's learning experience as unique. Another emerging perspective is that learning is not necessarily a linear progression of discrete skills (See for example Kolb (1985); Gardner (1983); and Dunn et al. (1989)). Study of learning has also suggested that learning styles vary in terms of memory, developmental rate, forms of intelligence, brain dominance, and degree of abstraction. Finally, research suggests that people perform better when they know the goal or see models and know how their performance compares to a standard (Bandura 1997). These developments in the understanding of learning call for assessment that matches these perspectives -- assessments that are individualised, standards-based, continuous, and collaborative.

Evaluation has usually occurred at the end of a learning episode. Its primary intent is to place a value on the student's work *ex post facto*.

* **Jean Donham van Deusen** is an Assistant Professor with the School of Library and Information Science at University of Iowa, IA in the United States. Jean may be contacted via email at <jean-vandeusen@uiowa.edu>.

Often, its ultimate purpose is to sort students according to their degree of success. Assessment represents a shift toward using a process to guide learning. As a participant in the process, students can develop skill in assessing their own progress -- an important aspect of becoming self-regulated, life-long learners. Another shift in assessment is toward comparing students' performances with performance criteria, instead of comparing one student's performance to that of another. Moving toward 'public' criteria, ie. telling students exactly what is expected before they begin their work is another trend.

The emergence of new thinking about assessment has brought with it a new set of terms, some of which are easily confused. Three terms often confused are alternative, authentic and performance when used to describe assessment. Alternative assessment can be any assessment that differs from objective measurements that characterise most standardised and many classroom tests. Authentic assessments engage students in applying knowledge and skills in the same way they are used in the real world. In performance assessment, students demonstrate their understanding with a tangible product or observable performance.

Purposes of Assessment
Assessment can serve any of four purposes. Two of these relate to the teaching process itself. The first is to monitor student progress. To achieve this purpose, assessment occurs as an integral part of teaching. A simple check-for-understanding constitutes such an assessment. Sometimes a checklist can be used so that students and teachers can refer to the checklist as the student is working to ensure that no components of the task are being omitted. Sometimes a journal or a rubric can be used for this purpose. The fundamental question is, "How is each student progressing in relation to the goals we have set and agreed on?" The purpose is to **improve growth.** Another purpose for assessment is to improve instruction. Again this type of assessment is ongoing, as the teaching and learning progress. Similar techniques can be used, eg. checking-for-understanding, journals, rubrics, checklists. The fundamental question is, "How can I use this evidence about students' progress to improve the teaching and learning?" The purpose is to **improve instruction** by modifying the teaching. The other two purposes of assessment are summative in nature: evaluating student achievement and modifying the instructional program. Periodically,

it becomes expected that teachers will synthesise student progress into a narrative commentary, a checklist, or a grade. the fundamental question is, "How is this student doing compared to our overall expectations?" The purpose is to **recognise accomplishment.** Educators look at overall student performance to help determine the efficacy of the educational program. Often such a review occurs as a part of an accreditation process, or a mandated program review. This assessment is often undertaken by an external review committee. The fundamental question is "How well is the program working in relation to the goals and expectations for all students?" The purpose is to **modify or improve the program.** The focus of this paper will be on assessment as a way to improve growth.

Assessment Techniques

Educators have a veritable arsenal of assessment techniques. They range from the simple question/answer routine that occurs when we check for understanding to the elaborate, norm-referenced standardised test. Some assessment techniques are particularly useful to the library program for information skills. Among those are journaling, rubrics, conferencing and checklists.

Journaling. During information processing, journaling can be a highly effective, open-ended approach to assessing. As students work at the research process, at the end of a day's work session, the teacher or librarian poses a question like, "What problems did I have today? How did I solve them? Which ones are still unsolved?" Or on another occasion, the question might be, "What did I accomplish today? What do I need to accomplish next?" The intent of this journaling is to urge students to focus, at least briefly, on the research process rather than on the content of their research. In addition, the brief entries can give the teacher and the librarian a sense of how students are doing; this may give clues to mini-lessons that need to be taught next. Finally, if students look at their journal entries at the beginning of the subsequent session, they are likely to know right where to begin next.

Rubrics. A much more structured approach to assessment is the use of rubrics. They are particularly useful when students need a precise and concrete description of successful performance. A rubric is a scaled set of criteria that clearly defines for the student and the teacher what a range of acceptable and unacceptable performance looks like. Its purpose is to provide a **description** of what good performance looks like. Often, we tell students their performance is excellent or that they get an A. This is not a description; this is **evaluative** language. It only tells the student our judgment, rather than describing what success looks like. To develop a rubric, first we must identify the attributes of a successful performance of the task. For successful note-taking, for example, attributes might include:

- the information written in the notes is relevant to the research question
- the information written in the notes is comprehensible by the student
- the information written in the notes is organised so that relationships between information is evident.

Once we identify these attributes of success, the next step in developing a rubric is to watch performances that represent varying degrees of excellence. This observation helps us recognise less-than-perfect performance so that we can describe it as well. the final step is to **describe** performances of varying qualities. For example, a rubric for note-taking with three dimensions, relevance, comprehension and organisation might be:

Relevance

Expert	The information in my notes relates directly to my research questions.
Proficient	I will probably not use some information in my notes, but most of my notes answer my research question(s).
Novice	The information in my notes does not answer my research questions.

Comprehension

Expert	I understand everything I have written in my notes; there are no words that I cannot define.
Proficient	There are words or ideas in my notes that I cannot explain myself, but I can get more information so that they make sense to me.
Novice	My notes are copied from my sources and I don't really understand them.

Organisation

| Expert | My notes are grouped according to each research question. |
| Proficient | My notes are organised according to the source where I found the information. |

| Apprentice | My notes are organised according to when I took them. |
| Novice | My notes are written as one continuous list of information. |

There are two crucial conditions for using rubrics:

1. Students must have the rubrics **before** they do the work in order to increase success.
2. **One-time use** of a given rubric is less than ideal; students need the chance to show improvement in performance.

The two most important points on the rubric scale are the top point and the cut point between acceptable and unacceptable performance. The top point on the rubric should describe truly excellent performance. And the cut point between acceptable and unacceptable should be easily discerned.

Conferencing. Either formal or informal conferencing can help students and teachers assess progress. Conferencing about research can be formal or informal. As students work, the teacher or librarian can move from student to student to inquire about progress. Important in the conferencing is that a simple "How are you doing?" followed by "OK" is not adequate. The questions in an informal conference must be more specific in order to really focus attention on the research process. So, in informal conferencing, the question may be, "What is your topic? And, what research questions have you written about it?", or "Have you composed a thesis statement?", or "What sources of information have you found?", or "How are you organising your notes?", or "How are you keeping track of your resources for your bibliography?" Questions like these call for the student to explain some aspect of the research process. Formal conferencing may be an appropriate assessment technique especially at the end of a research activity, so that students review their experience to see what they have learned about the process. A schedule of questions for a formal conference might look like this:

- How did you find your information?
- Can you think of any problems you encountered as you did your research? What was hard about doing research? Where did you get 'stuck'?
- What was most interesting to you about doing this research project?

Checklists can be one more useful tool for assessment. Similar to the rubric, the checklist should be given to students at the beginning of the research activity so that the criteria are clear from the beginning. A checklist is simply a guide that helps students attend to all aspects of the research process. It can include elements for the process as well as the product; for example:

> research question(s)
> thesis statement
> information from at least five sources
> notes organised around research questions
> rough draft
> final draft
>> thesis statement
>> supporting evidence
>> conclusion
>> bibliography
>> correct spelling and usage

Effective assessment to improve learning feature three critical attributes:

1. explicit criteria: The criteria provide enough description that students know what successful performance looks like.
2. structured feedback: The criteria show students how close to excellence they are; and
3. advance notice: The criteria for success are provided as the student **begins** the work, not at the end.

These four assessment strategies -- journaling, rubrics, conferencing, and checklists -- are particularly appropriate for one of assessment's purposes, promoting student growth. In this context, it is appropriate to think of assessment as providing a road map to success -- a guide to help all students succeed. Other assessment techniques may be more appropriate for other assessment purposes; for example, portfolios and standardised testing are particularly appropriate for recognising accomplishment. Analysis of standardised test results can also be helpful in improving a program, if item analysis indicates a consistent shortcoming among a group of students, for example. In determining what assessment technique to use, one must match the purpose to the technique. Rubrics, for example, are probably not the best technique for recognising accomplishment; by design they are intended to provide a pathway so that students can see where they are on a continuum and see what is necessary to move to the next step on that continuum. This is a formative process, whereas the purpose of recognising accomplishment is a summative process. The portfolio is an accumulation of student work that demonstrates progress; it could be used in a formative way to help students see what progress they have made, but it is also useful in recognising accomplishment. Matching purpose to technique is central to effective assessment.

References

Bandura, A. (1977). *Social learning theory.* Englewood Cliffs, NJ: Prentice-Hall.

Dunn, R., Beaudry, J., and Klavas, A. (1989). Survey of research on learning styles. *Educational Leadership*, 46(6), Mar: 50-58.

Gardner, H. (1983). *Frames of mind: The theory of multiple intelligences.* New York: Basic Books.

Kolb, D.A. (1985). *Learning style inventory.* Boston, MA: McBer and Company.

Pitts. J. (1992). Constructivism: Learning rethought. In *School Library Media Annual, Vol.10.* Littleton, CO: Libraries Unlimited: 14-24.

Topic I

Professional Electronic Networks for Teacher Librarians

KidsConnect: School Librarians in Cyberspace!

Blythe Bennett[*]

KidsConnect is a question-answering, help and referral service for K-12 students on the Internet. The goal of *KidsConnect* is to help students access and use the information available on the Internet effectively and efficiently. *KidsConnect* is a component of ICONnect, the technology initiative of AASL (American Association of School Librarians, a division of the American Library Association). ICONnect is designed to offer school library media specialists, teachers and students the opportunity to learn the skills necessary to navigate on the Information Highway.

KidsConnect is underwritten by the Microsoft Corporation and is hosted by the ERIC Clearinghouse on Information and Technology at Syracuse University. It is modelled after the AskERIC Internet Question and Answer service for educators.

KidsConnect goals are to:

- provide high quality information services in response to student needs
- help school library media specialists fulfill their roles as information skills teachers
- connect kids and information on the Internet.

The mission of the library media program is to ensure that students and staff are effective users of ideas and information.

(Information Power 1988)

The Distributed Model

Questions come to *KidsConnect* via email and are read by the Coordinator to be routed to the appropriate volunteer school librarian. These 'cybrarians' are on teams of 5-10 people who work and teach with students of the same age grouping.

---

[*] **Blythe Bennett** is the KidsConnect Coordinator and works closely with the ERIC/IT Clearinghouse at Syracuse University, New York, USA. KidsConnect is a question-answering and referral service on the Internet, provided by the American Association of School Librarians, a division of the American Library Association. Blythe may be contacted via email at **<blythe@ericir.syr.edu>**. The KidsConnect web site can be located at **<http://ericir.syr.edu/kidsconnect>**.

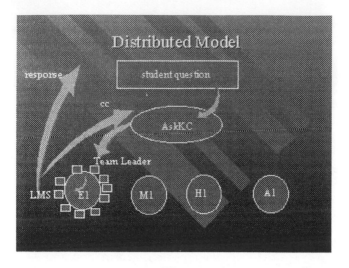

Currently there are five elementary school teams, two middle school teams, five high school teams, two teams who have K-12 schools and two Australian teams. Questions from elementary students are sent to elementary team members because their resources best reflect what the student would have in his or her own school library. When a cybrarian sends a response to a student, they also send a carbon copy to the *KidsConnect* archives for future reference and for receiving feedback from a team leader. Generally, students receive a response in two school days. These teams of cybrarians work on alternating month schedules, so they will take a maximum of a question per school day for one month, then have the next month off. Assets for Distributed Model include:

- a single *KidsConnect* address
- allocated questions to teams/specialties
- a 48 hour turn around
- CC replies are kept for archives and continuous improvement.

Cybrarians are spread across the United States and the world. Red team members would be on duty for odd months, for example, and the blue team members are off duty for that time period. Cybrarians, so far, are from 39 states and 8 countries including Australia, Canada, Indonesia, Israel, Japan, New Zealand, the Philippines, and the United States.

The following image shows a sample team of cybrarians in their teams:

The duties of Team Leaders are to provide feedback and support for team members; respond to questions in an emergency; and liaise between their team and the KC Coordinator.

The KC Service
KidsConnect has just completed its first year of service to students. In that first year, we have responded to 3041 questions:

half of April 1996	45
May	95
June	24
July	9
August	16
Sept	206
Oct	900
Nov	446
Dec	402
Jan 1997	472
Feb	448
March	430
half of April	348

Age Groups Using KC
Over the year, the age of the users has remained consistent, within a few percentage points with 44% elementary, 16% middle school, 31% high school, 6% adult (asking questions for their students), and 3% asking about *KidsConnect*.

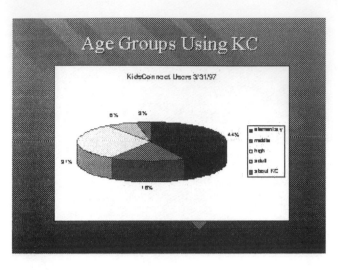

KC Questions

Most of the elementary questions are related to science, usually about animals. For example:

How many manatees are there left in the world?

Our 2nd grade students would like some information about Smoky Bear. Is he still alive? How old is he?

My class and the other 5th grade classes are needing some information on grizzly bears and wolves. The teachers said we could get it off the Internet to share with everyone.

Why do the bottoms of my hands and feet get wrinkly when they are wet for a long time, but not the rest of my skin?

Examples of secondary questions include:

We're making bridges out of toothpicks and I would like to know what bridge design should I use to make the strongest bridge.
I'd like to know at what rate the ozone layer around the earth is being depleted and when damage caused as a direct result of this depletion will be seen, and where.
I have been unable to find the names of Clinton's cabinet on the Internet, is this something that KidsConnect would be helpful with?

Examples of teacher questions include:

My fifth graders are studying the Oregon Trail. We are trying to get the dimensions of a Conestoga wagon to lay out on our floor...can you help?

I have a student who is trying to find national statistics on teenage mortality rates.

We also get the kind of question that makes us scratch our heads and say "hmmm...", for example:

I need a picture of Hades for my class.
Why don't dogs get poison ivy?
Please help me find information on insect bread.
Our class would like to know the name of Noah's wife.
Why are hotdogs packaged with 10 and hotdog buns packaged with 8?

Response to Student Questions
When we respond to student question, we include all of these components:

- Copy of the original question
- CC to *KidsConnect*/team folder
- Personalised greeting
- Internet/print resources
- Path/keywords
- Referral to Library Media Specialist
- Reference to *KidsConnect*.

KidsConnect DOES NOT: do analysis for a student; point to inappropriate web sites; serve as an interlibrary loan source; and replace the local library media specialist.

Sample Question
The following is an example of a typical question for *KidsConnect*:

Dear KidsConnect,

We are studying biomes in science the next two weeks. We have groups working on the different biomes such as tropical rain forest, deserts, deciduous forests, grassland, tundra, and taiga. We are having trouble with taiga, especially.
Thank you very much for your help.

Sincerely,

Mrs. Thorman's 5th grade science class.

Sample Response

After a Web search, the vounteer's response usually begins in this way. The original question is also included in replies. If there is a way to personalise the note, then names are used. The search engine and search terms are included to provide a model and a path for the student to follow. Short citations with the title and URL are included in the message. Print resources are also suggested in many cases. In closing, *KidsConnect* cybrarians also refer the students to their own school librarians, since they are the local experts. A mention of *KidsConnect* is made somewhere in the message, most often in the signature:

> *Dear Mrs. Thorman's 5th graders,*
>
> *Thanks for your question. I have a good biome site in my bookmarks:*
>
> *BIOMES*
> *This site contains links to other sites with information on wetlands, temperate forests, tundra, savanna and grasslands, tropical rainforests, and deserts.*
>
> *I also did a search on Alta Vista using the search string: +taiga +deciduous +biome.*
>
> *I found these sites for you:*
>
> *World Biomes*
> *It has a section on the taiga (scroll down the page to "Taiga"). There is no separate section for deciduous biome but mentions deciduous as a characteristic in plant life in some biomes.*
>
> *Tour of Biomes*
> *This site was created for middle school students. Pages are devoted to tropical rain forest, tropical savannah, mid-latitude deciduous forest, desert, subarctic taiga, and polar tundra.*
>
> *I hope these will help your students!*
>
> *Please ask your school librarian for more information about biomes that you might have in your own school library.*
>
> *Abby Kasowitz*
> *Graduate Assistant, KidsConnect.*

Thank You messages

We love getting mail back from the students we help:

> *THANK YOU SO MUCH!!!, This will really help my project get moving a little quicker. Thanx!!!*

Thank you for helping me find some information. Now I'll get help with the Internet sites. My Mom will have to check out the book at the city library, but on my birthday in May I will get my own card. I can't wait.

We also receive thanks from teachers:

The responses from KidsConnect have been WONDERFUL. 24 of my students are currently completing I-Search projects... the premise is that they will get away from the traditional report writing and really search...KidsConnect has been a helpful vehicle. The kids are so excited to receive responses, which have been very prompt. Thank you!

And parents:

Thank you very much for your information on animal facts on line and how to use AltaVista effectively. Many Thanks.

Volunteer Requirements/Commitments

Volunteers are required to:

* respond to 1 question per school day during 'on month'
* notify team leader if you are unable to respond to questions
* provide a 2 school day turn around response time
* have reliable email and Internet access
* have access to print resources.

Why are Library Media Specialists the best for this service?

* We are uniquely qualified to provide students with assistance due to our training and experience with students and the research process.
* We are the best trained group to help students use the Internet as an information resource.
* We will refer a student back to his/her own LMS for assistance at the school for further resources and professional assistance.
* *KidsConnect* serves as an extension of our library media centers.

Why Does It Work?

* Meets user needs: user based
* Know our audience
* Adds intelligence to the net

- Provides a comfort zone for users
- Resources reflect uses' needs and interests
- Explores innovative uses of technology
- Expects and accepts continual change.

The *KidsConnect* cybrarians also benefit from this project. Some comments from volunteers include:

I'm really learning a lot about the web because of these questions - stretches me. M.L.

I'm having fun! I wish I could do this for a living!! P.T.

I enjoyed the sense of collegiality with other librarians across the country. J.F.

I think it pushes me to be organised and do creative thinking. V.L.

Cybrarians' current professional needs fulfilled, such as collection development, increased interaction with school community, ability to incorporate knowledge of Internet into curriculum, increased confidence in locating Internet information for teachers and students, familiarity with useful Web sites, sense of contribution to field of Information Science, positive public relations, and an opportunity to serve as technology leaders for school and community. Personal needs are also fulfilled: a sense of accomplishment; intellectual stimulation; sense of community; and pride in participating in a 'cutting edge' project. One's skills are also improved in searching the World Wide Web, in general reference work and research skills. Long-term effects include: provision of experience for future positions; many include *KidsConnect* experience on resume; change in image of school library media specialist; and provides encouragement to pursue advanced graduate study.

What a wonderful image-booster for library media specialists!
KidsConnect Cybrarian

To send a question to *KidsConnect*, email the following address:

<AskKC@iconnect.syr.edu>

To find out more about the *KidsConnect* service visit the web site at <http://ericir.syr.edu/kidsconnect>.

Would You Like That a la Carte, Or Do We Need a Menu for Accessing Professional Resources on the Internet?

Gerald R. Brown[*]

Do you read the left column or the right column first when you pick up the menu?
The question is the same when we consider the development of school libraries. "Do we want to know what they can do for us?", or "Do we want to know how much they will cost us?" The answer, of course is "yes" in both cases. The wise purchaser will scan the offerings and see where are the best choices.

The good news is that technology is causing shifts in attitudes about information, knowledge, attitudes and behaviour in the school system, and in society in general. The good news is also that funding is available for implementation of the new technology in various forms and to varying degrees at all levels in education, whether in the developed or developing world.

The bad news is that the shifts in priority for information, knowledge, attitudes, and behaviour are causing drastic changes in some of our schools. Some people are traumatised by these change. Others grasp change and manage it to make a better environment for themselves and their students. With the proliferation of the new technologies, our traditional definition of "literacy" has changed. No longer does "literacy" refer expressly to the ability to read and write traditional print media. Due to the flood of information or data that technology enables, literacy now means the ability to filter and interpret that information. McLuhan's **medium = message** theory is blown away, but in its' stead is the necessity for people to build meaning - to glean the message (knowledge) from the medium (data/information).

Further, the addition of sounds, images, animations, videos to the context of a message also requires a kind of "literacy": the literacy to understand that those media are manipulable; that those media often involve iconic symbols and systems (Hazle 1997).

---

[*] **Gerald R. Brown** was at the time of writing Vice President of the International Association of School Librarianship, and Library Media Services Consultant in Winnipeg, Manitoba, Canada. Gerald may be contacted via email at <**browner@cyberspc.mb.ca**>.

Will the Head Waiter please step forward?
So what is the role of the teacher librarian in this changing environment? Elsewhere in this conference, there will be a discussion on the name for the person leading the parade in this new information age in the school or district. Suffice it to say, that whatever the new name might be/or the existing name re-burnished, the persons filling the positions will need to be of leadership quality and capacity.

Administrators are looking for quality teacher competencies, so that the manager of the resources can help teachers and students learn how to use both the new and tradition information technologies independently. Research has told us that the building level leader will need to be a strong integrationist for process learning and skill development in the curriculum context. We have barely survived two generations of teacher librarians who have emphasised collection development and isolated skill instruction at a terrible price to our credibility and visibility. So the new colleague must understand integrated skill development, collaborative planning, cooperative teaching, systematic assessment and evaluation, and the technology needed to access the resources both inside and outside the school buildings. When one looks back over the list, it is easy to see that one person is likely not going to be able to fill all these functions. Will the profession accept differentiated staffing?

Some of the leaders in this new role for teacher librarianship will be found at the school building level, others will work at district levels and still others will be found in training institutions for new teachers and administrators.

> *The principle forces which will motivate a leader in this new age are an incredibly high need for personal achievement and a different vision of the world - one who marches to a different drum beat, who does not see him/herself as party of the mainstream, is essentially an outsider. You don't necessarily have to be charismatic, you just have to believe in what you are doing so strongly that it becomes a reality. Your passion for life needs to permeate everything you do. The duty of leadership is also to put forward ideas, symbols and metaphors of the way it should be done, so that the next generation can work out new and better ways of doing the job.*

(Roddick 1993)

Leaders in school librarianship must have the best possible training for the changing roles that are being thrust upon the profession. At the same time, they needs a flair for dealing with people, ability to have fun with their working colleagues, and a Pandora's Box of ideas, offering others the means of taking an idea, opening a door and going through by themselves. We are in a situation where we must create new rules for the running of the information service centres that reach far beyond our building limits. The old stereotypes must be overthrown by our very ability to show that we are teachers, educators, administrators and leaders in the field of learning. A colleague recently observed, "It isn't always so much the work you do, but the way you do it, and how others see you doing it **with them**. It is often the quality of the person and the integrity of the idea that matters most."

New items on the menu?

As we adventure into these new challenges in the information service sector, we as teacher librarians have an obligation to work together and to share our success stories. We don't have to time to make the same mistakes over again, if someone else can share their leanings with us. And just because we make a mistake once, doesn't mean the world has come to an end. The wise person will learn from the mistake, and will try and try again, each time another way... until success is achieved.

Research is one of the vehicles for demonstrating what are the critical ways to achieve change. Action research at the work-face is imperative in rapidly changing times. Those in administration need to be encouraged to allow school staff to try experiments, and to report on the progress. Providing time to write up projects, or even better the editorial assistance to see that the articles are available is very important.

Postsecondary institutions are providing valuable documentation for successful programs through the research that they are requiring for graduate certification. It is imperative that these projects be written up in regular journals in such a way that workers in the field can appreciate the applicability of the results quickly and easily. The option to have the researcher speak to local groups is highly desirable. Professional associations are initiating 'Research Interest Groups' which can encourage, sometimes with funding grants, the dissemination of research results to wider audiences (often outside the school librarianship circles.) This year the first such international Research Forum will be held at the International Association of School Librarianship Conference in Vancouver, British Columbia,

Canada 6-11 July, 1997. Reports of research from several different countries will be featured.

The electronic medium has made it possible for school personnel to share ideas, information and resources much more quickly. This conference is a superb example of such sharing around the world. Australian teacher librarians are to be highly complimented for this leadership.

The main course includes
It is difficult to sort out which listservs are best. Each brings a bias from the creator in the same way that a school library collection usually reflects the bias of the collection development staff member (even though we loudly proclaim that we focus directly on the curriculum, a few favourite items always appear on the order sheet.)

Teacher librarians must keep current with the resources that are proliferating in the electronic field. The number of listservs and web sites that appear daily are mind-boggling. It would be a full time job for several people to keep checking them, updating the records and sharing the information. Few school staff members have this kind of time. Therefore it is wise to search out the quality listservs, subscribe for a while and see if that is the kind of information one really wants, and then unsubscribe if it isn't.

For the beginners Clyde (1995) provides a very valuable list, and some key items are cited below:

1. *IASL-LINK* is the listserv of the International Association of School Librarianship (IASL) is designed as a communication tool for members. Recently the Executive have initiated a number of Special Interest Groups in such areas as Advocacy, Children's & Young Adult Literature, Information Literacy, Information Technology, International Schools, Library Education, Library Research, and Literacy. In addition, it is also used for the dissemination of reports, documents, and conference information to approximately 150 subscribers. To subscribe, send an electronic mail message to <anne@rhi.hi.is> leave the subject line blank, and in the message include your name and country.

2. *LM_NET* is an international listserv where "school library media people" can talk to colleagues around the world, collect information, test ideas, and solve problems. There are more than 6,000 members and the list is managed by Professor Michael

Eisenberg of Syracuse University and Peter Milbury of California (a practising library media specialist.) This is a very active list, generating 35-50 messages a day. To join, send an electronic mail message to <listserv@listserv.syr.edu> with nothing in the subject line, and with the words <subscribe LM_NET> and your own name and address in the body of the message.

3. *ATLC FORUM* is the listserv of the Association for Teacher Librarianship in Canada (ATLC) carries announcements of interest to the school library community in general. To join, send an electronic mail message to <listproc@camosun.bc.ca> with nothing in the subject line, and with the words <subscribe atlcforum> and your own name in the body of the message.

4. *CSLA-L* is the listserv of the Canadian School Library Association, a division of the Canadian Library Association. To join, send an electronic mail message to <csla-l-request@mala.bc.ca> with nothing in the subject line, and the word <subscribe> followed by your own name, in the body of the message.

5. *OZTL_NET* -- Do I need to tell you about this one? I think it is terrific. One of the best out there today. The discussion is always of high calibre, and the information sharing is terrific. Keep up the good work. And for readers who don't know about *OZTL_NET*, it is based at Charles Sturt University, managed by Lyn Hay and Ken Dillon. Membership is open to teacher librarians and any other interested persons. To join, send an electronic mail message to <OZTL_NET-request@listserv.csu.edu.au> with the word <subscribe> in the subject line and nothing in the body of the message. [And I am sure you will be glad you did.]

6. *BIGSIX* is my favourite listserv devoted to a discussion of the *Big Six* skills approach to library and information skills instruction. I believe that this is one of the most important developments in school librarianship that makes it plausible to do collaborative planning and cooperative teaching in the new information services environments. There are usually 10+ messages a day from various parts of the world. To join the listserv which is also managed by Mike Eisenberg from Syracuse University, send an electronic mail message to <listserv@listserv.syr.edu> with nothing in the subject line, and with the words <subscribeBigSix> and your name in the body of the message.

7. *EDULIST* is an open and moderated list covering topics related to education and information technology in Mediterranean countries. It announces conferences, meetings on education, and deals with issues for teachers using technologies in education. It appears to be focused at this time at the secondary and postsecondary institutions. Messages are mostly in Spanish, Catalan, Italian and French. Occasionally English is used. To subscribe, send an electronic mail message to <listserv@listserv.rediris.es> with nothing in the subject line, and with the words SUBSCRIBE *EDULIST* your first and last name in the body of the message. The owner for the system is Victor Feliu, and he may be reached at <vfeliu@pie.xtec.es>.

8. *EDTECH* was conceived to bring together students, faculty, and "interested others" in the field of educational technology to share ideas and information. There are more than 3,000 subscribers from about 30 countries on the *EDTECH* list. Some topics discussed include: problems in using educational technology and how to solve them; articles and books that are stimulating and worthwhile, information about course offerings and *EDTECH* graduate program requirements in various schools, conferences and events, current dissertations and research projects in educational technology. The list is moderated. To subscribe, send an electronic mail message to <listserv@MSU.EDU> with nothing in the subject line, and with the words <*EDTECH*-Request your name> in the body of the message.

9. *EL-ANNOUNCE* is a new listserv of announcements about products and services by education and library vendors. This listserv was designed so that *LM_NET* and *BIGSIX* would not carry commercial announcements. You can choose to read-only Education and Library Announcements, from this moderated list. Most of the material covered on this list to date is available in the United States. A digest function is also available if you prefer to have your messages grouped. To subscribe to *EL-ANNOUNCE*, send an email message to <listserv@listserv.syr.edu> with nothing in the subject line, and with the words <subscribe *EL-ANNOUNCE* your name> in the body of the message.

Now if anyone subscribes to all those lists, he/she should also apply for a sabbatical. There will be too many messages to handle. Do check in on one or two of the lists at a time, and see if the range of discussion meets your needs. There are varying levels of sophistication across the range of listservs.

May I have some additional cutlery?

Yes, by all means. The listservs are only the tip of the iceberg in Internet land. First, one should be aware that electronic mail is a wonderful device for sharing information with colleagues and friends quickly and efficiently. Most people will have developed their own electronic mail address files and mailing lists.

Secondly, directories are created to store the files you choose to save. Your program will have specific directions on how to establish these files. They will save you many hours of searching for the message that you thought you sent last week... and you won't have the paper files to sort. And weeding the trash is so easy.

Third, come the wonderful world of web sites. There are experts who surf the Internet many hours a day just to keep up with the new sites. New publications are compiled and issued monthly in the regular market place which will tell you about the existing sites, the ones that have changed their names and addresses, and the ones that died in infancy. I would like to recommend the following as some choice sites. Please share yours with us as we discuss the value of web sites in your professional development.

1. *NEEDLE IN A CYBERSTACK - The InfoFinder*
   <http://home.revealed.net/~albee/index.html>
   Currently has 12 interlinked pages including the best of curriculum, research, reference, exploring, what's cool, Cybrarian's Favourites, etc. It is simple, powerful, quick-loading (Table Format - no graphics) and user friendly links to all the best Search and Info Tools in the world. [Check this one out; it is exceptional.] Created by John Albee, Teacher, Davenport Community Schools, Davenport, Iowa, USA.

2. *IASL WEB SITE*
   <http://www.rhi.hi.is/~anne/iasl.html>
   Now has many links to library related materials, including the favourite sites from many members around the world.

3. *ERIC*
   <http://ericir.syr.edu>
   Provides wonderful resources, and an incredibly fine archive of professional and practical information in education.

4. *EdDirect*
<http://www.eddirect.com>
Designed to cater for Australia's and New Zealand's teachers professional needs. It is watched by North Americans to follow the latest trends and issues in education that may find their way across the ocean.

5. *MAINLY FOR TEACHER LIBRARIANS*
<http://www.ozemail.com.au/~jhlee>
Contains a number of sections: information and hints on OASIS, the automated system; "Did you read this...?" gives a choice of synopses of recently published articles on technology, children's literature, the web and other matters of concern to teacher librarians; "Have you tried this...?" provides useful hints for all aspects of the role. It is maintained on a regular basis by John Lee.

6. *CMIS - WA*
<http://www.eddept.wa.edu.au/centoff.cmis/home/htm>
A dynamic web site from the Curriculum Materials Information Services, Education Department of Western Australia. There are many useful sites and lots of good links.

7. *CM magazine*
<http://www.mbnet.mb.ca/cm>
Canada's premiere electronic reviewing journal of books produced for children and young adults.

8. *WEB66*
<http://web66.umn.edu.statistics/>
Features the Internet's oldest and most comprehensive list of school web sites, with more than 6,000 school home pages listed in more than 60 countries. Other features on this site include:
- 'Web66 Internet Server Cookbooks'... step-by-step instructions for setting up an Internet server
- 'Mustang: A Web Cruising Vehicle' provides help for teachers on how to integrate the Internet into the classroom
- 'Web66 Network Construction Set', with information to help you understand network principles
- 'Web66 Mailing list', provides a discussion group of educators using the web.

9. *INTERNET LIBRARY FOR LIBRARIANS*
<http://www.itcompany.com/inforetriever/>

Combines Vianne Sha's *Internet Resources for Cataloging* and *Library and Information Science Toolbox* as a comprehensive web database designed to provide a one-stop shopping centre for library staff to locate Internet resources related to the profession. It provides links to hundred of Internet sites ranging from general to specific, from technical services to public services, from administration to library job opportunities, from publishers to library system vendors, and from library email lists to library grants and projects. All the Internet resources that are included in this site have been reviewed and described in the document. [Check this one out, it is exceptional.]

10. *CLASS IV NEWS & EDUCATIONAL RESOURCES*
<http://www.classIV.com/resource.html>
Created by teachers who were frustrated because they did not have time to keep up with the news related to the rapid changes in education. To make decisions educators need good information, but one simply does not have time to read twenty print sources and search the Net. To solve this problem, online education newsletters were created that consisted of a collection of brief summaries of education news stories. The newsletters were designed to be read in less than ten minutes, yet give the reader a reasonably complete overview of the week's important education news. [Well worth the time.]

11. *FILE ROOM CENSORSHIP ARCHIVES*
<http://fileroom.aaup.uic.edu/FileRoom/documents/homepage/html>
Offers detailed information and updates on censorship cases worldwide. Visitors can browse the illustrated archive of cases or submit their own tales of oppression.

12. *EDUCATION WORLD*
<http://www.education-world.com>
Offers educational professionals, parents, students and administrators around the globe a top quality search engine. [Your principal will like this one.]

13. *FILTERING THE INTERNET*
<http://www.libertynet.org/~lion/filtering.html>
Part of LION (Librarians Information Online Network), the web site for school librarians in the School District of Philadelphia, PA, USA., and gives a good perspective on the concern that some individuals have about the kinds of materials to which children might be exposed from random surfing on the Net.

14. *SOLARIS*
<http://www.info.unicaen.fr/bnum/jelec/Solaris/>
This is a French electronic journal about Library and Information Science, published annually by the Group Interuniversitaire de Recherches en Sciences de l'Information et de la Documentation. Articles are full-text and focus on the impact of new technologies on information retrieval systems from different perspectives: technical, political, economical and historical. Text is in French.

15. *INFORMATION TECHNOLOGY PLANS*
Jill Ball, Kent House MLC School, Burwood, NSW, Australia recommended these sites for people working on technology plans:

<gopher://gopher.msstate.edu:70/11/Online_services/nctp>
Provides samples of a number of technology plans for all levels .

<http://www.mtnbrook.k12.al.us/ss/bendset.htm>
The *Mountain Brook City Schools Technology Scope and Sequence* is a detailed document which provides a good basis from which to model a technology curriculum.

<http://www.dfee.gov.uk/nc/itindex.html>
The *National Curriculum for Information Technology* in the U.K.

16. *IFLA listserv and lists page*
<http://www.nlc-bnc.ca/ifla/>
Covers the whole scope of IFLA operations, resources and services.

17. *ORANA*
<http://www.alia.org.au/publications/orana/home/html>
or <http://babs.com.au/orana>
Australia's national journal of school and children's librarianship... a first of its kind.

18. *PICK*
<http://www.aber.ac.uk/~tplwww/e/>
A gateway to Internet resources in Library and Information Science and librarianship, with links to web pages of libraries, library suppliers and professional bodies, relevant texts and reports, mailing lists and electronic journals and newsletters. Also contains useful annotations and in-depth reviews. An initiative from Thomas Parry library, University of Wales, Aberystwyth and funded by HEFCW.

19. *LIBRARY CLIP ART*
<http://www.netins.net/showcase/meyers/library_clipart/clipart.html>
The title speaks for itself.

20. *LIBRARY JOURNAL (US)*
<http://www.ljdigital.com>
This online version of the print publication of *Library Journal* provides full-text news, opinion columns, book reviews, and articles about information technology and various multimedia; including WWW sites, CDROMs, audio books, and videos. Articles, columns, reviews, etc are excerpted from the current issue of the print magazine and are provided free-of-charge.

21. *DOGPILE SEARCH ENGINE*
<http://www.dogpile.com./>
This new search engine is amazing... simultaneously searches multiple search engines at once, and will check Usenet and then go on automatically to search the Web. It is better than *DejaNews* and *AltaVista* combined... because it includes searches on those engines and many more. It also checks mailing list archives. [Many positive responses.]

22. *COPAC*
<http://copac.ac.uk/copac/>
A new nationally accessible catalogue, based at the University of Manchester to provide unified access to the consolidated online catalogues of some of the largest university research libraries in the United Kingdom and Ireland through merged online library catalogues.

23. *VIRUSES*
<http://ciac.llnl.gov.ciac>
A great source for virus information is CIAC (Computer Incident Advisory Compability, US. Department of Energy). Not only do they maintain a database on the most current viruses and what to do about them but you can also subscribe to their notes and bulletins which keep you right up to date at your desktop.

Or for some other cool virus related stuff read:

<http://www.cnet.com/Resources/Tech/Advisers/Virus/index.html>
<http://www.hotfiles.com/hlpframe.html>
<http://www.kumite.com/myths/>
<http://www.nha.com>
<http://www.netwrx.net/raport2/cmptrs.htm>.

24. *NETFUTURE*
   <http://www.ora.com/people/staff/stevet/netfuture/>
   An eclectic newsletter about the relationship between technology
   and humanity which is distributed about once a week. It goes
   beyond the usual computer and networking issues to deal with
   how the interaction between human technology consciously and
   subconsciously shapes both. Newsletters are available back to
   1995, with a detailed topical index of 42 subjects ranging from
   alternative culture to the Year 2000 problem.

25. *THE UNPREDICTABLE CERTAINTY: INFORMATION
    INFRASTRUCTURE THROUGH 2000*
    <http://www.nap.edu/readingroom/books/unpredictable/summary/html>

And now that the main meal is served

The cost/bit of information is getting infinitely cheaper every day,
but the cost of useful bits is getting more expensive. Thus the
information poor, in many ways are worse off than before, but have
the illusion of having access to information. The answer to this
statement has little to do with technology. The Internet simply
makes more data available to the user who has access to the tools.
But the pertinent needs to be separated from the irrelevant. High-
valued insights have to be drawn from the info-dross. Originality
must be rescued from repetition. This has always been the case.
Teaching ourselves and our students to do the interpretative
processes is at the heart of adding value to information. When that is
done, we have added knowledge to our assets. This is where we as
teacher librarians come into our greatest strength as professionals.

For dessert, let us choose

> *Creativity is allowing yourself to make mistakes.*
> *Art is knowing which ones to keep.*
>
> Scott Adams

> *Wander, your footsteps are*
> *the road, and nothing more;*
> *wander, there is no road,*
> *the road is made by walking*
>
> Antonio Machado (1978)

And to the kitchen crew, a few sources of interest

Balaban, A.T. (1997). Mozart, Ford and the Information-Superhighway paradox. *Scientific American,* 85 (3): 207-209.

Clyde, L.A. (1995). Internet listservs for school librarians. *ATLC Impact,* Dec: 10-13.

Ellwood, W. (1996). Seduced by technology. *New Internationalist,* No. 286, Dec: 7-10.

Hannesdottir, S. (1997). Facing the changes. *IASL NEWSLETTER,* April.

Hazle, L.J. (1997). 'Including Local Knowledge.' Global Knowledge Development Conference 97 discussion email list, April.

Johnson, D. and Eisenberg, M. (1996). Computer literacy and information literacy: a natural combination. *Emergency Librarian,* 23 (5): 12 - 16.

Kawasaki, G. (1997). Hindsight. *Manitoba Library Association Newsline,* March: 1 - 3.

Loertscher, D. (1996). All that glitters may not be gold. *Emergency Librarian,* 24 (3): 231 -25.

Machado, A. (1978). *Selected poems.* Translated by Betty Jean Craige. Baton Rouge: Louisiana State University Press.

Marais, J.J. (1992). Evolution of information literacy as a product of information education. *South African Journal of Library and Information Science,* 60 (2): 75.

McCann, D. (1992). The paradigm shift in business. *Marketing Facts,* 11: 2.

Roddick, A. (1993). Leadership. *The Future of Business:* 3.

Roszak, T. (1996). Dumbing us down. *New Internationalist,* Dec: 12-14.

Small, G. (1994). Teaching and assessing information skills through the mainstream curriculum. *School Libraries in View,* 1: 11-14.

Talbott, S. (1997). 'The Future Does Not Compute: Transcending the Machines in Our Midst.' Global Knowledge Development Conference 97 discussion list email April, 1997.

Wood, F. et al. (1996). Information skills, searching behaviour and cognitive styles for student-centred learning: a computer-assisted learning approach. *Journal of Information Science*, 22 (2).

Wresch, B. (1996).   *Disconnected: Haves and Have Nots in the Information Age.* Rutgers University Press.

Wyllie, J. (1997) 'Content Analysis: a Methodology of Adding Value to Information by Systematic Interpretation.' Global Knowledge Development Conference 97 discussion list email April, 1997.

'...Participate, Motivate, Educate!!'

*Lyn Hay and Ken Dillon**

What is *OZTL_NET*?

OZTL_NET is the national listserv for the Australian teacher librarianship community. *OZTL_NET* stands for **OZ**(Aus)tralian **T**eacher **L**ibrarians Inter-**NET**-work: an Electronic Forum for the Australian Teacher Librarian Community. *OZTL_NET* was established to:

• support the professional information needs of Australian teacher librarians using an electronic communication forum
• enhance regular professional communication delivery and exchange between all members of the Australian teacher librarianship community, thus overcoming the professional isolation of teacher librarians, and
• effectively create an electronic community of Australian teacher librarians on the Internet which could potentially unite all parties interested in teacher librarianship issues.

OZTL_NET has become an important professional information service for practising teacher librarians, school library consultants, teacher librarianship academics and other professionals who are involved with or interested in teacher librarianship and school library issues. This listserv provides an online forum where teacher librarians can assess current school library practices on a daily basis with immediate feedback. Teacher librarians can:

• share ideas, problems, experiences and advice instantly
• develop common visions and work towards common goals

* **Lyn Hay** and **Ken Dillon** are the *OZTL_NET* Administrators and lecture in Teacher Librarianship with the School of Information Studies at Charles Sturt University, Wagga Wagga, N.S.W., Australia. Lyn may be contacted via email at <lhay@csu.edu.au> and Ken at <kdillon@csu.edu.au>. The *OZTL_NET* web site is available at <http://www.csu.edu.au/research/cstl/oztl_net/>.

- work together as a powerful political force to overcome professional and workplace issues and problems
- 'conference' at the point of need as issues and problems arise
- develop information technology skills with the support of their teacher librarian colleagues
- reduce their professional isolation and support one another more effectively and collaboratively, offering links to even the most remote teacher librarian in Australia with national and international colleagues
- receive professional advice from experts in primary, secondary and tertiary education and private institutions within an Australian context
- efficiently and effectively disseminate information from professional groups, associations and publications
- interact with academic and researchers, bridging the gap between theory and practice, eg. forum to conduct teacher librarianship research
- display leadership of the profession by placing the teacher librarianship community in the centre of a national networking movement
- support training teacher librarians completing tertiary study - who can draw from the collective knowledge of practitioners, ie. experience 'real life' teacher librarianship issues and problems and seek practical solutions.

OZTL_NET: a short history

While *OZTL_NET* was conceived as an idea as early as October 1994, the *OZTL_NET* list officially began in June 1995. In the first month we had approximately 30 members. As of April 28, 1997 *OZTL_NET* had 1202 members![†] While the majority of OZTLs are from Australia (1112 members), we also have colleagues from New Zealand (12), the United States (50), Canada (16), Asia (7), South America, UK and Europe. The graph in Appendix 1[†] charts the growth of the *OZTL_NET* population from August 1995 to April 1997.

[†] At the time of editing these proceedings, *OZTL_NET*'s subscription rate had increased to just over 2000 members.

Subscribing to *OZTL_NET*

One of the most common questions asked of us as list administrators is *"How much does it cost to subscribe to OZTL_NET?"* The answer is: subscription to *OZTL_NET* is free! What we do ask of our members, however, is that they participate in list discussion rather than 'lurk'. *OZTL_NET's* motto is *'...Participate, Motivate, Educate!!'*. In order to motivate and educate others, one must first participate in and contribute to the community's 'collective pot' of knowledge and expertise to help create a richer and more stimulating environment.

Subscribing and posting to *OZTL_NET* is simple. Just follow these instructions carefully:

1. post a message to the following listserv address:

   OZTL_NET-request@listserv.csu.edu.au

   Note the underscore between the 'L' and 'N', and the dash between the 'T' and 'r'. Unsuccessful subscribers usually misspell words or ignore the required punctuation.

2. in the subject line, type the command **subscribe**

3. do not include any information in the message field, ie. LEAVE IT BLANK and turn off your Internet signature, and

4. send your message. :-)

Your subscription is automatically processed by the listserv computer and you will receive an *OZTL_NET Welcome Message*. Please read and **save** the *OZTL_NET Welcome Message* upon receipt. This message is important because it contains the procedures for using this listserv as well as some Netiquette Guidelines.

Alternatively OZTLs can elect to subscribe to the ***Daily Digest option***. The Daily Digest consists of a compilation of all messages posted in one day forwarded to a member in one email message. This can assist members 'control' of their daily email traffic. Only about 9% of OZTLs subscribe to the Digest option. We suggest to those members who are starting to feel a little overwhelmed with the number of messages posted daily to consider subscribing to this option. To do this you need to post a message to the following digest listserv address: <OZTL_NET-d-request@listserv.csu.edu.au> (note the addition of the '-d' in this address) and in the subject line, type the command 'subscribe'. If you are still subscribed to the individual *OZTL_NET* list, remember to 'unsubscribe', other wise you will receive the Digest plus individual messages!

OZTL_NET Conversation

OZTL_NET conversation focuses on the latest issues and developments relating to school library and information services including:

- policies - library, school, departmental
- location/use of Internet resources
- information literacy - issues, programs, strategies
- reference questions for teachers/students
- children's/YA literature and reading
- resource sharing/networking
- products and services for school libraries
- general discussion of teacher librarianship issues
- technology problems and tips
- conference/workshop/association announcements
- regional teacher librarian group updates, eg. ACT Update.

The following is an example of one teacher librarian's information requests being met through *OZTL_NET*:

Date sent: Wed, 15 May 1996 18:59:24 +1000

...Through OZTL_NET I have asked a number of work related questions and received great replies from experts I would not normally come in contact with from within Australia and occasionally from overseas. My questions have included:-

* What is the best way to network CD ROMs through Windows for Workgroups instead of Novell? Is it feasible to install 2 CD ROM drives in each of say 3 Pentium Computers so that students can access up to 6 different CD ROMs without the need for change. (My school is poor and can't invest much money in networking)

* How can I get OASIS stocktake to accurately reflect my stock? My stocktake reports (current stock and stocktake statement) don't tally for 3 of my library's 6 locations!

...I have also helped to reunite a teacher-librarian in America with a local teacher and family in Sydney's Western Suburbs through a message request on OZTL_NET. (He was previously on exchange to the States and the TL had misplaced address)....

Mr. Darryll Hopkins
Teacher-Librarian

Subject Line Keywords and *OZTL_NET* Archives

Subject Line Keywords are used as a form of mail control assisting OZTLs to sort through their list mail based on content-related keywords. We recommend that all messages be prefixed with one of the following keywords in the subject line:

ADMIN: these are official messages sent from the OZTL_NET Administrators to the list

CH LIT: includes postings which focus on all aspects of children's literature, young adult literature, the reading process and related issues

COLL DEV: deals with postings which discuss collection development issues, topics relating to resource management and resource sharing

COMM: it is compulsory for all messages which include commercial product and service announcements to use this subject line keyword

GEN: includes postings of a general nature

GREET: used for requests from OZTLs for greetings to TL groups, staff meetings and conferences. Penpal requests are also listed here.

HUMOUR: messages including anecdotes, jokes, poems, etc.

INFO LIT: contain messages which focus on information literacy related issues, policies, programs, resources, etc.

INTRO: includes all introductory messages sent to OZTL_NET from members

JOBS: contains messages which deal with employment opportunities, both employers and prospective employees are welcome to post

REF: includes requests and responses for all types of reference questions

TECH: deals with postings about computer hardware and software, IT networking, library automation, Internet resources and assistance with a range of technologies

TL ROLE: postings which focus on issues pertaining to the role of the TL

WHAT'S ON: includes announcements of forthcoming conferences, seminars, etc.

All *OZTL_NET* messages that do not include one of the above prefixes are 'tagged' with the most appropriate subject line keyword before being stored in an archives. This allows OZTLs to retrieve past messages using a variety of search methods. The *OZTL_NET* Archive of previous messages is now available at <http://www.csu. edu.au/research/cstl/oztl_net/archives.html>.

OZTLs can keyword search for messages using the entire archives database or can restrict searches by subject line keyword. For example, if you were looking for messages on the Director of Information Services debate, you could select to search the TLROLE subject line field using the phrase 'Director Information Services'; or if you were looking for tips on stocktaking using OASIS library automation software, you could select to search the TECH field using the keyword 'OASIS' and 'stocktake'; or if you are looking for a specific person and you recall they have introduced themselves to the list, you could select to search the INTRO field using their first or second name, the name of their school, or any other word or phrase that you can associate with that person.

What do OZTLs talk about?
The following table presents the number of posts sent to the *OZTL_NET* list during 1995 and 1996 according to Subject Line Keywords:

ARCHIVE	No. Posts/Year	
Keyword	**1995**	**1996**
ADMIN	8	14
CH LIT	33	147
COLL DEV	31	222
COMM*	0	9
GEN	47	210
GREET	21	88
HUMOUR*	0	1
INFO LIT	25	108
INTRO	109	164
JOBS*	3	28
REF	32	149
TECH	106	289
TL ROLE*	7	65
WHATS ON	26	89
Yearly Sub-Totals	448	1583
Total Posts 1995-96 =	**2031**	

From this table we can identify the major professional information needs of OZTLs to date. Technology-related requests and replies have been the most prominent in number -- a total of 395 over the 1995-96 period. The list has also been used to assist teacher librarians with collection development-related requests (a total of 253 posts in this period). A substantial number of posts have also been sought in the areas of children's literature and information literacy, as well as reference-related queries. Based on the INTRO figures we can also conclude that over 25% of OZTLs have introduced themselves to the list during the 1995-96 period - leaving close to 75% of OZTLs 'lurking'!! (Remember out motto?) :-)

Note that the subject line keywords marked with an asterix (*) were not in the original archive list. These 4 additional subject line keywords were introduced to accommodate the information and netiquette needs of the list. At the end of 1995 we found a number of messages questioned or commented upon the teacher librarian role -- we were concerned that these messages were 'getting lost' in the GEN area, hence the creation of a TLROLE keyword -- this proved invaluable as the Director of Information Services and TL nomenclature debate 'heated up' in April 1996. In early 1996 concerns were raised by some OZTLs regarding commercial posts being sent to OZTL_NET -- we believe the creation of the COMM keyword can still allow commercial messages to be posted to the list (as many teacher librarians are interested in new resource/product announcements) while still conforming to list 'netiquette'. For OZTL_NET policy on commercial posts please refer to the Netiquette Guidelines in the OZTL_NET Welcome Message. During the 1995-96 period, OZTL_NET generated a total of 2031 requests, suggestions and announcements - that's a lot of information sharing among colleagues! We look forward to a lot more dialogue in 1997...

Community Services :-)
We do encourage members to request *greetings* and recommendations from OZTLs when they are introducing the power of email and listservs as effective communication tools to TL colleagues, school staff, parents or students - over 100 greetings have been requested to date! This is a 'community service' and TL advocacy function of OZTL_NET. When requesting greetings OZTLs can ask for messages to include special information to assist them in their presentation, for example:

From: "Lyn Hay" <lhay@csu.edu.au>
Organization: Charles Sturt University
To: OZTL_NET@harpo.riv.csu.edu.au
Date sent: Tue, 14 May 1996 10:34:40 GMT-10
Subject: Greetings to North West NSW TL Conference
Priority: normal

Hi OZTLs,

I am presenting a workshop at the North West NSW TL Conference in Tamworth this Friday (17th May) on 'Communicating with Colleagues in Cyberspace'. I would like to share with NW TLs the power of OZTL_NET as a professional support network, and would appreciate help in 'selling' OZTL_NET to our NW colleagues..

Could OZTLs from Australia and all those wonderful places around the world please send a greeting to the NW TLs? In your greeting could you include the names of the mailing lists to which you currently subscribe, and also a sentence about why you like communicating with colleagues in cyberspace.

Please send greetings directly to my email address, not that of the OZTL_NET list. Much appreciated.

Cheers,

Lyn Hay
<lhay@csu.edu.au>

Intro Welcomes - Creating a Welcoming Committee

All new members are encouraged in the *OZTL_NET Welcome Message* (received upon subscription) to introduce themselves to the list. This is one strategy used by us to help develop a 'sense of community' on the list - just like you would introduce yourself at a professional network meeting or conference workshop. Since the lists inception, once a new member posts their INTRO, Lyn forwards a personal Intro Welcome encouraging the new member to actively participate in list discussion, eg.

To: Pam Richardson <lltceo@iinet.net.au>
Subject: Re: INTRO: Pam Richardson
Date sent: Sat, 29 Jun 1996 15:23:26

Hi Pam,
Welcome to OZTL_NET. Please keep OZTLs updated on the work of the Library Liaison Team for the Catholic Education Office of WA, it sounds interesting. Do you know of similar initiatives in other states?

Good luck with your request for technology plans - if you receive some good ones, feel free to post them to the list for others to share.
I hope OZTL_NET keeps you in touch with old and new colleagues.

All the best,

Lyn.

With the growth of *OZTL_NET* and the expansion of *OZTL_NET* services to the WWW, we would like to establish a small 'Welcoming Committee' to coordinate INTRO replies. We envisage this committee to consist of 3 or 4 OZTLs who would be eager to go on 'INTRO duty' for 1 week of each month in the year. Committee members would be responsible for monitoring *OZTL_NET* INTRO posts during their 'On Week' and automatically reply to new members with a personal INTRO Welcome. Each INTRO Welcome message would also be CCed to the *OZTL_NET* archives. If any OZTLs are interested in providing this community service, please email Lyn Hay at <lhay@csu.edu.au>.[‡]

OZTL_NET Breakfasts

In 1996 we also organised some 'real-life' encounters in the form of *OZTL_NET* Breakfasts at conferences held throughout Australia. *OZTL_NET* breakfasts have been held at the ITEC'96 Information Highway conference in Sydney, the NSW Computers in Education Group '96 conference in Bathurst, the ASLA(NSW) Biennial '96 conference in Newcastle, and the ALIA'96 Conference in Melbourne. A less formal OZTL_NET 'brekkie' was organised during Easter 1997 in Perth, WA. We would like to see more 'real life' encounters happening throughout Australia and ultimately at international conferences [if more than 2 OZTLs attend!! -- IASL'97 in Vancouver looks promising :-)][§]. This is an opportunity for OZTLs to communicate face-to-face in a relaxed social atmosphere with their electronic colleagues -- it's great putting faces to names! Approximately 40 OZTLs have attended each breakfast, and we look forward to more 'real-life' networking with our cyberspace colleagues! Once again, the list administrators would like to call upon more active involvement in encouraging the development of the *OZTL_NET* community. If you would like to become part of a

---

[‡] Lyn is still interested in hearing from *OZTL_NET* members who would like to join the Welcoming Committee.

[§] The IASL *OZTL_NET* Dinner in Vancouver attracted over 35 international participants.

small *OZTL_NET* Hospitality Committee please email Lyn Hay at <lhay@csu.edu.au>. We intend the Hospitality Committee to essentially play a coordinating and marketing role in the organisation of *OZTL_NET* social gatherings -- it is not essential that members of this committee organise or attend *all OZTL_NET* social gatherings.

We look forward to OZTLs becoming involved in the community service activities of *OZTL_NET*.

OZTL_NET on the Web
As of April 1997 *OZTL_NET* has become more than just a discussion list. *OZTL_NET on the Web* located at <http://www.csu.edu.au/research/cstl/oztl_net/> has been established to provide teacher librarians with access to *OZTL_NET* archives and other professional information relevant to teacher librarianship.

Please note that this site is currently under construction, however, we intend *OZTL_NET on the Web* to be more than just a 'storehouse' of past list discussion, we have plans to create a gateway to electronic information sources and services that are of particular importance to the professional information needs of teacher librarians. Over the next few months a variety of services will be created on *OZTL_NET on the Web*.

Some examples include an *OZTL Mentors* program which will in effect be a Web-based professional 'bulletin board' linking practising teacher librarians wishing to acquire particular skills with TL 'experts' and a 'Profiles' database containing OZTLs contact details and interests. We would also like to establish an *OZTL Job Registry*, providing an employment reference service for teacher librarians, schools and educational authorities -- linking teacher librarians to vacant teacher librarian positions throughout Australia (and potentially worldwide)!

We also plan to develop a commercial announcement page creating links to library-related commercial product sites -- just imagine, an online shopping mall for teacher librarians!.

It would be too ambitious a claim to say that *OZTL_NET on the Web* will be like a 'one-stop shop' for Web services relating to teacher librarianship, however, we hope that *OZTL_NET's* web site will be a 'regular stop' for teacher librarians. Visit us regularly to keep up-to-date with teacher librarianship issues, developments and happenings.

Remember, teacher librarians are major stakeholders in the Information Age, and as key players must lead Australian schools -- teachers, students and their parents -- into the 21st Century. *OZTL_NET* is an electronic initiative that can assist teacher librarians in achieving this vision. Join us in shaping the electronic future of teacher librarianship in Australia.

'...Participate, Motivate, Educate!!'

---

† **Appendix 1**

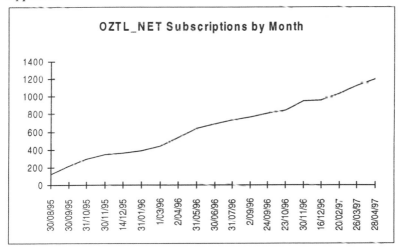

Topic J

The School Library Home Page

The School Library as Information Provider: the Home Page

Laurel A. Clyde[*]

Introduction

When teacher librarians first began to access the Internet, they were generally using it to communicate with colleagues, to discuss professional issues, and/or to locate information. The Internet was primarily a communications tool and a way of extending the range of information and resources that were available through the school library. Some teacher librarians also began to use the Internet with students, as a way of helping them to develop the information skills that will be the essential life skills of the information age. (Clyde 1996c)

From 1993/1994 onwards, some schools (or classes within schools) began to develop World Wide Web (WWW) sites. Apparently the first schools onto the Web were Grand River Elementary School in Grand River, Minnesota (USA), Hillside Elementary School in Cottage Grove, Minnesota (USA), and The Buckman School in Portland, Oregon (USA). In 1995 and 1996, the number of school Web sites increased enormously, and 'metasites' such as *Web 66* were developed to keep track of them. But while there were many WWW home pages, or even full Web sites, created by schools, there were, in comparison, relatively few school library home pages. A survey of the WWW home pages of Australian schools, carried out early in 1995 revealed that there were then more than 40 school home pages or Web sites -- there would, of course, be many more today (Clyde 1995a). However, of those 40, only two showed evidence of having been created by or with the involvement of the school library. Again, while the numbers would be much greater today, there are still many more school Web sites than school library sites or pages, and many school Web sites are still being created without any evidence of involvement on the part of the school library staff.

The creation of a home page involves information searching, information organisation, information evaluation, and information

---

[*] **Dr Anne Clyde** is Professor with the Department of Library and Information Science, Faculty of Social Science at the University of Iceland, Reykjavik. An online version of this paper is available at **<http://www.rhi.hi.is/~anne/slhomepage. html>**. Anne may be contacted via email at **<anne@rhi.hi.is>**.

presentation, all skills that are basic to the practice of teacher librarianship. While other skills, such as the ability to write HTML (hypertext mark-up language) documents, are necessary too, these skills can be learned fairly quickly -- I teach a one-day course on 'Creating the Library Home Page', (Clyde 1996d) which seems to be sufficient (according to evidence from the course evaluation forms and the results of class activities) to enable librarians and teacher librarians to acquire the basic HTML skills and to achieve a level of confidence that allows them to proceed further afterwards. Even if teacher librarians do not wish to acquire these skills, then people with HTML skills, including school students, may be willing to work on a home page project with a person who has the higher level professional information skills that are necessary for the creation of a successful Web page. There is certainly an abundance of evidence on the WWW to support the contention that good content and the ability to organise and present information are more critical to the success of a page than the ability to write fancy HTML.

It should be recognised from the beginning that the creation of a home page is not a 'once only' activity. It is rather the beginning of an ongoing process that lasts as long as the home page is available for public viewing. The page will need to be maintained and updated regularly, again perhaps as a cooperative venture involving students and teachers, and within the context of information skills work. Links to other pages will have to be checked regularly to make sure that they are still active, and the information about the library kept up to date. New links and new content will be needed to keep that the page interesting and relevant to the needs of users. Thus when resources (personnel, time, money, equipment) are allocated to this task, it should be on an ongoing basis. In addition, if a Web page is being developed as part of the school's educational programme, then students need to understand that these ongoing tasks are part of the process; through the ongoing maintenance of a Web page they gain a greater understanding of the volatile nature of the Internet.

Rationale: Why Have a Home page?
Through the home page, the school library moves from being a user of online information to being an online information provider, a significant change that is appropriate in today's context, but one that needs to be planned and managed so that educational goals are achieved through it. Why should a school library make this ongoing commitment? Why should the school library have a home page?

There are educational reasons, and reasons associated with management strategies. They include the following:

- The teacher librarian has an important role in information skills development in the school, and the creation of a home page incorporating work of students involves the exercise of high order information skills.

- The school library is the major information centre in the school, and so it is logical that the school library would be involved in any Internet-based information activities in the school, both in terms of information skills work and in terms of the skills that teacher librarians themselves can contribute to the development of what is really a school information service on the Internet.

- If the teacher librarian and the school library are not involved in the creation of home pages and school Web sites, then they are losing opportunities to promote the school library and the specialist skills of its staff. Having a home page indicates to everyone that the school library is moving with the times and adopting new technologies to provide information services. In fact, as the school's information centre, the school library should be taking the initiative in providing information in this way, through its own home page.

- The school library can use a Web page to promote its collections and services, and to promote any special library activities, such as Book Week activities. Students and teachers can be involved in these activities through the Web page as well as through visits to the library.

- Bibliographies, book reviews, guides to information sources ('pathfinders'), and other documents can be made available to the school community through the library's Web pages. Information being made available on school library Web sites includes information about citing references in assignments, guides to using the Internet, online tutorials, and databases created by students as well as library staff.

- Depending on the automated library system that is used in the library, it may be possible to make the library catalogue available for searching through the school library home page. This would have the further advantage of making the catalogue available to users (for instance, from a classroom, or from home, or through a public Internet terminal in the local public library) even when the school library is closed.

When a school library home page is being planned, many questions need to be addressed.

- What should be the purpose or aim of the page?
- What needs should it serve?
- Who would be the users?
- How should it be designed?
- Who should create it?
- Who should maintain it?
- What should be on it?

These questions cannot be addressed within the scope of a short discussion paper. Nevertheless, they are important if a home page is to serve to promote the mission of the school library and the school, to further the educational aims of the school, and to promote the school library as the information centre of the school.

Research Study: What is really happening?
In terms of the school library home page, the possibilities seem almost endless. But what is really happening, and what do school library home pages really look like? To begin to answer this question, I carried out a small-scale study of school library home pages and Web sites, in August 1996. (Clyde 1996a; 1996b). This involved a content analysis of 50 school library home pages (and any supporting pages) from nine different countries (including the United States of America, Canada, Australia, Sweden, Singapore, Iceland, Kuwait, New Zealand, and Norway). This project is described in more detail elsewhere; the most significant results will be outlined again here for the benefit of ITEC conference participants.

The content and format of the school library Web pages used for this study suggested that school libraries may have very different aims in developing their pages, though some pages had no apparent aim and no clearly-defined audience. Only a few pages actually identified the intended audience in some way, either by a statement of purpose or by obvious implication. Seven had been developed (at least in part) for students of the school, to help them to find Internet resources, and to incorporate them into their class work, while one was aimed at teachers in the school. One was developed for "students, teachers and visitors" -- a diverse group with very different needs; another was for "students, teachers and parents". Six were clearly intended for online visitors from outside the school, in that they were little more than sections from a school prospectus, made available via the Internet. The intended audience for the other school library pages was impossible to discern from the pages themselves, and it may be that they had been created with no particular audience in mind. It is very difficult to select and present information to meet the needs of users if neither the users nor their needs have been identified, and so these pages tended to include a miscellany of material and links, at a variety of levels, usually without any indication of purpose and without any linking theme. It is interesting that eight of the home pages provided links to Internet resources for school librarians, suggesting that the school library staff themselves were among the main users of the pages in some cases. The Table summarises the results of the content analysis of the 50 pages.

Table 1: Contents of School Library Home Pages
n=50

HOME PAGE FEATURE	NUMBER
Name of school and library	41
Links to selected resources on the Internet	31
Information about the school library	29
Interactive email contact address	28
Link to a school home page	24
Date of the last update of the page	19
Links to Internet search engines	15
Research skills information or guides	8
Links to Internet resources for teachers	8
Links to Internet resources for teacher librarians	8
Book reviews, lists of recommended books	7
Photograph of the school library	6
Information about citing Internet resources	6
Links to resources about the local area/region	5
News about the library or library activities	4
Information about the Internet for library users	4
Internet tutorial	4
Online reference desk for email enquiries	3
Information about school library Internet use policies	3
The library rules	2
Electronic magazines	1

Examples of School Library Home Pages

The following are examples of WWW home pages that have been created by school libraries in the United States of America, Canada, Sweden, and Australia:

Newark Memorial High School Library, Newark, California, USA.
<http://www.infolane.com/nm-library/>
This Web server incorporates an 'Internet Driver's License' section through which the school's students develop the skills that are necessary for independent use of the Internet for information gathering.

Hopkinton High School and Hopkinton Middle School Library, Contoocook, New Hampshire, USA.
< http://www.conknet.com/hhs/library/hhslib.html>
This Web site has links to 'useful sites' on the Internet, a collection of bookmarks for teachers, the text of the school's 'Guidelines for Student Use of the Internet', information about the library, 'Ideas for Reading', and Web versions of 'Library Survival Sheets' that have been created by the library ('Coping With the Incredibly Overdue Book', and information about referencing and bibliographies).

Chico High School Library, Chico, California, USA.
< http://www.chs.chico.k12.ca.us/libr/webres/helpful.html>
Peter Milbury's library page has bookmarks arranged by school subject, with an additional page of 'Teen Topics' leading to online magazines and other resources for teenagers. There are also 'Bookmarks for Educators', links to Internet search engines, and an Internet tour called 'Entering the Internet From the Chico High School Library'.

La Salle Secondary School Library, Kingston, Ontario, Canada.
<http://www.icactive.com/jwz/>
The home page of La Salle Library, billed as a "library without walls, accessible by computer modem 24 hours a day, 7 days a week", is designed to guide "students, teachers, and visitors to information in our library and in cyberspace". It was created by Jerry Zawisza, a member of the library staff.

The Library at Östrabogymnasiet, Uddevalla, Sweden.
<http://www.ostrabo.uddevalla.se/bib/bibleng.htm>
The library of this Swedish secondary school has a home page in English as well as one in Swedish. There is information about the

library, and links to Internet resources. The home page was created by the Librarian, Ann-Charlotte Backlund.

Loreto College, Coorparoo, Queensland, Australia.
<http://www.uq.edu.au/~zzloreto>
Kathy Hedemann, teacher librarian at Loreto College, has created and maintains her school's Web site. The 'Loreto Web' from the school library has been designed to help users "to use the Internet effectively for educational purposes". Among other topics, it covers 'Sites for School Subjects', 'How Good is Internet Information?', 'Finding What I Need', and 'Citing Internet Sources'.

Cannington Senior High School, Perth, Western Australia.
<http://www.vianet.net.au/~cshs/>
There is a link to the school library pages from the school's home page, plus links to Internet projects and resources.

Kilvington Baptist Girls' Grammar School, Melbourne, Australia.
<http://www.kilvington.schnet.edu.au>
From the home page, there is a link to the school's Information Services Centre, with a page of links to Internet resources (arranged by broad topic). The home page also has a link to a 'Book Reviews' page with reviews by the Information Services Centre Book Club.

Walton Library, Methodist Ladies' College, Kew, Victoria, Australia.
<http://www.mlckew.edu.au/library/>
Suzette Boyd, Director of Library Services, and her staff, have created a colourful Web site for the Walton Library. There is information about the Library, an electronic form for teachers who are planning to set research assignments for their students, information about a course called 'Wired for Information' that is offered to Year 8 classes (with samples of home pages created by the students), and links to Internet resources.

Smiths Hill High School Library, Wollongong, New South Wales, Australia.
<http://foyer.uow.edu.au/schools/shhs/library/libmain.html>
Created originally by Georgia Phillips, this school library Web site has pictures of the library, a link to the school library catalogue (not operational as this paper was being prepared), and links to Internet resources for teachers and students. A section called 'Research Help' provides students with a guide to carrying out research, using the 'Be DEFINITE' approach.

The following Web sites provide links to many school library home pages:

School Libraries on the Web: A Directory
<http://www.voicenet.com/~bertland/libs.html>
Compiled by Linda Bertland, a school library media specialist in the United States of America, this site provides a listing of school library pages on the Web, covering the United States of America (organised by state), Australia, Canada, Sweden, New Zealand, Singapore, Norway, the United Kingdom, and other countries.

School Library and School Librarian Web Pages
<http://cusd.chico.k12.ca.us/~pmilbury>
Compiled by Peter Milbury, a school library media specialist at Chico Senior High School in California, and co-owner of the *LM_NET* international listserv for 'school library media people', this site provides a listing of pages that have been created by school librarians. Peter Milbury suggests that other school librarians might like to use some of these as models or as sources of ideas for their own library pages.

Getting Help
For teacher librarians who are interested in developing a home page for their school library, there are many sources of information available on the Internet. Among the most useful is an online textbook, *Writing for the Web: A Primer for Librarians* by Eric H. Schnell at <http://bones.med.ohio-state.edu/eric/papers/primer/webdocs.html>.

I have created a page, *The Internet Course* <http://www.rhi.hi.is/~anne/internet.html>, as a resource for students in a course that I teach in the Library and Information Science Programme at the University of Iceland, a course in which students are required to create a home page. One section of this page, *Recommended Internet Sources - Guides to Creating World Wide Web Pages* <http://www.rhi.hi.is/~anne/internet.html#sources>, has links to a wide variety of online resources, including HTML manuals and guides, collections of images and icons, and information about advanced techniques for Web page construction.

References

Chu, K. and Chin, F. (1996). *HTML publishing on the Internet*. New York: McGraw-Hill.

Clyde, L.A. (1995). The Internet and Australian schools, *Access*, 9 (2), June: 26-28.

Clyde, L.A. (1996a). School libraries: at home on the World Wide Web?, *Scan*, Nov: 23-26.

Clyde, L.A. (1996b). The library as information provider: the Home Page, *The Electronic Library*, 14 (6), Dec: 549-558.

Clyde, L.A. (1996c). *School libraries and the electronic community: the Internet connection*. Lanham: Scarecrow Press.

Clyde, L.A. (1996d). *Creating a World Wide Web Home Page: a course manual*. Perth, WA: Netweaver.

Collins, S.E. (1994a). 'First elementary school on the Web.' (online). Message posted to *Net-Happenings* listserv, 16 March.

Collins, S.E. (1994b). Hillside Elementary WWW events.' (online). Message posted to *LM_NET*, 27 April.

Garlock, K.L. and Piontek, S. (1996). *Building the service-based library Web site: a step-by-step guide to design and options*. Chicago: American Library Association.

Morris, M. E.S. (1996). *HTML for fun and profit*. Mountain View, CA: Sunsoft Press.

Weinman, B. and Crall, S. (1996). Design a Web page: a basic tutorial, *The Net*, 2 (3), Aug: 55-57.

Westbury, M. and Bertsten, R. (1996). What you Web is what you get: HTML authoring packages, *internet.au*, May: 50-56.

'Promise... is the soul of an advertisement.'

Considerations while Planning a School Library Home Page

Sharron Hewer[*]

So, you're looking for a way of raising your library's profile within your school and beyond, while emphasising the wide reaching and influential role of the teacher librarian. You're looking for a different way of advertising the library and its services. I have an answer for you. Design, and where possible write, a home page for your library.

I intend this paper to be one with more questions than solutions, and more decision making challenges than proformas, while raising issues for consideration rather than being a 'how to' paper on writing school library home pages. This is because individual situations differ, but we all have a common aim - to provide ways for our users to find information. By providing access through a home page, we are just using a different tool to achieve this.

Should Teacher Librarians be involved in writing home pages?
Of course we should. In many schools, the library has been sidelined in the school's technological advances in teaching and learning, often through no fault of the teacher librarian. Now is the time for us to regain the high ground in technology and learning, and to put the library at the forefront of educational technology in our schools.

Consider your own school staff. How many, other than the TL, have the big picture of school wide activities and student needs? How many have Internet knowledge and familiarity, and understand how it can fit into the learning outcomes of students, and aid the work of teachers? We recognise this ourselves, but we need to let other people know it too. We need to emphasise our leadership skills and role and we should be using the latest technology to do it.

---

[*] **Sharron Hewer** holds the position of Librarian (School Libraries) for the Tasmanian Department of Education, Community and Cultural Development in the Library and Information Centre in Hobart, Tasmania, Australia. Sharron can be contacted via email at <slt_hewer@ecc.tased.edu.au>. Visit the website <Sharron. Hewer@Central.tased.edu.au>.

Role/s the Teacher Librarian can take

The ideal is for the teacher librarian and the library to take complete control of the design and writing of the library's home page. However, in many schools this will not be possible because of technology and/or time restraints. At the very least, the teacher librarian needs to be the **facilitator** and **designer** of the library's home page. After all, the searching, organisation and evaluation of information which is required to create a home page matches our areas of expertise. Producing a library home page is just a different way of providing knowledge of library resources, bibliographies and access to wider resources.

The Preliminary Stage

Before pursuing the design of your home page, or lobbying the power brokers in your school to allow you to take your rightful technology leadership role, spend plenty of time exploring. Familiarise yourself with yours and the school's technology, read articles and books, explore the Internet, track down as many library related addresses and home pages as possible. *And be critical.* Feel comfortable and confident with your own use of the Internet before moving into an advisory role within the school and expanding the library's role as an information provider.

Planning considerations

The following can also be used as a checklist while planning your library's home page. The decisions which need to be made are really very much the same as those made before writing any document.

We need to be aware of, and make decisions about:

Task	Person Responsible	Done ✔
The intended audience. What information is required, and how should it be presented. Remember that apart from your known local (school family) audience, you may be being read by a worldwide audience. But don't let that cramp your style, just discipline it.		
What is the purpose and aim of the page?		

What is the character of the school's home page? Take this into consideration when deciding on the character of the library's.		
What character would you like your page to have - bright, serious, professional. Or would it be appropriate to have different characters for different sections of the page?		
Do you want the library home page to have a clear library-classroom link?		
What colours, or wallpaper would be appropriate for the page? Some colours and patterns are better than others. Can you, or should you, use a school symbol/emblem?		
What would/should your readers get from it?		
How will users access the library's page? If they come from the school's home page, ensure that the library's link is prominent.		
Ensure that the school's name and address are somewhere on the library page. Some users may not access the library page through the school's home page, and you want them to know where you (and they) are.		
Decide on the position of graphics or photographs on the page. Remember that the use of graphics will not suit the machine of every user. Having to download graphics where they have been incorporated as an integral part of a section may slow the process down so much that it will only frustrate the user. It may be better to have text based pages with links to supporting graphics which the user can choose to use.		
Do you wish to build in opportunities for student input to the page? And how? Can you use it to display students' work?		
Can the page be used for communication with parents regarding library procedures or resources?		
Can the library's page be used as an intranet within the school, or between a network of schools?		
Can or should users access the library's catalogue through the home page?		
Do you want to include a map of the library layout?		

It is always useful to include a library staff list.		
Do you want to include the library's rules and a statement of the library's philosophy, or mission?		
Should a list of services provided by the library be included?		
Do you want to build in email links to the library?		
Do you want to provide scope for direct feedback about the page?		
Consider including guidance for students on preparing bibliographies, and citing Internet resources which are being used in school projects.		
What are the type of links you see as important to have **from** the library's page?		
Are you going to provide links to search engines. And if so, which ones?		
Should you bookmark Internet resources useful for topics which are covered by different classes throughout the year?		
Should you provide Internet links which are organised under the 8 Key Learning Areas?		
Do you want to provide links **to** school/classroom projects which are on the school's page while they are active within the school. Or could the library provide links to Internet sites which will support these projects?		
Do you want to provide links to other resource areas eg. museums and other libraries?		
Do you want to provide links to PD and resource information for teachers as a separate section of the page?		
Timetable for constant maintenance and updating of information on the page.		
Incorporate a counter to monitor the number of visitors. Useful for ongoing evaluation.		
Put a **Return to Home Page/Top of Page** at the bottom of each page so users can easily backtrack if they are getting lost.		
Double check how your home page looks on other machines. Your users may not have systems as sophisticated as yours, so something which looks good on your machine may fall apart, look dreadful, or take a long time to load on others.		

Moving towards designing your home page

Look at some exemplars. Seek out, visit and observe home pages from other school libraries where you will find many sites to inspire you. You may wish to put a link in your home page to theirs, and you will certainly want to learn from their designs.

Maintenance

This is the more difficult part of the operation. Planning and designing a home page is fun and challenging, but it is important that it is maintained, ensuring that everything on it is current and still relevant to your users' needs. If there are interactive sections, ie. email or feedback, ensure that these are answered promptly, or acknowledged. Constant maintenance of the page can be very time consuming, but having produced a home page, you will have created increased expectations among your users for immediacy of information. Nothing looks so old as old home page information.

Once your home page is completed, advertise, advertise, advertise - mention it in every possible situation and at every possible opportunity. Add the address to your library stationery.

So… 'Trailing clouds of glory do we come.'

Remember when designing your school library's home page, the first section of the page is like a job interview - the first few seconds are the most important for first impressions and to keep your users returning. Ensure that they open up a neat, uncluttered, attractive (colourful, maybe), and **useful** opening page.

Your school library page can promise (and deliver) access to the library's own resources and to those available world wide. That promise, if fulfilled, is the soul of a good advertisement.

References

Internet sites
The following are pages which I like and visit fairly regularly to catch up on new things there, and just to see if there are any interesting links listed.

Bendigo Senior Secondary College
<http://www.bssc.edu.au/>

Elizabeth College
<http://www.eliz.tased.edu.au/>

John Paul College
<http://proteas.client.uq.edu.au/index.htm>

Methodist Ladies' College (Vic.) - Walton Library.
<http://library.mlckew.edu.au/>

St. Michael's Collegiate School
<http://www.stmic.tas.edu.au/>

Schools-on-the-Net
<http://www.chaos.com/learn/Schoolnet.html>

Resources for background reading:

Carroll, F. and L. Brady. (1997). 'Does the yellow brick road really lead us to the Land of Oz?' EduNet97@stmichaels.vic.edu.au.

Clyde, L.A. (1996). School libraries: At home on the World Wide Web? *Scan*, 15 (4): 23-26.

Kinch, G., G. Caudrey and D. Nettlebeck. (1997). 'The implications of web pages for school libraries.' EduNet97@stmichaels.vic.edu.au.

Morrison, A.M. (1997). Creating a library home page - ready or not! *Scan*, 16 (1): 31-34.

Quik Pro: Your guide to the Internet. An interactive Internet training package on CDROM. (1997). University of Queensland.

Weinstein, P. (1997). Tips and tools for building a school website. *Technology & Learning*, Jan: 25-38.

Developing the School Library Home Page

Pru Mitchell[*]

Creation of a library web page was an attempt to solve the following Internet related problems at La Salle College during 1996, when our Internet capable workstations increased from one to five.

The Problems

Students	Teachers	Teacher Librarians
• problems navigating • running out of time • not coping with instructions • errors typing URLs • Netscape - confusion between Find and Net Search buttons • Search engines – clicking advertisements instead of results list • limited ability to evaluate quality of sites • slow loading speed with students trying different sites.	• limited knowledge of what was available on Internet • limited time to learn to search and use the Internet • limited time to locate and evaluate useful sites • limited opportunity to share selected sites with colleagues • problems transferring bookmarks between home, faculty office & classroom workstations • access to Telnet difficult (Nexus, library catalogues).	• time spent helping students on users • preparation, searching for sites wasted when bookmarks lost • maintaining bookmarks on 5 machines • unable to add worthwhile description or comment to bookmark • ensuring each machine in school was set up the same way.

Sites such as the *Bellingham Schools' World Wide Web pages* <http://www.bham.wednet.edu/www.htm> guided our philosophy and practice.

> *This page provides WWW 'windows' to support curriculum - windows leading the student or staff member straight to good content, cutting past needless menu levels and providing annotations to support the user in making wise choices.*

---

[*] **Pru Mitchell** is a teacher librarian, and holds the position of Head of the Jan Jolley Library at La Salle College in Midland, Western Australia. An html version of this paper is located at **<http://www.lasalle.wa.edu.au/itec97.html>**. Pru may be contacted via email at **<pru@lasalle.wa.edu.au>**.

The Process: 1. Defining

Audience

Defining the target audience and their needs is the first step for any Web site planner. The following table is an attempt to brainstorm possible information needs which could be addressed by school web pages. It illustrates the reality that users' needs may change according to whether they are accessing the World Wide Web from the Library building, in a classroom or increasingly, at home.

Information Needs of School community which may be addressed via a World Wide Web site.

	Library Building	Elsewhere in School	Remote
Students	Curriculum Research	Catalogue Curriculum Research	Catalogue Curriculum Research School-Administration
Teachers	Curriculum Professional Research	Catalogue Curriculum Professional Research	Catalogue Curriculum Professional Research School-Administration
Library Staff	Administration Curriculum Professional Research		Administration Catalogue Curriculum Professional Research
Parents			School - Administration School - Public relations
Community			School - Public relations

Personnel

Ideally a school's web site will be the responsibility of a team which includes a representative from the library team. Web pages concerned with Parents/Community News, Public Relations and Administrative information should not normally the responsibility of library staff, but in most other areas there is a role for the 'information specialists'. While faculty pages should be 'owned' by Heads of Department, library staff can accommodate teachers' curriculum, study and research needs by adding links to these pages. Library Staff also benefit from a custom-made home page on their workstations. A basic example of this can be found at: *Library Officers Page* <http://www.lasalle.wa.edu.au/liboffs.html>.

Content
I started my library web page planning with a clear definition:

> *The library catalogue is the tool for organising access to the library's physical resources, the library web page is a tool for organising access to electronic information.*

This definition served me well while we had limited Internet access points in the library, and student access from outside the library was rare. Now that many students and teachers use remote Internet access as their primary information source, I have questions not definitions.

Should the library catalogue be accessible on the library's web page, as is the case in most tertiary education library web pages? *Bendigo Secondary College Library* <http://www.bssc.edu.au/library/index.htm> is one school with Web access to its catalogue. If the catalogue is not accessible, should details of relevant library resources be included on the Web page? See *Genazzo F.C.J. College Senior School Library homepage* <http://www.genazzano.vic.edu.au>.

Which curriculum or assignments links should be included in these pages? At first the library assignments page included links only if existing library resources for that topic were scarce. As use of the assignments page from home increased, the advantages of including links to reference sources such as the *Cambridge Biographical Dictionary* <http://www.biography.com/find/find.html> increased. For single volume reference items, five Internet workstations provide better access for students in the library than one copy on the shelf. Now convenience, number of students, due date, and likelihood of topic being repeated next year have become criteria for inclusion on assignment pages.

The Process: 2. Locating
Locating WWW sites to support curriculum needs involves interrogating a variety of search engines, following links from other

sites, checking suggestions from listservs and journals, browsing and luck. Find teachers who are recent Web converts and get them to email you any sites particularly useful to their area. Ask students to document their successful searches at the beginning of a major new topic or assignment.

One strategy for recording at this stage is to maintain a word processor document or template which contains the major web page headings. This document is open on the desktop during all email reading, WWW searching or surfing, and allows for quick pasting of suggested sites, URLs, and annotations for later action. Sites from this document are later checked, and either transferred into the relevant web page or deleted.

It is a guiding principle to locate 'actual' information for the library web page, as opposed to lists. *Chico High School Library Web page* <http://www.chs.chico.k12.ca.us/libr/webres/heal.html> has a great description of the *Hardin Meta Directory of Internet Health Sources* at <http://www.arcade.uiowa.edu/hardin-www/md.html>:

> *They "list the sites that list the sites"... pages have pointers to the most complete and frequently cited lists in each subject. This site is three or more levels removed from actual information.*

The Process: 3. Selecting
Evaluation of Web sites is a paper in itself, and guidance can be found online at:

Softweb Guide for students Evaluation Questions
<http://www.dsc.vic.gov.au/netiqet2.htm#3>

Grassian, Esther. (1995). *Thinking Critically about World Wide Web Resources.* UCLA College Library.
<http://www.library.ucla.edu/libraries/college/instruct/critical.htm>

McLachlan, Karen. *WWW CyberGuide Ratings for Content Evaluation.*
<http://www.cyberbee.com/guide1.html>.

It is certainly a challenge to juggle conflicting criteria, selecting sites for relevance, for primary rather than secondary source material, for material not available in the library, appropriate audience level, Australian, fast to download, easy to reference, and answering the set questions.

The Process: 4. Organising

Lack of organisation initially resulted in waste of time and effort as there was no clear map of the web site before we started creating, naming and linking pages. Before we knew it there were 40 pages, with no logical naming structure, little consistency in formatting, plenty of repetition and tedious navigation routes. There was also a need to separate text which was relatively constant (eg. policy statements) from information which requires frequent updating.

A major breakthrough was the realisation that different groups could have different entry points to the web site. The glossy College home page was irrelevant to those already at the College, so library and classroom workstations now have Netscape's home option set to the *Reference Page* <http://www.lasalle.wa.edu.au/links.html> Workstations in staff areas are set to the appropriate Department page, eg. *Social Studies Home Page* <http://www.lasalle.wa.edu.au/dep-soc.html>.

Organising the content of each web page requires decisions on the order of information and how much detail to include in annotations. For assignment pages an agreed format simplifies editing, by listing under first Year level, and then Subject, eg. the *Social Studies Assignment Page* <http://www.lasalle.wa.edu.au/ss-ass.html>. As each page grows decisions have to be made about deleting past topics, or moving them to a holding page in case they are needed in the future.

Web page design is important, and is covered well in other resources. Looking at other sites helps clarify web page designs which appeal, and viewing the document source provides a useful template. An important disclaimer at this point: As a teacher librarian my responsibility is the content of the web page. Schools need to consider the services of a design specialist for Web documents in the same way as for other publications. For example:

Schnell, E.H.(1997). *Writing for the Web: A Primer for Librarians Design Considerations.*
<http://bones.med.ohio-state.edu/eric/papers/primer/design.html>

Bellingham Schools Designing School Home Pages
<http://www.bham.wednet.edu/homepage.htm>

EduWeb Design Issues
<http://www.netspot.unisa.edu.au/eduweb/Practice/practice.htm>.

The Process: 5. Creating and Sharing

Creating web pages requires some form of publishing tool. For those starting from scratch, the newer range of applications such as Office 97, Publisher 97, and the latest Netscape provide templates and tools for web publishing. Many webmasters use html editors such as Hotdog, reviews of which are available from *Stroud's Consummate Winsock Applications List* <http://cws.iworld.com/32html-reviews.html>.

HTML tutorials are readily available on the Web or through short courses. Internet Service Providers such as *iinet technologies* also provide assistance *iinet html tutorial* <http://www.iinet.net.au/support/tutorial/html/index.html> and *FAQ on setting up own webpage* <http://www.iinet.net.au/support/homepages/>.

Availability of the web page is an important consideration, especially if the school operates an Intranet. Is the web page going to be accessible to students from home? Use of the Web page needs promotion to students and teachers, and the address should be published in accessible places such as the student diary and school newsletters.

The Process: 6. Evaluating

The evaluation criteria listed above must be applied to one's own web site. Currency and accuracy testing everything works, checking links are active, is assignment still active. Regular link checks can be done by students or volunteers. The Internet does not allow anyone to rest on their laurels for long. New developments mean changes to web publishing techniques and tools, and to keep your site looking good and working well it is important to keep an eye on the enhancements occurring.

Use of the web pages is a critical consideration. Who is using the service? How do students use the World Wide Web for assignment-related study at home? Research is needed into these issues to ensure that library web page creation is indeed a valuable use of library staff time (remember the Vertical file!), and to maximise the benefits of this service to our users. There are those who argue that instead of 'spoon feeding' in this way, energy would be better spent on training users to become competent searchers and evaluators of information.

References

Clyde, L.A. (1996). School libraries: At home on the World Wide Web? *Scan*, 15 (4):23-26.

Vezey, G. (1997). Using the Internet: Genazzano College Library. *Access*, 11 (1):34-36.

About the Editors

Lyn Hay is Lecturer in Teacher Librarianship at the School of Information Studies, Charles Sturt University. She has studied and worked in the field of teacher librarianship for seventeen years. Lyn is co-administator of the OZTL_NET and InfoLit_Aust listservs, coordinates virtual conferences for the teacher librarianship community, and is the recipient of a number of professional awards including the ASLA(NSW) John Hirst Award for 1997, the IASL/SIRS Commendation Award for 1997, and the IASL/SOFTLINK 25th Anniversary Grant for 1996.

James Henri is Senior Lecturer and Sub Dean Marketing in the Faculty of Science and Agriculture at Charles Sturt University. He is Director of the Centre for Studies in Teacher Librarianship and coordinator of graduate programs in teacher librarianship. James has held a number of visiting professorships in Canada and Hong Kong. He has authored and edited over forty works and published widely in the field of teacher librarianship.